VIA FERRATAS OF
THE ITALIAN DOLOMITES
VOLUME 1

VIA FERRATAS OF
THE ITALIAN DOLOMITES
VOLUME 1

by James Rushforth

JUNIPER HOUSE, MURLEY MOSS,
OXENHOLME ROAD, KENDAL, CUMBRIA LA9 7RL
www.cicerone.co.uk

© James Rushforth 2018
First edition 2018
ISBN: 978 1 85284 846 0
Reprinted (with updates) 2019, 2023

This guide further develops and replaces the previous guide by Graham Fletcher and John Smith with the same title published under ISBNs 9781852843625 and 9781852845926 in 2002 and 2009 respectively.

Printed in Singapore by KHL Printing on responsibly sourced paper.
A catalogue record for this book is available from the British Library.
All photographs are by the author unless otherwise stated.

Route mapping by Lovell Johns www.lovelljohns.com
Contains OpenStreetMap.org data © OpenStreetMap
contributors, CC-BY-SA. NASA relief data courtesy of ESRI

Updates to this guide

While every effort is made by our authors to ensure the accuracy of guidebooks as they go to print, changes can occur during the lifetime of an edition. Any updates that we know of for this guide will be on the Cicerone website (www.cicerone.co.uk/846/updates), so please check before planning your trip. We also advise that you check information about such things as transport, accommodation and shops locally. Even rights of way can be altered over time.

The route maps in this guide are derived from publicly available data, databases and crowd-sourced data. As such they have not been through the detailed checking procedures that would generally be applied to a published map from an official mapping agency, although naturally we have reviewed them closely in the light of local knowledge as part of the preparation of this guide.

We are always grateful for information about any discrepancies between a guidebook and the facts on the ground, sent by email to updates@cicerone.co.uk or by post to Cicerone, Juniper House, Murley Moss, Oxenholme Road, Kendal, LA9 7RL.

Register your book: To sign up to receive free updates, special offers and GPX files where available, create a Cicerone account and register your purchase via the 'My Account' tab at www.cicerone.co.uk.

Front cover: Negotiating the steep and crux traverse at the start of Via Ferrata Cesco Tomaselli (Route 37)

CONTENTS

Acknowledgements

The creation of this guidebook was only made possible by the enormous and generous support of a great many people. First and foremost, thanks to John Smith and Graham Fletcher for entrusting me to continue their work, updating and building upon the previous editions of this guide. They set the bar high, crafting the first English-language guidebook to via ferratas in the Dolomites and creating a comprehensive resource and list of routes that would be used and referenced by a multitude of nationalities. Their hard work and commitment over the years were invaluable and it is a privilege to be entrusted with the task of taking their guidebooks forward for new generations.

My thanks to CAI, the Alpine guides and local populace who work tirelessly to construct and maintain the huge variety of routes we enjoy today; without their dedication and enthusiasm there would be precious little to write about!

During the last decade spent in the Dolomites, Collett's Mountain Holidays have very kindly supplied me with accommodation, support and drinking partners in-between many extended stints living out of a van. A huge thanks to all the resort and office staff who have always treated me as one of their own.

My thanks to everyone who has accompanied me on countless adventures in the Dolomites, whether on routes included in this guide or not. It has been a true privilege exploring the mountains with you.

As ever, my family provided excellent support, guidance and encouragement throughout the project. Thanks, as always, to Lynne Hempton for accompanying me on many of the routes, for assisting with all aspects of the book and for turning my inarticulate musings into something resembling intelligible text.

Finally, my thanks to all the staff at Cicerone who have assisted, steered and helped shape the evolution of this project, from the initial print run in 2002 to the book you now see before you.

Route closures

While the information given in this guidebook was accurate at the time of writing, via ferrata routes may subsequently close due to rockfall, maintenance or other such circumstances. As with any excursion in the mountains, it is recommended that you obtain up-to-date information with the local guides offices, CAI branches or tourist information offices to ensure the viability of the routes and check the mountain conditions. Except for any liability that cannot be excluded by law, neither Cicerone nor the author accept liability for damage of any nature (including damage to property, personal injury or death) arising directly or indirectly from the information in this book

Symbols used on route maps

~	route
······	alternative route
Ⓢ	start point
Ⓕ	finish point
ⓈⒻ	start/finish point
	glacier
	woodland
	urban area
	regional border
	international border
▬■▬	station/railway
▲	peak
▲▲	group of peaks
🏠 🍴	hotel/restaurant
⬆	manned/unmanned refuge
P	parking
Ⅹ	campsite/bivouac
■	building
⚇	chapel
❶	information
)(	pass
≂	bridge

Relief
in metres

3400–3600
3200–3400
3000–3200
2800–3000
2600–2800
2400–2600
2200–2400
2000–2200
1800–2000
1600–1800
1400–1600
1200–1400
1000–1200
800–1000
600–800
400–600
200–400
0–200

SCALE: 1:50,000

0 kilometres 0.5   1

0 miles   0.5

Contour lines are drawn at 25m intervals and highlighted at 100m intervals.

All maps are at 1:50,000 except for Routes 26–27, 73, 74–75 which are at 1:40,000.

Evening light illuminates Rifugio Locatelli in the Sesto Dolomites (Route 64)

Mountain safety

Every mountain walk has its dangers, and those described in this guidebook are no exception. All who walk or climb in the mountains should recognise this and take responsibility for themselves and their companions along the way. The author and publisher have made every effort to ensure that the information contained in this guide was correct when it went to press, but, except for any liability that cannot be excluded by law, they cannot accept responsibility for any loss, injury or inconvenience sustained by any person using this book.

International distress signal *(emergency only)*
Six blasts on a whistle (and flashes with a torch after dark) spaced evenly for one minute, followed by a minute's pause. Repeat until an answer is received. The response is three signals per minute followed by a minute's pause.

Helicopter rescue
The following signals are used to communicate with a helicopter:

Help needed:
raise both arms
above head to
form a 'Y'

Help not needed:
raise one arm
above head, extend
other arm downward

Emergency telephone numbers
Italy: Emergency Services: tel 112

Weather reports
Italy: tel 0165 44 113

Mountain rescue can be very expensive – be adequately insured.

ROUTE SUMMARY TABLE

No	Route name	Mountain group	Start	Distance	Time	Grade	Wire length	Page
Val di Fassa/Canazei								
1	Sentiero Massimiliano	Massiccio dello Sciliar	Campitello di Fassa	24km	6–10hr	2B	200m	45
2	Via Ferrata Laurenzi	Catinaccio	Campitello di Fassa	29km	9–12hr	4C	850m	49
3	Via Ferrata Passo Santner	Catinaccio	Top of Laurin chairlift	8km	6hr	2A	300m	53
4	Via Ferrata Roda di Vaèl	Catinaccio	Top of Paolina chairlift	6.5km	4–5hr	1B	350m	56
5	Via Ferrata Masare	Catinaccio	Top of Paolina chairlift	7km	4hr	2B	400m	58
6	Via Ferrata Catinaccio d'Antermoia	Catinaccio	Rifugio Gardeccia	10km	6–8hr	2B	600m	61
7	Via Ferrata Franco Gadotti	Marmolada	Malga Crocifisso chapel	12.5km	7–8hr	2C	400m	66
8	Via Ferrata I Magnifici Quattro	Marmolada	Malga Crocifisso chapel	8km	4–5hr	6B	400m	69
9	Via Ferrata Kaiserjäger	Marmolada	Val San Nicolo car park	14km	6–7hr	4C	260m	73
10	Sentiero Attrezzato Bepi Zac	Marmolada	Top of Costabella chairlift	13km	9–10hr	2C	300m	76
11	Via Ferrata Paolin-Piccolin	Marmolada	Colmean	10.5km	7–8hr	3B	300m	80
12	Via Ferrata dei Finanzieri	Marmolada	Top of Ciampac cable car	5.5km	4–5hr	3C	300m	83
13	Via Ferrata Hans Seyffert	Marmolada	Top of Pian del Fiacconi lift	6.5km	4–5hr	4C	400m	86
14	Via Ferrata Eterna Brigata Cadore	Marmolada	Rifugio Fedaia	8km	6–7hr	4C	1000m	91
Selva								
15	Via Ferrata Sass Rigais Est/Sud	Odle-Puez	Top of Col Raiser gondola	11km	7–8hr	1B/2B	800m	97
16	Sentiero Attrezzato Piz Duledes	Odle-Puez	Top of Col Raiser gondola	11km	7–8hr	1A	150m	101

No	Route name	Mountain group	Start	Distance	Time	Grade	Wire length	Page
17	Via Ferrata Sandro Pertini (closed and wire removed)	Odle-Puez	–	–	–	–	–	102
18	Via Ferrata Oskar Schuster	Sassolungo	Top of Sassolungo gondola	12km	5–6hr	3B	350m	103
19	Via Ferrata Col Rodella	Sassolungo	Hotel Passo Sella Dolomiti Resort	5km	2–3hr	3A	175m	108
20	Via Ferrata Mesules (Pössnecker)	Sella	Passo Sella	12km	6–7hr	4C	500m	111
Badia/La Villa								
21	Sentiero Attrezzato Günther Messner	Odle-Puez	Croce Russis	15km	7–8hr	1B	200m	117
22	Sentiero Attrezzato Sass de Putia	Odle-Puez	Passo delle Erbe	10km	5–6hr	1A	150m	121
23	Via Ferrata Sasso Santa Croce	Fanis	Top of Santa Croce chairlift	15km	7–8hr	1B	150m	123
24	Sentiero Attrezzato Piz de les Conturines	Fanis	Capanna Alpina	17km	7–8hr	1B	100m	126
25	Via Ferrata Furcia Rossa	Fanis	Capanna Alpina	19km	7–8hr	2C	300m	128
Corvara								
26	Via Ferrata Piz da Cir V	Odle-Puez	Passo Gardena	3km	3–4hr	2A	100m	135
27	Sentiero Attrezzato Gran Cir	Odle-Puez	Passo Gardena	3.5km	2–3hr	1A	100m	140
28	Via Ferrata Brigata Tridentina	Sella	Tridentina car park	5km	5–7hr	3B	400m	141
29	Via Ferrata Vallon	Sella	Top of Vallon chairlift	8km	5–6hr	2B	200m	145
30	Via Ferrata Piz da Lech	Sella	Top of Vallon chairlift	4km	3–4hr	3B	200m	148
31	Sentiero Attrezzato Sassongher	Odle-Puez	Top of Col Pradat gondola	7km	3–4hr	1A	100m	150

13

No	Route name	Mountain group	Start	Distance	Time	Grade	Wire length	Page
Arabba								
32	Via Ferrata Cesare Piazzetta	Sella	Passo Pordoi	9km	5–6hr	5C	500m	155
33	Via Ferrata delle Trincee	Marmolada	Top of Porto Vescovo cable car	7km	6–7hr	4B	300m	159
34	Via Ferrata Sass de Rocia	Marmolada	Ronch	1km	1–2hr	1A	30m	162
35	Sentiero Attrezzato Col di Lana	Fanis	Lasta	11km	4–5hr	1A	100m	163
Falzarego								
36	Sentiero Attrezzato Sass de Stria	Fanis	Passo Valparola	2.5km	1–2hr	1A	20m	170
37	Via Ferrata Cesco Tomaselli	Fanis	Top of Lagazuoi cable car	7.5km	6–7hr	5C	600m	172
38	Sentiero dei Kaiserjäger	Fanis	Top of Lagazuoi cable car	3km	2–3hr	1B	100m	175
39	Sentiero Attrezzato Galleria del Lagazuoi	Fanis	Passo Falzarego	3km	2–3hr	1A	200m	178
40	Via Ferrata degli Alpini al Col dei Bos	Tofane	Bar Strobel	5.5km	3–4hr	3B	350m	181
41	Via Ferrata Averau	Nuvolau	Top of Cinque Torri chairlift	4km	2–3hr	2A	75m	184
42	Via Ferrata Ra Gusela	Nuvolau	Top of Cinque Torri chairlift	7km	3–4hr	1A	125m	189
Cortina								
43	Via Ferrata Scala del Menighel	Tofane	Rifugio Dibona	11.5km	5–6hr	1C	70m	197
44	Via Ferrata Giovanni Lipella	Tofane	Rifugio Dibona	12km	7–8hr	4C	600m	200
45	Sentiero Attrezzato Grotta di Tofana	Tofane	Rifugio Dibona	3km	2–3hr	1A	100m	203
46	Sentiero Astaldi	Tofane	Rifugio Dibona	3km	2hr	1A	400m	205
47	Via Ferrata Punta Anna and Gianni Aglio	Tofane	Rifugio Pomedes	10km	7–8hr	5C	800m	208

No	Route name	Mountain group	Start	Distance	Time	Grade	Wire length	Page
48	Via Ferrata Lamon and Formenton	Tofane	Top of Freccia nel Cielo cable car	5.5km	3–4hr	2B	200m	212
49	Sentiero Giuseppe Olivieri	Tofane	Rifugio Pomedes	3km	2–3hr	1B	300m	216
50	Via Ferrata Maria e Andrea Ferrari	Tofane	Rifugio Duca d'Aosta	1km	1–2hr	3A	380m	217
51	Sentiero Attrezzato Giovanni Barbara/Lucio Dalaiti/Cengia de Mattia	Fanis	Ponte Felizon car park	12km	4–5hr	2B	100m	220
52	Via Ferrata Ettore Bovero	Tofane	International Camping Olympia	10.5km	5–6hr	3B	300m	224
53	Via Ferrata Michielli Strobel	Pomaganon	Hotel Fiames	8km	5–6hr	3B	600m	227
54	Sentiero Attrezzato Terza Cengia del Pomagagnon	Pomaganon	Col Tondo	11km	5–6hr	2C	250m	230
55	Sentiero Attrezzato Renè de Pol	Cristallo	Cimabanche	11.5km	6–7hr	2B	500m	232
56	Via Ferrata Ivano Dibona	Cristallo	Rifugio Son Forca	13km	7–8hr	2B	500m	235
57	Via Ferrata Marino Bianchi	Cristallo	Rifugio Son Forca	6.5km	5–6hr	2B	200m	238
58	Via Ferrata Sci Club 18	Cristallo	Midstation of Faloria cable car	3km	3–4hr	5C	400m	240
59	Via Ferrata Giro del Sorapiss	Sorapiss	Passo Tre Croci	26km	12–16h	3C/1C/3C	700m	243
Misurina								
60	Sentiero Attrezzato Capitano Bilgeri/Monte Piana/Monte Piano	Monte Piana	Rifugio Angelo Bosi	2km	2–3hr	1B	250m	251
61	Via Ferrata Merlone	Cadini di Misurina	Lago d'Antorno	9km	4–5hr	3B	300m	254
62	Sentiero Attrezzato Alberto Bonacossa	Cadini di Misurina	Top of Col de Varda chairlift	10km	5–6hr	1A	400m	260

No	Route name	Mountain group	Start	Distance	Time	Grade	Wire length	Page
63	Sentiero delle Forcelle	Paterno – Dolomiti di Sesto	Rifugio Auronzo	12.5km	5–6hr	1B	800m	262
64	Via Ferrata De Luca/ Innerkofler	Paterno – Dolomiti di Sesto	Rifugio Auronzo	9km	5–6hr	2B	1000m	265
65	Via Ferrata delle Scalette/ Curato Militare Hosp	Paterno – Dolomiti di Sesto	Rifugio Auronzo	10km	5–6hr	3B	150m	268
Sesto								
66	Via Ferrata Strada degli Alpini	Popera – Dolomiti di Sesto	Hotel Dolomitenhof	18km	8–9hr	2B	2000m	273
67	Via Ferrata Nord	Popera – Dolomiti di Sesto	Top of Cabinovia Croda Rossa gondola	8km	5–6hr	2B	100m	276
68	Via Ferrata Mario Zandonella	Popera – Dolomiti di Sesto	Rifugio Lunelli	10km	8–9hr	4C	1500m	279
69	Via Ferrata Aldo Roghel/ Cengia Gabriella	Popera – Dolomiti di Sesto	Rifugio Lunelli	20km	10–12hr	4C/3C	400/ 1500m	283
70	Via Ferrata Mazzetta	Popera – Dolomiti di Sesto	Acque Rosse, Padola	11km	7–8hr	2C	150m	288
Auronzo								
71	Sentiero Cengia del Doge	Marmarole	Somadida Forest Nature Reserve car park	17km	7–8hr	1C	150m	294
72	Sentiero degli Alpini	Marmarole	Ristorante alla Pineta, Val d'Oten	17km	8–9hr	2C	450m	297
73	Sentiero Attrezzato Amalio da Pra	Marmarole	Pian dei Buoi, Lozzo di Cadore	7km	4–5hr	2B	200m	299
74	Via Ferrata Sartor	Peralba	Near Rifugio Sorgenti	8.5km	4–5hr	2B	250m	301
75	Via Ferrata Via di Guerra/ CAI Portogruaro	Peralba	Near Rifugio Sorgenti	8km	4–5hr	3B/2B	700m	304

FOREWORD

It's almost 20 years since we first went to the Dolomites and started our addiction with via ferrata climbing. Following our realisation in 1998 that the previous English-language guidebook (a translation from an old German guidebook, *Via Ferrata: Scrambles in the Dolomites*, Cicerone Press) was out of date, we initially made notes for our own use before deciding to take things a step further and write a new guidebook.

Our first guide was first published in 2002 as a two-book series covering the complete area of the Italian Dolomites, taking in some wonderful mountain groups with a wide range of via ferrata climbing routes from the very easy to the most difficult. One thing we had found unsatisfactory was the various grading systems in use at the time, which didn't seem to fully address the technicality and/or remoteness of each individual route. Many hours were spent debating how we could differentiate between a hard technical route with easy escape possibilities and easier routes in remote high-mountain situations which can present a potentially more serious undertaking. The system we evolved was a dual grading approach, taking into account both the seriousness and technical aspects of each route. This seems to have stood the test of time and continues to be accepted as a standard across the United Kingdom.

As the popularity of via ferratas grew and changes occurred (the creation of new routes, closure of some old ones and various modifications to existing routes), we released revised editions of Vol 1 in 2004, 2006, 2009, 2012 and 2014. Vol 2 (first published in 2003) covering the southern Dolomites, Brenta and Lake Garda was also revised in 2005, 2008, 2012, and 2015.

Over the years we have continued our love affair with via ferrata climbing, and Graham actually lived in the Dolomites for a while. At our initial meeting with Jonathan Williams at Cicerone Press, we were told that writing a guidebook was like having children – back then we were at the conception of the idea, and we have since had the pleasure of watching the books grow up to where they are now coming of age. A meeting with James Rushforth at a friend's wedding in Corvara in 2012 sowed the seeds for him taking on the task of bringing our guides into the 21st century, where we hope they will continue to flourish and inspire. A professional writer and photographer, James has worked with our guidebook content to produce this new exciting edition, which we are sure will inspire new generations to visit and enjoy the delights of the Dolomites.

John Smith and Graham Fletcher,
2017

First snow is encountered on a late-season ascent of Possnecker (Route 20)

INTRODUCTION

Superb views over to Sassolungo, the Sella and Lago di Fedaia (Route 14)

The Dolomites are often cited as the most unique, dramatic and beautiful mountains in the world. The splendour of the scenery is undeniable; the explosive shapes of the peaks and ridgelines, the ever-changing colours of the rock and the stunning contrast between the seasons are just some of the factors that make this mountain range stand out from its alpine counterparts and have led to the well-deserved award of UNESCO World Heritage status.

In addition to the natural wonder, one of the most intriguing and captivating aspects of this beautiful region is the culture; the Dolomites offer an insight into a truly fused society, with Italian and Austrian influences found throughout the area. Furthermore, and most pertinent to this guide, the Dolomites are home to the greatest concentration of via ferratas in the world.

First constructed in the early 1900s, these cabled routes originally followed traditional climbing lines and were initially conceived as a form of recreation for visiting tourists. When the First World War broke out, the front line between the Italian and Austro-Hungarian troops ran through the middle of this mountainous region and the via ferratas took on a new role; existing routes were expanded and many new cables were installed to aid the movement of alpine military troops through the mountains.

After the war many old routes were restored, expanded and rerouted, and as popularity grew new via ferratas were added, creating a vast network of cabled climbs which today is one of the Dolomites' major attractions for summer tourism. The sheer concentration of via ferratas ensures there is something for every ability, from family-friendly mountain days, to exposed ridge routes, to physically demanding climbing. The scenery is world-class and the landscape studded with idyllic mountain towns and villages, serving as excellent bases to explore this beautiful region and provide access to some of the most breathtaking via ferrata routes in the world.

WHAT IS A VIA FERRATA?

Literally meaning 'iron way', the term *via ferrata* refers to a mountain route or climb that is protected by a series of cables, stemples (metal rungs), pegs and ladders. Originally equipped with iron, today routes tend to use modern, more lightweight steel cable, which is bolted to the rock at intervals using robust resin pegs or rings. Often, less sheer routes which are more akin to exposed mountain traverses or protected walks are known as *sentieri attrezzati*, meaning 'equipped paths', although to a point the terms are used interchangeably as there are some sentieri attrezzati that are notably more difficult than easier routes given the term 'via ferrata'. However, as a rule, via ferratas tend to be more mountainous and challenging than sentieri.

Ascending the initial ladder from Rifugio Lorenzi on Route 56

Traversing one of the many ledges on Route 21

Routes are regularly checked, maintained and waymarked by the Italian Alpine Club, CAI (Club Alpino Italiano). CAI has hundreds of geographical sections, the largest of which is SAT (Societa degli Alpinisti Tridentini), which alone has more than 20,000 members. CAI owns nearly 500 rifugios and shelters in the Dolomites and maintains many thousands of kilometres of paths and via ferratas.

USING THIS GUIDE

There are 10 chapters containing route descriptions for 75 via ferratas and protected paths, organised by geographical location and proximity to the nearest valley base or town. Route descriptions were accurate at the time of writing and are accompanied by an information box giving the start and finish points, the route length and time (without stops), the grading of the route, the total ascent and descent, the length of the wire, and the GPS coordinates of the recommended parking location.

An additional section, 'Other possibilities', is included to highlight any possible alternatives and extensions that may be of interest. Place names on the maps that are significant for route navigation are shown in **bold** in the text.

Each route is complemented by a 1:50,000 overview map extract (except for routes 26–27, 73 and 74–75 which are at 1:40,000), which is intended for use in conjunction with a 1:25,000 Italian Tabacco map (the correct map number is provided in the information box at the beginning of each route). Additionally, where possible, an annotated photo topo has been included to show the entire route or a section of the route that is particularly difficult to navigate.

This guidebook covers the north, central and eastern Dolomites, while Volume 2 covers the southern regions, Pala, Brenta and Garda.

WHEN TO GO

Tourism in the Dolomites is typically seasonal and the summer season runs from June to late September. However, route conditions are heavily dependent on the previous winter season; significant snowfall in late spring can result in a late start to the summer, particularly when it comes to some of the harder, high-level ferratas. Equally, snow can fall year-round (although it's rare in high summer) and temperatures tend to drop considerably towards the end of September.

Some of the routes in this guide are accessed by cable car, chairlift or gondola; the running periods vary from valley to valley, but as a guide most lifts operate from late June to the start of September.

August is the busiest period of the summer and queues become common on the roads, below routes and on the via ferratas themselves. Accommodation also tends to be more expensive (and elusive) during this month. However, if you're willing to venture off the beaten track onto some of the more remote routes in this book, solitude and mountain tranquillity can still be found.

Tofana di Rozes as seen from Lago Limides (Route 44)

Festa d'Istà in Canazei celebrates the end of summer

The weather in the Dolomites varies from year to year, but generally speaking June and September are the most stable months, with July and August being more prone to afternoon thunderstorms.

October is perhaps the most beautiful month of the year here, as the leaves turn golden and a dusting of snow often graces the tops of the peaks. However, it can also be very cold, the tourist infrastructure shuts down and many of the routes will drop out of condition.

GETTING THERE

The Dolomites are located equidistant between Venice (and Treviso), Innsbruck and Verona – all of which can be reached from the UK by budget airline. Other options are Munich, Brescia and Bergamo. It is possible to continue to the Dolomites by public transport and private shuttle services, but given the difficulties in accessing the routes in this guide by bus, it is recommended to hire a car at the airport and complete the journey by road. Rough driving times from the airports are given below:

Innsbruck 2hr 15min
Treviso 2hr 40min
Venice 2hr 40min
Verona 2hr 50min
Munich 3hr 40min
Brescia 3hr 15min
Bergamo 3hr 50min

If you wish to bring your own vehicle, the fastest route is through France and takes around 12hrs from Calais. However, the French motorway tolls make this a very expensive option and as such a route through

The autumn sun rises behind the five towers of Cinque Torri (Routes 41 and 42)

Belgium, Germany and Austria is a slightly longer but more affordable alternative – allow 14hrs. Italian motorways are tolled while Austria operates a Vignette system – this can be purchased at petrol stations and motorway services and is valid for 10 days, 2 months or a year. The Brenner Pass – the main road in from Austria – has a separate, fixed toll of around €10.

GETTING AROUND

While hiring a car is highly recommended for getting the most out of a trip to the Dolomites, in high season public transport in the major valleys is reasonably good and cheap, and with some prior planning many of the routes in this guide can be accessed by bus. Three main operators serve the area – Dolomitibus, SAD and Trentino Transporti Esercizio – with a few smaller companies running services in specific valleys. It's worth familiarising yourself with the timetables even if bringing a vehicle (website addresses are given in Appendix A) as some routes involve extensive mountain traverses and a bus is often the most convenient way to return to your car. Most services operate seasonal variations and it can be difficult to rely on public transport early and late in the season.

Thanks to the extensive winter ski network, the Dolomites is well served by lifts, gondolas and cable cars. Although many lifts are winter-only operations, those in the more popular areas operate throughout the summer months – albeit often with reduced services at the beginning and end of the season. As a general rule, most services operate from July to August, and remain in place into the beginning of September, with a handful continuing into October. Local tourist offices can advise on timetables, and it's worth checking the services in advance if you're intending to use any of the lifts during your trip.

ACCOMMODATION

There is no shortage of accommodation in the Dolomites, and all the main towns and villages offer a variety of options ranging from basic to the most luxurious. Hotels of all standards abound and there are numerous *garnì* (bed and breakfasts) and self-catering apartments. Hotels styling themselves as 'Sport' or offering 'Wellness' usually have spa facilities such as saunas, steam rooms and Turkish baths. In addition to the accommodation in the valleys, there are countless *rifugios* in the mountains themselves; literally meaning 'refuge', these are more akin to plush alpine hotels offering good sleeping quarters (sometimes with a choice between private rooms or dorms), a decent breakfast and a three-course evening meal.

Accommodation in most places in the Dolomites is available with three options: *solo pernottamento* (overnight stay), *con colazione* (bed and breakfast) and *mezza pensione* (half-board). If opting for the bunk-room option in the rifugios, a sleeping bag liner is usually expected.

Torrente Avisio waterfalls on the Passo Fedaia (Val di Fassa/Canazei)

There are also quite a few campsites dotted around the Dolomites, many of which have developed into quite luxurious sites with good facilities – but unfortunately this means they are not the budget option they once were. If you visit the Dolomites in a campervan, the cheapest option is to make use of an *area attrezzata* or *stellplatz* – these are effectively car parks where campervans are allowed to park for a small fee. There is often running water and sometimes a wastewater disposal area. Finally, if you really are on a shoestring, there's ample parking at the top of most of the passes and although overnight stays are not officially permitted, you may find safety in numbers with many other campervans, particularly in high season.

In some of the more remote mountainous areas there are a number of *bivacchi* or shelters. These are rarely more than just that, with facilities limited to bunks and blankets, but can be a novel way of spending a night when attempting some of the longer or more isolated routes. Use is on an honesty basis and it is not possible to guarantee a space, although despite this they are rarely crowded.

Nearly every town or village in the Dolomites has a tourist information office (*ufficio turistico*) that provides good, up-to-date information on accommodation, as well as information on lifts, public transport and cultural events. English is usually spoken in the larger offices, while the offices in the smaller villages may require a little more gesticulating.

Inside Bivacco Slataper on the Sorapiss circuit (Route 59)

Architecture typical of South Tyrol

TELECOMMUNICATIONS

Northern Italy has an excellent mobile phone network and coverage in the Dolomites is surprisingly good for a mountainous region. If making calls within the country from a UK or non-Italian phone, the international dialling code for Italy is +39 and the initial zero of the phone number should not be dropped. There are a few public payphones dotted around the towns and these usually operate with a phone card, which can be purchased from most newsagents and tabacs.

Useful emergency numbers:
Carabinieri/rescue 112
Police 113
Fire service 115
Road rescue 116
Mountain rescue/ambulance 118

MAPS AND PLACE NAMES

There are two main maps used in the Dolomites: Italian-made Tabacco (www.tabaccoeditrice.it), and the German equivalent Kompass (www.kompass.de). Both manufacturers cover the Dolomites with 1:50,000 and 1:25,000 maps, with little variation between the two. For the purposes of this guide, the Tabacco maps are recommended as place names (like the guidebook) appear in Italian first. Although waymarking is generally excellent throughout the region, for the routes in this guide a 1:25,000 map for the relevant area is recommended.

In recent years, online mapping has become much more prevalent, and both map companies now offer mobile apps which can be used in conjunction with the GPS function on a compatible device. It's worth checking the operating system requirements for these if you intend to use them. Maps can be bought easily online before your trip from suppliers such as Stanfords (www.stanfords.co.uk), or otherwise locally at most newsagents, gift shops and supermarkets.

One of the most complicated aspects of navigation in the Dolomites is the confusion surrounding place names. Because many areas were historically Austrian, almost all towns, villages, valleys and mountains have an Italian and a German name, both of which are still in common usage. To further add to the confusion, a local dialect, Ladin, is still widely spoken, often resulting in a third name. While these are often easy to correlate, sometimes the names are wildly different in two or all three of the languages and may be signed differently depending on where you are. For ease and consistency of use, Italian place names have been used throughout the guide, with the German or Ladin equivalent provided for major features when required.

WEATHER

As in all mountain areas, the weather in the Dolomites can be unpredictable. As a rule, the months of July and August are the warmest and follow a general pattern of a clear start followed by increasing cloud in the afternoon and a thunderstorm. Rain (and even snow) can occur at any time of year, although September tends to be more stable in terms of storms. Daily forecasts are available

Chiesa di San Vigilio in the village of Colfosco

A storm approaches Sassolungo as viewed from the Alpe di Siusi (Route 18)

online at www.arpa.veneto.it, www. provincia.bz.it/meteo and www. meteotrentino.it – usually a short summary is given in English, with a much more detailed version in Italian and German. Forecasts are also available from tourist offices and the local mountain guides offices.

It's worth getting into the habit of checking the forecasts regularly; they are usually updated around midday and again later in the afternoon, and act as a reasonable guide when planning a via ferrata. An early start is almost always recommended, as the weather typically deteriorates in the afternoon. Conversely however, if the day starts badly there are some shorter, more easily accessible routes that can be completed in the afternoon.

While wet rock is not ideal, via ferratas – especially easier ones – can be climbed in the rain, but bear in mind that in low temperatures icing can occur throughout the summer.

Thunderstorms should be avoided in all cases. It is not uncommon for lightning to strike the peaks, and being caught out in an exposed mountain situation can quickly become very serious. If you are caught in a storm and are unable to escape from a route, there are some simple rules to minimise the potential risk:

- If a storm is approaching, evaluate potential escape routes as soon as possible.
- If it is safe to do so, unclip from the cable and move a safe distance away. If an escape route is available, then use it. If you have

29

no option but to sit it out, a wide ledge might provide an adequate safety zone on a cliff face. If on a ridge, however, try to get off it as soon as possible.

- In a storm, stay out in the open if you can – do not seek shelter under boulders or overhangs or go into caves, as these can be the natural spark points as lightning tries to find its way to earth.
- Keep as low as possible: sitting on your rucksack minimises both your profile and your contact with wet ground.
- Keep your core dry by putting on your waterproofs without delay.

Above all, stay calm; lightning strikes natural projections, such as mountain tops or rock pinnacles, so if you are unlucky enough to be caught in a storm, don't panic, make measured decisions and follow the tips listed above.

ROUTE GRADINGS

There are currently many different grading systems used to denote the difficulty of a via ferrata and, much like with rock climbing, a European standard has yet to emerge. This guide uses the Smith/Fletcher dual grading system of the original guides, which has been widely adopted in recent publications.

It should be noted that grading is subjective and will vary on the same route depending on the conditions encountered on that particular day.

If in doubt, start easy and work your way up to harder routes.

The Smith/Fletcher system

This system uses a dual numeric and alphabetic grading classification.

The number denotes the technical difficulty of the route, from a scale of 1 to 6 (the original Smith/Fletcher scale ran from 1 to 5 but the construction of modern high-grade via ferratas such as I Magnifici Quattro (Route 8) has led to the introduction of a sixth grade). Grade 1 is the easiest and 6 the most difficult.

The second, alphabetic grade represents the 'seriousness' of the route and runs from A to C, with A being the least committing and C the most serious. This grade is based on the mountain commitment (the distance to facilities that could offer aid and support) of the via ferrata and the possibility to retreat or escape from the route if circumstances require.

Technical difficulty

1   Gentle routes without technical difficulties, often taking the form of a path with a wire and an exposed drop on one side. A head for heights and sure-footedness is still required.

2   Straightforward routes for the experienced mountain walker or scrambler with a head for heights. Short passages of climbing required.

3   Rather more difficult routes with short sections of vertical climbing

and sustained passages of wire. At this level, complete freedom from vertigo and sure-footedness are required.

4   Demanding routes, frequently involving steep rock faces and requiring a fairly high standard of technical climbing ability.

5   Serious routes with difficult climbing moves, sustained ground and occasional overhanging passages.

6   Routes of the highest technical standard encountered in via ferrata climbing with strenuous climbing throughout.

Seriousness

A   Straightforward outings in unthreatening mountain terrain. Routes will have easy access and/or escape opportunities.

B   Itineraries with access that might be more difficult – opportunities to escape from the route will be limited, so minor mishaps could develop into quite serious situations. A change in the weather could potentially be more than merely inconvenient.

C   Remote and isolated routes in a serious mountain environment that could present major logistical problems in the event of an emergency. Often with exposed terrain and unprotected passages.

For example: Route 2 – Via Ferrata Laurenzi (4C). This route is graded 4 in terms of technical difficulty as the route contains sustained periods of wire with technical climbing; the descent from Molignon di Dentro to

Looking out over Cortina d'Ampezzo from the upper part of Route 50

Lago d'Antermoia in particular presents some difficult down-climbing. The 'C' seriousness rating provides an indication of the route's remote nature on the northern edge of the Catinaccio Group, the exposed mountain-top environment making retreat and escape difficult, and the existence of several unprotected passages.

Mountain conditions

Both the gradings and the descriptions in the guide are written on the assumption that the routes are in good condition, free of ice and snow and not affected by rockfall or other unforeseeable events. However, weather and conditions can be extremely variable at any time of year and sudden thunderstorms, snowfall, ice formation or flash flooding can all occur unexpectedly, as can rockfall or damage to the cabling. Up-to-date route information can be obtained at local tourist information and mountain guides' offices.

EQUIPMENT

The following equipment should be taken on every via ferrata.

Helmet

Perhaps the single most important piece of equipment. This must conform to UIAA (Union Internationale des Associations d'Alpinisme) standards to protect the climber against rockfall. However, to be effective it should be on your head, not in your rucksack, so be sure to put it on as soon as the risk of stone-fall is present.

On Alfonso Vandelli (Route 59)

Harness

A climbing sit or full body harness should be used, depending upon personal preference. Full body harnesses are generally recommended for young children.

Via Ferrata lanyard or self-belay system

This is the principal method of attaching yourself to the wire via two lanyards. It is imperative that you buy or rent a set that is UIAA rated and fit for purpose. Do not attempt to make your own lanyards out of climbing rope, slings and standard climbing carabiners. Rock climbing falls normally have a fall factor of around 0.5 and even a serious fall from just above the belay on a multi-pitch climb 'only' generates a fall factor of 2 or 3. However, a 5-metre fall on a vertical or overhanging section of via ferrata can result in fall factors into double figures due to the huge impact forces associated with such a short length of lanyard.

Modern via ferrata sets are therefore incorporating a 'screamer' or shock absorber into the system, where multiple strands of sewn webbing rip and extend during a big fall in order to help reduce the impact forces and spread the shock over the whole system rather than just the attachment points.

Other variations involve the use of a KISA (Kinetic Impact Shock Absorber) – a friction device that allows climbing rope to be pulled through in the event of a fall.

It should be noted that a number of via ferrata lanyards from differing companies have featured in the news over the last few years following a series of product recalls. The engineering difficulties of coping with such massive impact forces can't be overstated, and the onus therefore is on the user to fully research various via ferrata set options, in what is very much developing technology that may change in the future.

CABLE ETIQUETTE

In high season, many of the routes in this guide can become extremely busy with climbers of all nationalities and levels of experience, and there can be great variations in cable etiquette.

It is not uncommon to find yourself behind a slower group or being hassled from behind; use common sense and overtake only when it is safe to do so, and allow people to pass when you are able. It's good practice to try to keep to one person per section of wire in order to avoid the so-called domino effect should someone fall, but realistically on busy routes this is rarely possible as many people will simply clip on to your section without too much consideration.

In terms of cable use, in addition to providing the anchor to the rock, the cable also acts as a constantly available handhold. Using it as an artificial aid for upward progress is both expected and, on the harder routes, required, although many of the via ferratas offer excellent climbing on the rock alongside which can often be less strenuous (and certainly more aesthetic) than hauling on the wire. A common technique is to climb with one hand on the rock and the other on the cable, with the carabiner lanyards resting over the cable arm.

While falling is common in climbing and in fact necessary to push your grade, this mentality should be very much avoided on via ferratas. Due to the potential for huge fall factors and proximity of other climbers, though it may sound obvious the risk of falling should be minimised wherever possible. This includes using the cable for support whenever climbing on the rock is difficult, and using a short rope to assist any members of the party who are struggling and at risk of falling.

Finally, be sure to warn climbers below you in the event of rockfall:

English – 'Below!'
Italian – 'Sassi!'
German – 'Achtung!'

WHAT TO WEAR

When preparing for a via ferrata, it's important to consider both the weather conditions and the characteristics of the route itself. Travelling light and carrying a small pack makes for a more enjoyable day on the hill when the weather is warm and settled. However, as in all high mountain environments the weather can change dramatically; a warm, sunny day can quickly become cold and bleak, while hail or snow can be encountered at any time of year. North-facing routes and those involving enclosed chimneys tend to be colder and damper, while south-facing routes can become veritable suntraps on hot days. During the summer it's worth keeping a lightweight waterproof in your rucksack whatever the forecast.

In terms of footwear, walking boots or approach shoes are generally the tools of choice; climbing shoes are not required and will look a little out of place!

ACCIDENTS AND MOUNTAIN RESCUE

If you are unlucky enough to be involved in an accident, the emergency contact number for mountain rescue is 118. Mobile phone coverage is generally very good in the Dolomites, although there are occasional black spots in the more remote areas. While UK citizens currently have reciprocal health rights in Italy it is strongly recommended you take personal travel insurance and mountain rescue insurance with a provider such as the BMC (www.thebmc.co.uk/insurance) or Austrian Alpine Club. Be sure to check that the policy covers your intended activities. Additionally, it is always worth carrying your European Health Insurance Card (EHIC) with you at all times (www.ehic.org.uk).

A BRIEF HISTORY

The military campaigns of the First World War helped shape the landscape of the Dolomites. However, in 1914, Italy – still a young country and with an ill-prepared army – chose not to enter the war. Instead it spent the first year of hostilities negotiating with the two sides to see which would offer the best terms in any post-war settlement. In 1915, judging that its interests would be best served by throwing in its lot with the allies, it declared war on its old adversary, Austria.

The Mountain War

Judging that the maintenance of its historic borders was unrealistic, Austria retreated to more readily defensible positions in the mountains. By the summer of 1915, previously Austrian towns such as Cortina and

San Martino di Castrozza were occupied by Italian forces. The so-called Mountain War had begun.

This was a war between two ethnic groups: German-speaking mountain folk fought in the Austrian Alpenjäger, while their Italian-speaking neighbours, sometimes friends, opposed them in the ranks of the Alpini. Here was the particular poignancy of a civil war.

Initially, the Italian army advanced slowly, giving the Austrians time to organise their defences, and from late spring 1915 to November 1917 the two sides fought a war of fixed positions, with the front line remaining essentially stationary. Troops slept within earshot of their enemy, and hand-to-hand combat was common. In this war of attrition, both sides sought to establish positions as high as

A soldier stands guard at Cinque Torri during a 'touching history' event

There are many remains from the war to be found scattered around the Dolomites

possible, often on mountain summits. Fortifications established in spring, summer and autumn were maintained through the harsh winters at great cost. The winter of 1916 proved to be particularly bitter, with a record snowfall of 10 metres. More than 10,000 men lost their lives in avalanches that winter. In one incident, at the Austrian barracks below the summit of Gran Poz on Marmolada, some 400 soldiers died in a single avalanche.

Neither side was able to break the stalemate, so an extraordinary underground war of tunnelling and mining ensued. Thousands of metres of tunnels were constructed, designed to undermine enemy positions, which were then destroyed with massive amounts of explosives. At Col di Lana (Route 35) an Italian mine forever altered the shape of its summit, while at Lagazuoi Piccolo (accessed from Route 40) above Passo Falzarego, three huge explosions changed the mountain face dramatically. The cost in human lives was overwhelming, with at least 60,000 soldiers killed in avalanches alone.

The Mountain War ended when, in late 1917, Austrian and German forces broke through the Italian lines at Caporetto, north of Trieste. The Italians, desperate to defend Venice, retreated from the mountains to form defensive positions on the River Piave. This line was held, with the assistance of British and French troops, but the Italian front was now little more than a sideshow, with the major events being played out elsewhere, and which resulted in the armistice in 1918.

The aftermath

Peace was cemented in 1919 by the Treaty of San Germain, which established the national boundaries seen today. Territorially, Italy was a major beneficiary of the peace settlement: in addition to the whole of the Dolomite region, it also secured part of the Dalmatian coast and the port of Trieste. Altogether, some 1.6 million new Italian citizens were acquired, many of whom could not speak Italian. Many families tell of older relatives who were born Austrian, but died Italian.

Despite their Italian nationality, the people of the northern Dolomites still prefer to speak German and demonstrate many expressions of their cultural traditions (including preferring to call their province Sud Tyrol). Unsurprisingly, separatist sentiment can be found not far beneath the surface within the German-speaking community. The government has responded by granting a high degree of autonomy to the Trentino-Alto Adige region, reinforced by generous tax benefits, making the region one of the richest in the country. Unsurprisingly, this creates considerable resentment elsewhere.

History of CAI and rifugios

Prior to the First World War, mountain huts were built across the Alps, including in South Tyrol, by the then German and Austrian Alpine Club (DÖAV). When the area was absorbed into Italy after the war,

these huts were taken over by the Club Alpino Italiano (CAI), becoming rifugios. Sadly, many were subsequently destroyed, or used by Italian soldiers in their attempts to stop insurgency, and from 1922 to 1973 the Austro-Italian border was effectively closed to climbers. Happily, since 1973 many huts have been rebuilt or renovated and now provide an excellent network of facilities throughout the region.

GEOLOGY

The name 'Dolomites' is derived from a French geologist, Déodat Guy Sylvain Tancre de Gratet de Dolomieu – a scholar who, in 1789, was so fascinated by the carbonate rock that he sent samples to Switzerland for classification. When they were classified as being of a previously unknown composition, the rock was named after him. In the 19th century it was mainly British mountaineers who applied the name 'Dolomia' to the area in recognition of his discovery.

Dolomite rock is made up of stratified calcium magnesium carbonate, with some areas of true limestone, some containing more stratified and folded rock than others, depending on the area. For example, in certain areas of the western Dolomites a layer of strata known as the Raibl or Travenanzes Formation can be observed – a characteristic of the significant marine regression typical of the late Triassic period that

Spectacular geology on Sentiero Astaldi (Route 46). The crimson-red coloration is due to the presence of the Raibl layers

contributed to the geological formation of the Dolomites.

Limestone has a reputation for loose rock, the Dolomites being no exception, and the colour of the rocks gives an indication of the firmness or friability: generally, grey and black rocks are water-worn and solid, yellow-coloured rock is only reasonably firm, and red rock is the loosest.

PLANT LIFE

The unique and remarkable geology of the Dolomites gives rise to a rich variety of mountain plants, with some species that can't be found anywhere else in the world. The diverse rock types, from the volcanic ridgeline of Padon to the limestone of the Marmolada, combined with variations in climate and soil fertility at different altitudes, have resulted in a spectacular array of plant life with over 1400 different species recorded across the range. The window of opportunity to view many of these mountain flowers is relatively short and the best time to find them is between June and July when they've emerged from the layers of winter snow that remain on the high mountain peaks.

The valley meadows, which have been cultivated for centuries by farming and grazing and are well supplied with water, are home to an abundance of flowers such as the fragrant orchid (*Gymnadenia conopsea*) and the vibrant orange lily (*Lilium bulbiferum*), also referred to in German as the 'fire lily', which can be seen blooming brightly in the lower meadows in early spring.

The woodland areas mainly consist of conifers, larch, beech and other deciduous species and the tree line is often sharply demarcated, with forest-covered slopes abruptly giving way to the high-altitude alpine terrain above. A variety of species thrive here in the moist, rich soil, including the rare and exquisite lady's slipper orchid (*Cypripedium calceolus*).

The high alpine meadows above the tree line provide the habitat for a different variety of species that flower later in the year, and the density of this biodiversity can be attributed to the fact that these fields have never been ploughed. Spring gentians (*Gentiana verna*) can often be seen scattered across these rocky meadows, as can

Lady's slipper orchid

the famous edelweiss (*Leontopodium alpinum*), which thrives in the thin stony soil. The edelweiss has become an emblem of the Alps but is in fact originally from the steppes of Asia. Due to its association as a 'token of love', the edelweiss almost became extinct in Europe at one stage, with young men risking their lives to climb dangerous slopes and ledges to pick a bunch of the flowers for their loved ones. It is now a protected species and can often be found in the high alpine terrain from July until August.

Perhaps some of the most impressive examples of wildflowers in the Dolomites are the ones that grow in the most unlikely of places and survive in extreme environments. Some plants, like the yellow Rhaetian poppy (*Papaver rhaeticum*), grow on the constantly moving scree slopes with little to no soil, sending deep roots down into the earth to source water and nutrients. Others cling to tiny cracks and crevices high in the cliff face, such as the striking devil's claw (*Physoplexis comosa*), the roots of which are used in herbal medicine as a natural painkiller.

WILDLIFE

Chamoix, ibex, deer and marmots are just a few of the animals you may see during your trip. The chamois, a breed of alpine goat, inhabits the scant grass above the tree line, as does the less common long-haired ibex, which has recently been reintroduced. Roe deer are widespread at lower altitudes in, or close to, tree cover. Colonies of marmots, living in burrows above 1500m, are one of the most common creatures spotted in the Dolomites and are usually heard before they're seen due to their high-pitched whistle.

Until the end of the 19th century, bears were reasonably common in the forests of the Dolomites, but hunting and deforestation led to many years of extinction. However, some were reintroduced into the wild as part of an international 're-wilding' project over the course of the late 1990s. Despite the reintroduction taking place in the hills of south-west Brenta, one of the released bears was found wandering as far afield as Bavaria. It is, however, very rare for bears to be seen in the central and northern Dolomites.

A low-flying buzzard swooping over the Passo Falzarego

Commonly sighted birds include eagles, buzzards, alpine choughs (keep an eye on your packed lunch), woodland grouse or capercaillie (at home in woods and undergrowth), white ptarmigan (which changes its plumage in summer to brown), crows, woodpeckers, owls, alpine tree creepers, jays, skylarks and many species of finch.

Snakes are often encountered basking on paths on warm, sunny afternoons. Most of these are harmless but adders are easily recognised by their chevron patterning; tread carefully so as not to disturb.

A marmot surveys the surrounding area

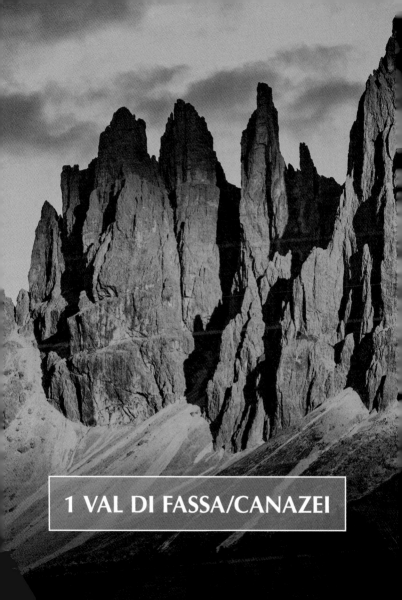

1 VAL DI FASSA/CANAZEI

Last light on the Vajolet Towers as seen from Tires (Routes 3, 4 and 5)

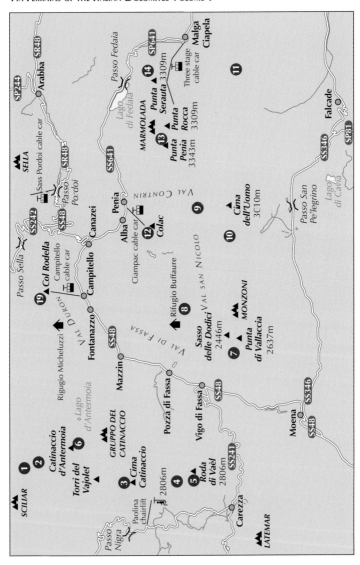

VAL DI FASSA/CANAZEI

Canazei is an attractive and thriving village at the head of Val di Fassa, a classic V-shaped valley. Flanked on all sides by mountain ranges, including the Latemar to the south-east, the Marmolada further to the east, the Catinaccio (Rosengarten) peaks to the west and the Sella group at its head, it is a dramatic and quintessentially dolomitic location and as such an ideal base for many of the routes in this guide.

The valley runs from east to west and is studded with a number of bustling villages, and while Canazei is arguably the most ideally located, Moena, Pozza, Vigo and Campitello are all well situated. Most of the villages boast a good range of shops, including several selling sports equipment, as well as cafés and restaurants of all standards, a tourist office and banks.

Accommodation is readily available and there are options to suit most budgets, whether in the form of luxury hotels, bed and breakfasts, campsites or even *Stellplätze/aree di sosta*, campervan parking areas. As with most alpine areas, the tourist network is very seasonal; prices and availability differ significantly between low and high season, and August in particular can be very busy.

The valley is reasonably well served by public transport, with several buses a day travelling up the valley from Bolzano and back, and the occasional service serving the Pordoi, Sella and Fedaia passes. Unfortunately however, these services are only in operation during high season (late June to the start of September), and given that the described routes are scattered throughout the region, a car is highly recommended to get the most out of the area. Similarly, the wide geographic distribution of the routes in this region involves several different mountain groups.

Some of the via ferratas in this chapter can be approached using the summer cable car (or chairlift) services, reducing the physical effort required; again, these tend to run in high season and it is well worth checking the dates before planning a trip (see Appendix A for contact details). Another useful transport service is a return minibus shuttle between Pera di Fassa to Rifugio Gardeccia, providing easy access to the Catinaccio group.

There is a wide range of routes accessible from Val di Fassa. Many are amongst the easier grades and offer excellent if technically straightforward mountain days, while others are more serious undertakings and may be dependent on good weather, mountain conditions and familiarity with remote mountainous terrain.

Located between **Val di Fassa** and the **Sciliar Natural Park**, Routes 1 and 2 may be accessed from Val di Fassa in the south or Alpe di Siusi in the north. Regardless of the chosen approach, both routes involve fairly long days in the mountains: Route 1 provides an exposed yet relatively low-grade itinerary while Route 2 is one of the more serious via ferratas found within the Dolomites. The routes may also be enjoyably combined with an overnight stay at the well-located Rifugio Alpe di Tires.

Passo Costalunga (also signed as Karerpass and Passo Carezza) marks the southern limit of the Catinaccio Group. In winter the pleasant skiing area is part of the Dolomiti Superski network and as such there are numerous accommodation options clustered around the top of the pass. Routes 3, 4 and 5 are best accessed from Passo Costalunga. While not especially hard, all three provide interesting outings and are fine mountain days in a spectacular setting.

A thriving little village in the centre of Val di Fassa, **Pozza** affords excellent access to Routes 6 to 9. Each of these routes has a very different character; Route 6 takes place in the heart of the Catinaccio and reaches the summit of Catinccio d'Antermoia, the only 3000-metre peak in the group, while Routes 7, 8 and 9 explore the beautiful Val San Nicolo. There is something for most abilities and tastes, with Route 7 offering a technically easy but long day while the more modern Route 8 is the hardest via ferrata in the Dolomites.

Routes 10 and 11 are rather remote, located between the towns of **Moena** at the southern end of Val di Fassa and **Falcade** to the east. If approaching from the east, Passo San Pellegrino can also be accessed from Agordo or Belluno – there are several other routes in these areas which are covered in Volume 2 of this guide.

The two via ferratas described in this area are not particularly difficult but nonetheless offer excellent mountain days, while the fact that these mountains are not quite as popular as some of the better-known groups in the Dolomites means that they are often much quieter. Route 10 is also particularly interesting for its historical significance.

Just to the south-east of **Canazei** stands Marmolada, the highest mountain in the Dolomites. Route 13 reaches the summit at 3343m, while Route 14 tackles the broad slabs and ridgeline of its eastern side. Given the high altitude of these routes, not to mention the length and serious terrain, both routes on Marmolada should be attempted in good weather with good visibility. Although included in this section, Route 12 does not take place on Marmolada but on nearby Colac, as such affording excellent views into the group.

ROUTE 1
Sentiero Massimiliano

Start/Finish	Val Duron valley entrance, Campitello di Fassa
Distance	24km
Total ascent/descent	1300m
Grade	2B
Time	6–10hr (or 3hr round-trip from Rifugio Alpe di Tires)
Wire length	200m
Map	Tabacco 06
Parking	Val Duron valley entrance: 46.47807, 11.74087

Although not technically challenging, this route unfolds along the spectacular Terrarossa ridgeline and offers some sections of unprotected and rather exposed scrambling. The panorama over the Catinaccio group and the Alpe di Siusi is superb and the rock offers enjoyable yet straightforward progression. The route can be climbed in either direction, although the east to west direction described here is recommended.

Driving approach
Enter the village of Campitello and follow signs for Val Duron/Rifugio Micheluzzi to reach a parking area at around 1500m (the unsurfaced road beyond this point is closed to private vehicles). Begin the approach from here, or alternatively make use of an inexpensive taxi shuttle which connects the parking area to Rifugio Micheluzzi, taking around 10 minutes and saving about an hour's walking (Taxi Prinoth tel +39 339 2796383 or Taxi Volpe tel +39 336 352881).

From the parking area, follow the unsurfaced road towards Val Duron, following signs and waymarks to Rifugio Micheluzzi. There are several parallel paths which avoid walking on the road, rejoining at various points. On reaching **Rifugio Micheluzzi** take the path to the right of the building, signed for Alpe di Siusi/Antermoia, passing **Baita Lino Brach** (a chalet/rifugio) in 15min.

Continue on the track (waymarked 532), passing the junction for path 578 (the return from Route 2) in a further 10min. The track continues to ascend the pretty Val Duron, dominated by the walls of Molignon rising vertically at the head of the valley. Pass the beautifully situated **Malga Docoldaura** (a farmhouse that sells home-made produce) to reach **Passo Duron** (2204m) and then continue along the track (waymarked path 4) to reach **Rifugio Alpe di Tires** (2441m) about 2hr after passing the junction for path 578.

Sentiero Massimilliano is signed from the back of the rifugio; follow the sporadic waymarks up a loose gully to reach the first short section of cable, then continue alternating on and off the wire to reach a col, affording a dramatic view down to Alpe di Siusi. From the col, follow the cables up to the left to gain the unprotected airy crest leading to the summit of **Dente Grande di Terrarossa** (2653m), again offering superb views.

From the summit, take the switchbacks down to the west to pass through a characteristic rock archway, then downclimb a steep protected section for 25 metres to continue along the exposed and unprotected ridge. Descend a short but steep chimney on good rock protected by a single metal ring, then continue to the end of the ridge to pass a sign marked 'Notausteig/Rientro d'Emergenza' – this is an unpleasant escape route down to Rifugio Alpe di Tires and should only be

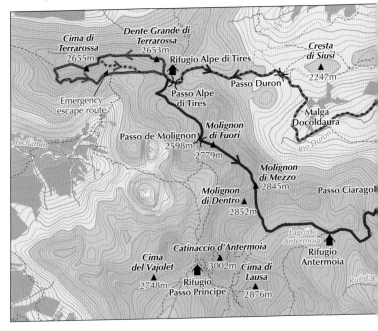

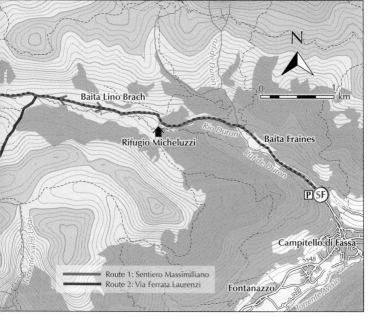

On the final section of Sentiero Massimiliano with Rifugio Alpe di Tires visible in the bottom of the valley.

descended in an emergency. From here a mixture of unprotected scrambling and wire protection ascends to the summit of **Cima di Terrarossa** (2655m), reached just over 1½hr after Rifugio Alpe di Tires.

The descent from the summit is unprotected and reaches the junction for path 3/4 in around 5min. To return to Rifugio Alpe di Tires, follow this southeast, descending a further 100 metres and traversing back to the **rifugio** in around 30min. Here it is possible to either stay the night and complete Via Ferrata Laurenzi (Route 2) the next day, or return directly to Val Duron by retracing the ascent route down paths 4 and 532. The descent from Rifugio Alpe di Tires to the **car park** takes around 2½hr.

Other possibilities

There are a number of alternative approaches to Rifugio Alpe di Tires:

- from the west, via Tires/Lavina Bianca and Val Ciamin/Tschamintal (3½–4hr, 9km, 1310m ascent);
- from the north, using the Panorama chairlift (June to September, 9am to 5pm) from Compaccio in the Alpe di Siusi (parking fee) (2½hr, 5km, 500m ascent);
- from the south, from Rifugio Vajolet in the Catinaccio group (2½hr, 5.5km, 750m ascent).

ROUTE 2
Via Ferrata Laurenzi

Start/Finish	Val Duron valley entrance, Campitello di Fassa
Distance	29km
Total ascent/descent	1350m
Grade	4C
Time	9–12hr
Wire length	850m
Map	Tabacco 06
Parking	Val Duron valley entrance: 46.47807, 11.74087
Note	For route map see Route 1

A long and very remote mountain day, Via Ferrata Laurenzi traces the dramatic and airy Molignon ridge, offering stunning situations and challenging climbing – not least because of the amount of down climbing involved. The route has recently been re-equipped, reducing the exposure and making the climbing easier, although it should still not be underestimated. Less confident parties may still benefit from taking a safety rope. The route can be climbed in either direction, although a traverse from north to south is recommended. Although reasonably well marked, the route can be difficult to navigate in poor weather.

Driving approach
Enter the village of Campitello and follow signs for Val Duron/Rifugio Micheluzzi to reach a parking area at around 1500m (the unsurfaced road beyond this point is closed to private vehicles). Begin the approach from here, or alternatively make use of an inexpensive taxi shuttle which connects the parking area to Rifugio Micheluzzi, taking around 10 minutes and saving about an hour's walking (Taxi Prinoth tel +39 339 2796383 or Taxi Volpe tel +39 336 352881).

From the parking area, follow the unsurfaced road towards Val Duron, following signs and waymarks to Rifugio Micheluzzi. There are a number of parallel paths which avoid walking on the road, rejoining at various points. On reaching **Rifugio Micheluzzi** take the path to the right of the building, signed for Alpe di Suisi/Antermoia, passing **Baita Lino Brach** in 15min.

Continue on the track (waymarked 532), passing the junction for path 578 (taken on the return) in a further 10min. The track continues to ascend the pretty Val Duron, dominated by the walls of Molignon (where the route develops) rising vertically at the head of the valley. Pass the beautifully situated **Malga Docoldaura** to reach **Passo Duron** (2204m) and then continue along the track (waymarked path 4) to **Rifugio Alpe di Tires** (2441m).

From the rifugio, head south on path 3B-554 and continue up the easily angled wall protected by a rather unnecessary cable. At the top of the slab, follow the track left (south-east) to continue along a broad, rounded ridge. At **Passo de Molignon** (2598m), ignore the main path leading south into the heart of the Catinaccio group and instead follow the sign left (east) towards Via Ferrata Laurenzi. An easy scramble leads to the start of the route, marked with a CAI sign detailing safe use of equipment. The approach from Rifugio Alpe di Tires takes around 45min.

The route begins with an easy scramble up a broken rib, protected by a short section of cable. As the angle eases, continue on unprotected but easier terrain to reach the airy ridge above. This soon widens out into a broad plateau of **Molignon di Fuori**; continue to follow the waymarks and cairns to reach two closely adjoining subsidiary summits rising out of the plateau.

Descend an exposed yet technically straightforward section protected by cable to reach the saddle below the second peak, then continue to gain the ridge beyond. Here the exposure is particularly pronounced with excellent views of the Marmolada south face; make use of the good footholds and avoid the temptation to climb too high. Continue on easier ground, now with intermittent protection but still very airy in places.

A section of cable protects a more challenging undulating traverse through a succession of small broken pinnacles, some of which are bypassed on the east and others on the west side of the ridge. This section culminates in the descent of a 30-metre buttress; the climbing is steep and the holds not always obvious. The protection is reasonable but relatively inexperienced climbers might welcome the security of a top rope for this rather awkward descent.

From the narrow gap below, continue along a broken slab protected only by a line of metal hoops drilled into the rock. A shallow cave shortly after contains the route book. A slope of broken rock now leads to another passage of relatively easy, but strikingly exposed ridge walking. Although unprotected with cable, occasional steel bolts provide belay points if required.

An easy walk up to the summit of **Molignon di Mezzo** (2845m) follows, with fantastic views in all directions. The highest point, Molignon di Dentro (2852m), can be reached via a short stroll past the waymarked descent route leading right (south-west).

To begin the descent, follow this path down steep and exposed switchbacks then continue onto a very broken and broad rib, protected by cable along the most difficult sections. Descend a steep and rather challenging buttress on excellent rock and good cable protection to reach another CAI sign marking the end of the via ferrata.

The descent route now follows path 584 to the broad Vallon de Antermoia below. This runs eastwards to Lago de Antermoia and its adjoining rifugio, although neither is visible from this point. Follow the waymarks down a broken rib alongside an easy-angled scree gully to the left. Where the rib steepens uncomfortably, move into the gully and descend to the valley bottom, aiming for the large, prominent boulder alongside the main track.

Continue to descend easily past the **lake** and on to the **rifugio**. Follow the signs for path 580 to reach **Passo Ciaragole** (2282m), then take either path 555 or path 578 to return to the floor of Val Duron. From here either continue right to the **car park** above Campitello, or left if returning to Rifugio Alpe di Tires.

Other possibilities

There are a number of alternative approaches to Rifugio Alpe di Tires, as follows:
- from the west, via Tires/Lavina Bianca and Val Ciamin/Tschamintal (3½–4hr, 9km, 1310m ascent);
- from the north, using the Panorama chairlift (June to September, 9am to 5pm) from Compaccio in the Alpe di Siusi (parking fee) (2½hr, 5km, 500m ascent);

Superb compact rock on the middle section of Via Ferrata Laurenzi, with views of Marmolada's south face

- from the south, from Rifugio Vajolet in the Catinaccio group (2½hr 5.5km, 750m ascent).

It is recommended to complete this route in conjunction with Route 1, spending the night at Rifugio Alpe di Tires (2440m, tel +39 0471 727958).

ROUTE 3
Via Ferrata Passo Santner

Start/Finish	Top of Laurin chairlift
Distance	8km
Total ascent/descent	900m
Grade	2A
Time	6hr
Wire length	300m
Map	Tabacco 06
Parking	Frommer Alm and Laurin chairlift: 46.44379, 11.58907

Despite the limited wire protection and relatively straightforward grade, this is a good mountain excursion that can be completed as a day route in around 6hr. It offers excellent views into the heart of the Catinaccio group and benefits from chairlift access, making it an accessible and consequently very popular route. The chairlift runs in high season (June to mid October) and closes for an hour around lunchtime.

Driving approach
From Canazei, follow the SS48 west past the villages of Campitello and Pozza di Fassa to reach the outskirts of Vigo di Fassa. Here turn right, following signs for Passo Costalunga/Karerpass. Continue beyond the top of the pass then shortly afterwards keep right to take the road for Passo Nigra, parking in the ample spaces below Frommer Alm (restaurant) at the base of the Laurin chairlift. Take the chairlift (a return ticket is recommended to avoid the long descent) to arrive at Rifugio Fronza in around 20 minutes.

From the top of the chairlift follow path 542/550 directly uphill, with some scrambling and a very short section of wire, to quickly reach a fork. Keep left, following path 542 north for around 30min to reach an ascending ramp with some fairly exposed and straightforward scrambling. The route is well-marked and logical, climbing through a series of interesting gullies and ascending a short ladder to reach a section of more continuous wire protection.

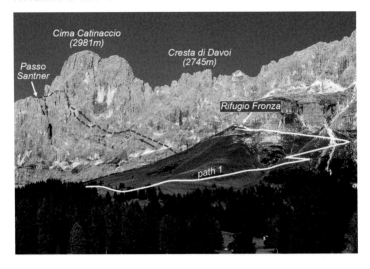

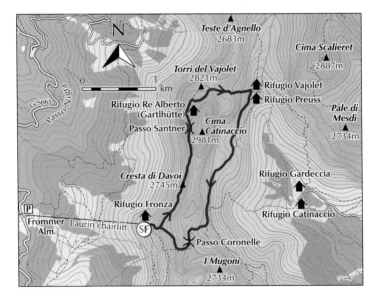

Continue through a cleft between two rock walls then descend to cross a wide gully; late-lying snow is possible here. From the gully, ascend the final section of wire to gain **Passo Santner**, reached in around 2hr from the start.

From the col, descend path 542 to quickly reach **Rifugio Re Alberto (Gartlhütte)**, with panoramic views of the famous Torri del Vajolet above. Continue downhill towards Rifugio Vajolet, descending a steep and unpleasant gully protected in part by cable. After descending for 35min rifugios Preuss and Vajolet should come into view. Don't follow path 542 down to the rifugios but instead branch right onto an unsigned path (unmarked on the map), traversing below a rock buttress around to the southern side of Catinaccio. This path is narrow and exposed at first, passing an airy corner before ascending through boulders to join path 541.

Follow path 541 uphill (south) to join path 550 at a signpost for Passo Coronelle. Follow this up steep switchbacks to reach the **col**, then continue steeply down the other side to **Rifugio Fronza** and the chairlift. The return from Passo Santner takes around 3–3½hr.

Other possibilities

If undertaking the route in low season or to save the chairlift fare, it is possible to walk up to Rifugio Fronza from Frommer Alm, ascending paths 15 and 1 to reach the rifugio in around 1½hr.

For a shorter but less satisfying day, it's possible to reverse the route from Rifugio Re Alberto (Gartlhutte).

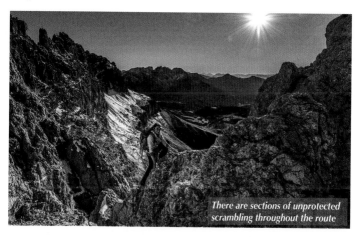

There are sections of unprotected scrambling throughout the route

ROUTE 4
Via Ferrata Roda di Vaèl

Start/Finish	Top of Paolina chairlift
Distance	6.5km
Total ascent/descent	700m
Grade	1B
Time	4–5hr
Wire length	350m
Map	Tabacco 06
Parking	Paolina chairlift: 46.40773, 11.5916
Note	For topo see Route 5

Despite the low grade, the cabled route to Roda di Vaèl (Rotwand) is an enjoyable excursion and highly rewarding in terms of scenery, offering spectacular glimpses into the heart of the Catinaccio group. The ascent is straightforward and the cables protecting the final ascent to the summit are well placed. The route is also easily combinable with Via Ferrata Masare (Route 5) to create a complete and exciting ridge traverse.

Driving approach
From Canazei, follow the SS48 west past the villages of Campitello and Pozza di Fassa to reach the outskirts of Vigo di Fassa. Here turn right, following signs for Passo Costalunga/Karerpass. Follow the road to the top of the pass, passing Hotel Savoy and keeping left at the junction with the Passo Nigra road to descend to the large parking areas either side of the road below the Paolina chairlift on the right. Take the chairlift (open June to October) to Rifugio Paolina.

From the top of the chairlift turn left to follow path 552 along the hillside. Where possible, take a path leading right which switchbacks up to join path 549 then continue left (north) along this to reach the junction with path 551 below a steep scree gully.

Turn right onto path 551 and ascend steep terrain to reach **Passo di Vaiolon**, in around 1½hr from the top of the chairlift. On reaching the pass turn right (south) and follow a waymarked path on steep but well-protected terrain. A final inclined section leads to the summit of **Roda di Vaèl** at 2806m.

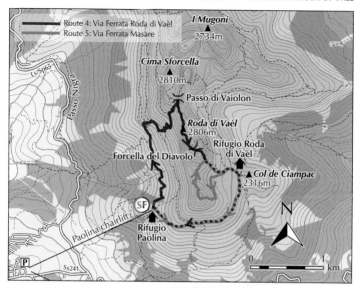

To descend, continue over the summit to follow the south side of the ridge, descending a steep open slope before reaching a junction at the end of Via Ferrata Masare (Route 5). Keep left here and descend more easily to reach **Rifugio Roda di Vaèl** below in just under an hour from Passo di Vaiolon.

From the rifugio follow signs for path 549 and contour the hillside first south and then west, eventually branching left onto path 539 to return to the top of the **Paolina chairlift**.

Other possibilities

Although a worthwhile excursion in itself, Roda di Vaèl is arguably best climbed in conjunction with Via Ferrata Masare (Route 5). To do so, complete Route 5 as described until the end of the via ferrata and the sign for Roda di Vaèl. Here turn left and continue upwards along the path to reach **Forcella del Diavolo** (2560m), characterised by a distinctive hole in the rock wall to the right. At the top of the grassy slope to the left of the hole, follow the cable as it descends steeply, with some testing moves, to reach a col with dirty, broken rock and steep gullies to either side.

After an awkward first move out of the col, climb a short ladder then continue following the path with intermittent wire protection before the angle of ascent

57

eases. Continue easily to the summit of **Roda di Vaèl** (2806m), reached in around 1–1¼hr from the junction with the standard descent.

From the summit, continue north to reach Passo di Vaiolon in about 30min. From here descend west on path 551; this zigzags down a gully before turning left and traversing below some impressive rock walls. Continue to follow way-marks downhill and generally west to reach path 549. Follow this south, making a panoramic undulating traverse. Branch right onto a path zigzagging down a grassy slope to return to the top of the **Paolina chairlift** (about 1hr from Passo di Vaiolon).

ROUTE 5

Via Ferrata Masare

Start/Finish	Top of Paolina chairlift
Distance	7km
Total ascent/descent	900m
Grade	2B
Time	4hr (7–8hr when combined with Route 4)
Wire length	400m (750m when combined with Route 4)
Map	Tabacco 06
Parking	Paolina chairlift: 46.40773, 11.5916
Note	For route map see Route 4

A superb ridge on the edge of the Catinaccio group, Via Ferrata Masare is a short but excellent mountain day with stunning situations and enjoyable if unchallenging climbing. It is best combined with an ascent of Roda di Vaèl (Route 4), enabling a long and airy traverse taking in a variety of views.

Driving approach

From Canazei follow the SS48 west past the villages of Campitello and Pozza di Fassa to reach the outskirts of Vigo di Fassa. Here turn right, following signs for Passo Costalunga/Karerpass. Follow the road to the top of the pass, passing Hotel Savoy and keeping left at the junction with the Passo Nigra road to descend to the large parking areas either side of the road below the Paolina chairlift on the right. Take the Paolina chairlift (open June to October) to reach Rifugio Paolina.

From the top of the chairlift follow signs for Rifugio Roda di Vaèl along path 539/549. From the rifugio, Via Ferrata Masare is clearly signposted; follow the path up towards the left (south) end of Punta Masare, passing through a large boulder field before ascending switchbacks to the end of the ridge and the start of the cable (reached in about 30min from the rifugio).

While the via ferrata route is easy to follow, protection is not continuous and there are some unprotected moves in quite exposed, airy situations. After about 2hr and a significant loss of height, reach the end of Via Ferrata Masare and continue on a path traversing a steep grassy hillside. Soon after, Via Ferrata Roda di Vaèl is signed uphill to the left (see 'Other possibilities'); otherwise, to complete Via Ferrata Masare as a standalone route, keep right and downclimb a section of cable to join the path leading back to **Rifugio Roda di Vaèl**, reached in around 30min. From here reverse the approach route back to the **Paolina chairlift**.

Other possibilities

- This route is best combined with an ascent of Roda di Vaèl (Route 4). From the fork at the end of the Masare ridge, keep left and continue upwards along the path, following signs for Via Ferrata Roda di Vaèl to reach Forcella del Diavolo (2560m), characterised by a distinctive hole in the rock wall to the right. At the top of the grassy slope to the left of the hole, follow the cable as it descends steeply, with some testing moves, to reach a col with dirty, broken

4: Via Ferrata Roda di Vaèl 1B
5: Via Ferrata Masare 2B

Roda di Vaèl
(2806m)

4

Rifugio Roda di Vaèl

5

Following the undulating ridgeline of Masare

rock and steep gullies to either side. After an awkward first move out of the col, climb a short ladder then continue following the path with intermittent wire protection before the angle of ascent eases. Continue easily to the summit of **Roda di Vaèl** (2806m), reached in around 1–1¼hr from the junction with the standard descent. From the summit, continue north to reach Passo di Vaiolon in about 30min. From here descend west on path 551; this zigzags down a gully before turning left and traversing below some impressive rock walls. Continue to follow waymarks downhill and generally west to reach path 549. Follow this south, making a panoramic undulating traverse. Branch right onto a path zigzagging down a grassy slope to return to the top of the **Paolina chairlift** (about 1hr from Passo di Vaiolon).

- If undertaking the route in low season or to avoid paying the chairlift fare, it's possible to turn right just before reaching the chairlift onto the Passo Nigra road and drive for a further 1.5km to a parking area alongside the road. Walk up the vehicle track leading towards the rock walls above, following this around to the right as it becomes path 1A. Shortly after crossing under the chairlift, turn left onto path 6A and continue more steeply uphill to join with path 552, following this for a final steep section to the top of the **Paolina chairlift**. This adds around 350m of ascent over 2km.

ROUTE 6
Via Ferrata Catinaccio d'Antermoia

Start/Finish	Rifugio Gardeccia
Distance	10km
Total ascent/descent	1150m
Grade	2B
Time	6–8hr
Wire length	600m
Map	Tabacco 06
Parking	Pera-Gardeccia bus navetta car park: 46.43868, 11.69333

Reaching the highest peak in the group, this relatively easy via ferrata encounters some exposed and unprotected sections, particularly the final 50 metres along the ridge to the summit. However, the route is in a truly grand mountain setting and the effort is rewarded by superb views and the satisfaction of gaining a 3000-metre peak. Given the drama of the surrounding scenery and the ease of access from the taxi service, this area can be very busy in high season.

Driving approach
From Canazei, follow the SS48 west to reach Pera, parking in the well-signed Pera-Gardeccia bus navetta car park to the left of the main road, located just below a pedestrian walkway over the road serving the winter ski lifts. Take the taxi shuttle to Rifugio Gardeccia; tickets can be bought at the wooden ticket office in the car park and while it is generally not required to pre-book, the service does get busy in high season. The taxi runs from mid June to early September, with the uphill service operating from 7.55am–6.25pm and the downhill service from 8.30am–12.30pm and 2.30pm–7pm. A return ticket is well worth the extra money to avoid a long and laborious descent.

From Rifugio Gardeccia, follow path 546 to **Rifugio Vajolet** and then continue up the valley on path 584 to **Passo Principe**, reached in around 2–3hr. Follow an arrow on the right to ascend the path to quickly reach the start of the via ferrata.

Walk left along a ledge below an overhang then continue up unprotected and exposed ground until reaching a short ladder. Downclimb this, then continue following intermittent cable and waymarks to reach the exposed summit ridge. Follow this to quickly gain the summit of **Catinaccio d'Antermoia** (3002m), reached in 1–1½hr from Passo Principe.

To descend, continue down the easy ridge, protected in part by cable and well waymarked throughout, to reach the end of the via ferrata at the head of Val d'Antermoia in just under 1hr (optional descent now possible using Sentiero Attrezzato Scalette – see below). From here, ascend path 584 south-west to **Passo Antermoia** then contour below the rock walls to return to **Passo Principe**, reversing the approach route to return to **Rifugio Gardeccia** (2–3hr).

Other possibilities
For a longer but more complete day, it is also possible to combine this route with Sentiero Attrezzato Scalette (grade 1A, 400m of additional ascent and 60m of cable) – a protected path affording a scenic and quieter alternative to the more popular return via Passo Principle.

From Val d'Antermoia, continue descending then follow path 583B – an obvious but poorly waymarked path – to **Passo di Lausa**. On reaching the pass, follow path 583 down into an expansive glacial valley enclosed by rocky ridges, crossing a bridge (dam wall) and ascending briefly to reach **Passo Scalette** just under an hour after Passo di Lausa

Catinaccio d'Antermoia
(3002m)

path 584

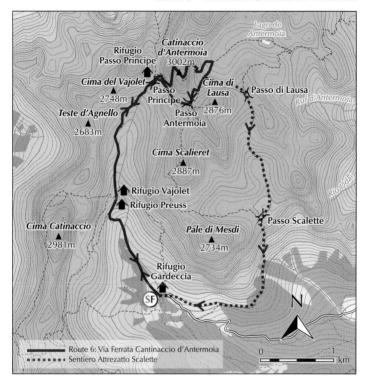

The descent continues down a wide, rocky gully with a very short protected section; this is not particularly exposed and is quite easy to descend. At the end of the gully, ascend slightly then traverse through pine woods back to **Rifugio Gardeccia**, reached in about 1½hr from Passo Scalette.

Excellent views towards the north and Sassolungo (Route 7)

THE CATINACCIO (ROSENGARTEN) MOUNTAINS

According to local folklore, the Catinaccio group was once ruled by the dwarf leader Laurino, who tended a beautiful rose garden at the heart of his domain. The surrounding land was ruled by King Adige, who one day announced his beautiful daughter Similde was to be wed. Adige threw a great feast in order to find his daughter an appropriate suitor, to which all the neighbouring nobles were invited; all the nobles except for Laurino that is. However, the dwarf leader decided to attend in secret, hiding beneath an invisibility cloak. On arrival he immediately became infatuated with Similde and stole her onto his horse, riding back to the relative safety of the Catinaccio mountains. The other nobles gave chase and Laurino, soon heavily outnumbered, sought refuge in his beloved rose garden, but his enemies spotted the roses moving and Laurino was captured. Furious at being taken prisoner, he cursed the rose garden, vowing that no human would ever see its beauty again, by day or night – and so it was that the alluring roses turned to stone. However, Laurino forgot one thing: twilight. So it is that every evening the roses shine pink through the rock, giving the mountains their famous hue.

ROUTE 7

Via Ferrata Franco Gadotti

Start/Finish	Malga Crocifisso chapel
Distance	12.5km
Total ascent/descent	1100m
Grade	2C
Time	7–8hr
Wire length	400m
Map	Tabacco 06
Parking	Malga Crocifisso chapel: 46.41666, 11.71936

This is a fairly easy via ferrata but a really good mountain day, offering superb panoramas of Catinaccio, Val di Fassa, Marmolada and the Sella massif. The grade of the route is more indicative of the strenuous and sometimes exposed nature of the route as opposed to any true technical difficulty.

Driving approach

From Canazei, follow the SS48 west to the roundabout outside Pozza di Fassa and turn left into the village, following signs for Val San Nicolo. Follow the road out of the village to reach Malga Crocifisso on the right and park by the chapel just before the road splits.

Walk back down the road below Malga Crocifisso for 200 metres to reach path 615 bis (not marked on some maps). Begin to ascend this steeply to the south, following abundant waymarks through the pine trees to reach the more major path 615 coming up from Soldanella (it is also possible to access the route from here).

Around 45min after leaving the car park, continue to ascend directly uphill, crossing path 635. Pass a number of large boulders to reach a short cabled section (wet after periods of rain) serving as a useful handrail. After a further 20min arrive at **Bivacco Donato Zeni** then continue for 5min beyond this to the start of the via ferrata, reached in 1½hr from Malga Crocifisso.

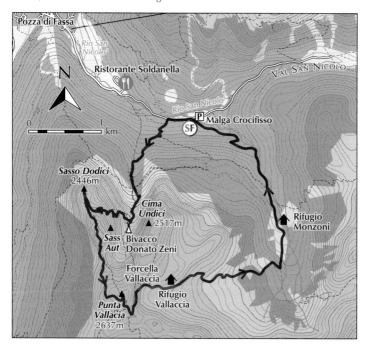

The route is characterised by intermittent wire and sections of unprotected walking on steep ground. There are a number of exposed moves but the route is technically easy and the protection is very good.

On reaching a col, descend slightly to the left before following a rising traverse path around a classic glacial bowl, reaching the ridge below Sasso Dodici in around 1hr from the start of the via ferrata. On a clear day, the additional 10min to the summit cross of **Sasso Dodici** (2446m) located to the north are well worthwhile for the wonderful views down to Val di Fassa, across the Sella, to Sassolungo and beyond.

Return to the ridge and follow signs for 'Forcella Vallaccia', crossing a series of ledges intermittently protected with cable to reach the grassy slope below **Sass Aut**. Either ascend to the summit direct or alternatively take a traversing path leading to the eastern side of the peak to avoid the summit entirely.

From the summit of Sass Aut, follow waymarks leading south to a large muddy gully with wire protection on its right. Descend for about 100 metres then continue through a spectacular hole on the left to descend a steep but well-protected enclosed gully beneath large wedged boulders. Continue to descend for a further 100 metres to the end of the wire protection, reached in just under 1hr from the summit of Sasso Dodici.

Now make a rising traverse south, passing large rock walls on the left, to reach a col. From here follow the path left (east) to ascend to the summit of **Punta**

Vallaccia (2637m) in about 45min from the end of the via ferrata, again with superb panoramic views. The total time of the route to this point is 4–5hr.

Descend to path 624, at first retracing your steps then continuing east down a ridge to a signpost. Continue to follow path 624, descending north into the open grassy bowl on the left. After a short while pass **Rifugio Vallaccia** then continue to join path 603. Follow this past **Rifugio Monzoni** and continue easily along the road back to **Malga Crocifisso**, reached in under 2hr from Punta Vallaccia.

ROUTE 8
Via Ferrata I Magnifici Quattro

Start/Finish	Malga Crocifisso chapel
Distance	8km
Total ascent/descent	600m
Grade	6B
Time	4–5hr
Wire length	400m
Map	Tabacco 06
Parking	Malga Crocifisso chapel: 46.41666, 11.71936

Constructed in 2009 in memory of four mountain rescue workers who lost their lives in a tragic rescue attempt in Val Lasties, I Magnifici Quattro is a challenging via ferrata that ascends the dramatic Maerins towers. Very much of modern conception, the climbing relies heavily on artificial holds and is superbly protected with wire and stemples. The exposed and strenuous traverse is undoubtedly the highlight of the route.

Driving approach
From Canazei, follow the SS48 west for 12km to reach a roundabout outside the village of Pozza di Fassa. Turn left here into the village and follow signs for Val San Nicolo. Continue to reach Malga Crocifisso and park on the verge by the chapel.

From the chapel, follow the road up the valley for a short way to reach a fork; keep left and cross a bridge. Continue up the road above to reach two bridges followed by a wooden hut bearing signs for the via ferrata. Follow the signs right

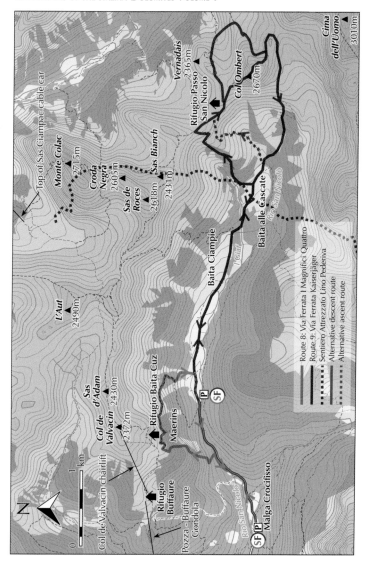

Route 8: Via Ferrata I Magnifici Quattro
Route 9: Via Ferrata Kaiserjäger
Sentiero Attrezzato Lino Pederiva
Alternative descent route
Alternative ascent route

alongside the stream to reach a fork and keep left, still following signs. At the next junction continue straight on and ascend a series of steep switchbacks to exit the trees by the rock face.

A plaque and information board mark the start of the route itself, reached around 30min after departing the parking area. Follow the wire steeply to the back of the damp cleft then make an ascending traverse left and then right. Continue more easily to reach a corner and ascend stemples to reach the strenuous traverse that characterises the route.

The traverse itself is exposed but exceptionally well protected, with the most tiring aspect being the continual clipping over each short section of wire. The wire then leads vertically up to enter back into trees and into a section of easy and unprotected walking with good views of the two Maerin rock towers to the right.

Follow the obvious path below the rocky cliffs for a short distance before encountering sections of intermittent cable which lead over straightforward terrain to the base of a distinctive tower. Here more continuous wire ascends the rounded arête of the tower steeply, finally reaching easier ground and a series of ledges. Head left around a corner to reach stemples leading up to a small niche housing the route book, then traverse left before exiting onto the plateau above by Baita Cuz, rewarding you with views over Val di Fassa to the Catinaccio group.

To descend, follow a small path right (east) towards the head of Val San Nicolo, following signs to Punta Panoramica Maerins and Val San Nicolo. Where the path splits, keep left (right leads to a scenic viewpoint overlooking the valley

Making the characteristic, memorable and exposed traverse in the middle of the route

below) and descend through the woodland to exit into the wide valley bottom. Here turn right and follow the large track back to **Malga Crocifisso**.

Other possibilities

For those wanting a longer itinerary, it is possible to link this route with an ascent of Via Ferrata Kaiserjäger on Col Ombert (Route 9). From Baita Cuz traverse the northern edge of Val San Nicolo, following path 613 and then 613B along Sentiero Attrezzato Lino Pederiva to reach **Rifugio Passo San Nicolo** and **Col Ombert**. This makes for an exceptionally long day and should only be attempted by suitably fit parties. (From start to finish linking the two routes: 10–12hr, 15km, 1100m ascent.)

ROUTE 9
Via Ferrata Kaiserjäger

Start/Finish	Val San Nicolo car park
Distance	14km
Total ascent/descent	1050m
Grade	4C
Time	6–7hr
Wire length	260m
Map	Tabacco 06
Parking	Val San Nicolo visitors' car park: 46.4239, 11.74099
Note	For route map see Route 8

This via ferrata was built in 1915 by the Austrian Kaiserjäger troops (hence its name), and was rebuilt in 1996, with many remnants of the original protection still visible alongside the new cabling. The route reaches the scenic summit of Col Ombert and although the via ferrata itself is relatively short, there are several quite strenuous passages to overcome which may feel challenging for the grade. The rock is friable for much of the ferrata and as such the route is a fairly serious undertaking.

Driving approach
From Canazei, follow the SS48 west to the roundabout outside Pozza di Fassa and turn left into the village, following signs for Val San Nicolo. Follow the road out of the village to reach Malga Crocifisso and where the road splits keep left to reach the large car park at the foot of Val San Nicolo (a parking charge applies in high season).

Follow the main path waymarked 608 up through the valley for 40min, passing **Baita Ciampi** to reach a left turn just before **Baita alle Cascate** (the old route followed the vehicle track past the hut itself). Turn left onto this newly made path, following signs to the via ferrata and Rifugio Passo San Nicolo.

Ascend steep switchbacks to reach the ridgeline above, with dramatic views of Col Ombert ahead, and join path 613. Follow this right for 200 metres to **Rifugio Passo San Nicolo**, reached in just under 2hr from the car park.

Follow the rather superfluous sign for the via ferrata to reach the prominent bulk of Col Ombert. A short 15-minute scramble leads to the start of the cable, marked by a route plaque and a section of an original ladder. The climbing is immediately steep and quite challenging, with the first of the strenuous passages reached within 15 metres.

After overcoming the first section the climbing eases for a time, although the rock is now very friable. Continue up another steep and strenuous passage to reach an easier-angled area of slabby rock, roughly the halfway point of the climb. From this point progression is considerably faster; continue up a succession of steep walls before making an airy rightward traverse on a broad ledge to reach easier ground.

Climb a steep but technically straightforward shattered corner to reach the last of the steep walls and continue for a few metres to the end of the cable. A short 20-metre scramble leads to the cross on the summit of **Col Ombert**.

On the final section of ascent just below the summit of Col Ombert

The descent takes an unpleasant-looking path down to the south-east; follow switchbacks down eroded ground to reach a huge and desolate bowl. Here the path forks and you must choose which descent option you wish to take.

The left-hand route provides the most direct route if you wish to return to Rifugio Passo San Nicolo. The path descends through scree (not obvious) until it joins path 609. Follow this east for 300 metres until a connecting path leading north joins path 608, which you follow left back to **Rifugio Passo San Nicolo**.

The right-hand route provides the best continuation of a circuit back down into Val San Nicolo and arguably the most interesting descent. Turn right, following a faint path around the scree bowl past several caves and war remains. The path isn't immediately obvious but you're aiming for a large gap through the cliff walls on the right, marked by cairns. Turn right through the gap, passing a small cave and following the subsequent path west through meadows until you reach a junction. Right takes you under the west face of Col Ombert via the Sentiero di Guerra back to Rifugio Passo San Nicolo. However, unless you need to return to the rifugio, it is better to turn left onto path 609, which leads scenically down to **Baita alle Cascate** from where you can retrace your steps back to the **car park**.

ROUTE 10
Sentiero Attrezzato Bepi Zac

Start	Top of Costabella chairlift
Finish	Bottom of Costabella chairlift
Distance	13km
Total ascent/descent	1000m
Grade	2C
Time	9–10hr
Wire length	300m
Map	Tabacco 06
Parking	Costabella chairlift: 46.379, 11.78487

Sentiero Attrezzato Bepi Zac follows the line of one of the main Austrian front lines of the First World War, where thousands of lives were lost as the Austrians succeeded in halting the Italian advance into Val di Fassa. The route given here takes in Cima di Costabella and culminates in an optional ascent of Cima Uomo, enabling a thrilling if technically straightforward ridge traverse offering excellent views and an insight into alpine warfare. The complete route is, however, a very long and serious undertaking, and as such there are a number of options to shorten the day if desired.

Driving approach

From Canazei in Val di Fassa follow the SS48 west and then south-west to the town of Moena and turn left towards the Passo San Pellegrino. Follow the road for 10km to reach a parking area on the right just below the Costabella chairlift on the other side of the road. This area is also easily accessed from Falcade in the Agordino valley, ascending to the Passo San Pellegrino from the south-east and continuing beyond the pass to reach the chairlift. Take the Costabella chairlift to the top station.

From the top of the chairlift, follow a good path west across the hillside to join with path 604. Continue to **Passo le Selle** and **Rifugio Passo le Selle**, currently still managed by the family of Bepi 'Zac' Pellegin after whom the route is named.

From the rifugio, ascend the well-signed path 637 north and then east, passing the first section of cable. The terrain here is straightforward and the exposure

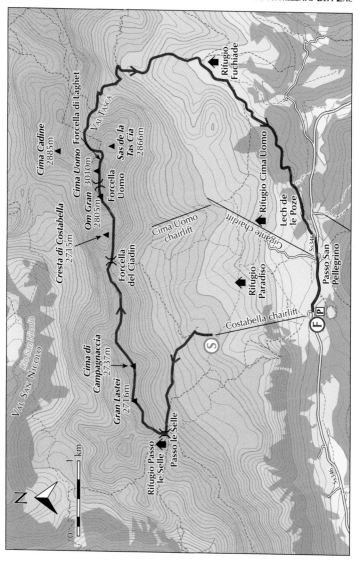

limited, so the wire serves as a handrail at most. The route now continues easily along the ridge to **Gran Lastei** (2716m) and on towards **Cima di Campagnaccia** (2737m), passing through a short tunnel (torch useful but not essential). In a further 10min, pass through a second tunnel to reach a ledge by a restored wartime shelter.

An exposed descent leads down to a section of easy walking, following way-marks and passing extensive areas of wartime trenches to reach a longer tunnel in about 45min from the shelter. Pass through this then descend 50 metres of cable to reach a sign to Cresta di Costabella (2715m).

Ignore path 637 descending north into Val San Nicolo and instead continue along the ridge towards Forcella del Ciadin. After a couple of minutes the path splits below a characteristic rocky buttress; an easier path leads left around this, however it is more interesting to ascend the via ferrata signed '637 bis Variante Osservaterio S di Costabella' up a gully on the right, reaching an old wartime observatory excavated into the buttress itself. From here follow the via ferrata down the other side to reach a steep tunnel descending a series of wooden stair-cases at the base, eventually rejoining the easier path.

Descend easily to a junction at **Forcella di Ciadin** (reached in about 2½hr from Passo le Selle), where path 637B offers the first of the shorter returns (see 'Other possibilities'). To continue along the main route, keep left here and follow signs for P02 Sent. Esperti. Forc Uomo, Forc Laghet and Valle di Tasca. The route from here is intermittently protected, undulating along ledges and through a narrow gap to reach a very unpleasant gully on the left, about 20min after leaving Forcella del Ciadin.

A couple of lengths of new cable protect a section of enjoyable climbing up the wall on the left of the gully, but there is still some loose scree and rocks to climb to reach the saddle at the top of the gully. Continue straight on across fairly level terrain (late-lying snow possible) to reach a shoulder.

Follow the path as it switchbacks up the shoulder to reach the crest of the ridge, rewarding you with stunning views of Piz Boè, Marmolada, Sassolungo, Catinaccio and even the Brenta range.

A short descent now leads into a broad saddle, followed by an easy walk up to the crest of the ridge to the minor summit of **Om Gran** (2805m), characterised by several small fortified positions. Follow signs for Forc. Uomo, Forc. Laghet and Val di Tasca, soon passing a large flake of rock studded with climbing bolts.

Continue along a slightly exposed and eroded path to ascend a steep gully equipped with a zigzagging cable. Follow the undulating path at the top of the gully to reach **Forcella Uomo** by a small wooden shelter about 1½hr from Forcella Ciadin. Continue to a junction just beyond where a possible escape route leads right down a gully (another shorter option; see 'Other possibilities'). This is also where the ascent to the summit of Cima Uomo begins (a 2hr out-and-back ascent of unprotected scrambling and easily climbing; see 'Other possibilities').

To continue the main route, descend to an obvious ledge below and cross a plank bridge (an escape route is signed right here to the Passo di San Pellegrino, leading down a heavily eroded gully; this is best avoided). Continue to a large boulder with 'PO2 Tasca/Cirelle, Fulciade' grafittied on it and follow the path around the front of a buttress.

Descend a short, narrow chimney protected with cable to reach an exposed and scree-covered ledge, then squeeze through the boulders to reach the edge of a large scree bowl. Follow the path to the centre of the bowl then ascend slightly to a short section of cable. Enter an eroded gully to reach a saddle, then begin the long descent towards Passo San Pellegrino. Follow cables easily for about 40 metres into the large depression of **Forcella di Laghet** (2765m, 1hr from Forcella Uomo), marking the end of the wire protection.

Continue down the waymarked path leading north-east to Val Tasca, soon degenerating into a steep scree slope. Pick the best line to reach the valley floor, then follow the path south-east down the valley to reach path 607. Turn right onto this and continue more easily across meadows to reach the luxuriously appointed **Rifugio Fuchiade** (1982m, about 1½hr after leaving Forcella di Laghet). From here follow the well-marked gravel road to return back to Passo San Pellegrino and the **car park**.

Other possibilities

There are a number of ways to shorten Sentiero Attrezzato Bepi Zac.

- It's possible to exit the route shortly after the wartime observatory, rejoining the main path and descending to the junction just below. Turn right here and descend a steep path joining with path 637B and leading to **Rifugio Paradiso**. From the rifugio turn left and follow path 604 easily down to **Passo San Pellegrino**.

- At **Om Gran**, take the path leading south to descend to Om Picol by the top of a chairlift, then descend the good path leading down to **Rifugio Cima Uomo**, continuing along a track back to **Passo San Pellegrino**.

- Shortly after Forcella Uomo, take the gully leading south to descend scree before bearing west on easier ground to join the descent route from Om Picol given above, continuing to **Rifugio Cima Uomo** and **Passo San Pellegrino**.

A worthwhile option to extend the day is the ascent of Cima Uomo, a relatively straightforward but unprotected scramble with some short sections of easy climbing. The round trip involves a further 200m climbing, taking about 2hr, and is well worth the effort:

- From the junction just beyond **Forcella Uomo**, follow the sign for 'C. Uomo Alpinistica' straight ahead to make an easy traverse, then continue to reach broken and steep rock. There are three short passages, each no more than

2–3 metres in length, which require some easy climbing, while the rest of the ascent is a straightforward scramble. While there is no cable, there are numerous pegs and belay points along the way, and a rope may be advisable if ascending with inexperienced or nervous parties. The view from the summit of **Cima Uomo** (3010m) is well worth the effort and the top is dominated by a small shrine built into the tail fins of an old bomb. To descend, reverse the route to the junction.

It is also possible to create a shorter itinerary while still taking in the summit of Cima Uomo, tackling the eastern part of Bepi Zac from Forcella del Ciadin onwards:

- From the top of the Costabella chairlift, follow a path leading north-east to join with path 637B. Ascend this to **Forcella del Ciadin**, reached in around 1½hr, and continue as per the main route above.

ROUTE 11
Via Ferrata Paolin-Piccolin

Start/Finish	Bar Colmean, Colmean
Distance	10.5km
Total ascent/descent	1300m
Grade	3B
Time	7–8hr
Wire length	300m
Map	Tabacco 15
Parking	Bar Colmean: 46.37743, 11.89136

Although the ferrata section of this rather remote route is relatively easy, this is a long and rewarding mountain day involving a steep ascent and a long and exposed descent. The view from the summit is sublime, providing a rare glimpse of the Marmolada south face.

Driving approach
From Moena take the SS346 towards Cencenighe, crossing the Passo San Pellegrino. Turn left at Caviola, following signs to Colmean, and park in the ample clearing at the end of the road by Bar Colmean.

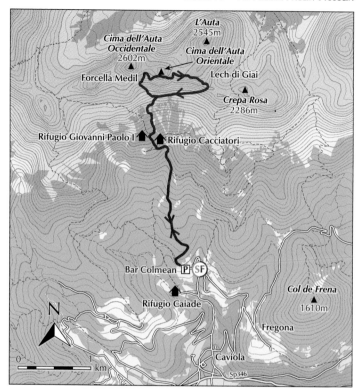

From the car park follow path 689 steeply through the pine forest to **Rifugio Cacciatori** (open in August), reached in just under 1hr. Continue on the path to the left, following signs for 'Cima dell'Auta Via Ferrata e Via Normale M2602'. Reach the simple log cabin of **Rifugio Giovanni Paolo I** in another 10min and take the path leading right just below the hut.

Ascend steeply for 45min to reach a fork and keep left, signed for the via ferrata and Forcella Col Becher. Continue for a further 20min, first up a tedious scree slope and then contouring left below the rock walls, to the start of the wire, reached in around 3hr from the car park.

Ascend the initial ladder and a series of stemples, overcoming a couple of awkward moves on a steep wall. The rock is initially good before the route follows the left side of the loose scree gully, requiring care and awareness to avoid dislodging debris onto those below.

Follow the cable off the scree on the left side of the gully to ascend a steep and often damp chimney, then continue on good rock to exit at **Forcella Medil**, reached in 45min from the start of the wire. From the saddle, follow the waymarks leading east along the ridge towards Cima dell'Auta Orientale; this leads quickly to a short ladder and further ferrata protection to climb directly up slabs on good rock until a ledge leads to the left, past a small cave, to a small saddle. The summit of **Cima dell'Auta Orientale** (2602m) is reached up to the right; allow 4–5hr for the total ascent from the car park to the summit.

The descent takes the normal route, returning to the saddle and crossing over a small summit on the right. There is some wire protection as the route descends to the east on the north side of Cima dell'Auta; this is a steep, narrow path and feels quite exposed in places.

After about 30min a helicopter pad is passed on the left, and the path continues with a short ascent before going to the right of some crumbling towers. Continue to follow signs for the Via Normale, descending right along 'Sentiero Attrezzato Attilio Bortolli 1983', initially down a steep, loose slope and then along a narrow path under large rock walls to the right.

Around 50min after leaving the summit, rejoin the ascent route and retrace the approach to return to the **car park** in a further 2hr.

ROUTE 12
Via Ferrata dei Finanzieri

Start/Finish	Top of Ciampac cable car
Distance	5.5km
Total ascent/descent	700m
Grade	3C
Time	4–5hr
Wire length	300m
Map	Tabacco 06
Parking	Ciampac cable car: 46.45816, 11.78822

Benefitting from a cable car approach and a short walk-in, this via ferrata reaches the scenic summit of Colac and provides a relatively short but rewarding day. As the ferrata faces north-west the rock can be icy early in the season, although the shade can make it an ideal choice for hot summer afternoons. Unfortunately, despite the numerous ascents the rock is still fairly friable in places and as such rockfall can be an unwelcome feature of this otherwise excellent route.

Driving approach
From Canazei in Val di Fassa, follow the SS641 leading south-east towards Passo Fedaia for 2.5km to reach the hamlet of Alba, parking in the large car park below the Ciampac cable car on the right. Take the Ciampac cable car (open late June to early September) to the wide bowl above.

Exit the cable car station and follow the ski piste on the left to reach a path on the right leading towards the rock walls. Follow signs for the via ferrata to pass a small (and often empty) reservoir, then ascend a short scree slope to reach the base of the route.

Follow the initial short section of cable and subsequent path to reach the true start of the route; here a cable leads up a slabby corner, often on wet rock, before rounding the corner to reach a steep slab studded with stemples. Climb these to a second series of stemples, now on steeper and exposed ground, before exiting onto easier terrain.

Ascending the steep, stemple-studded slab in the middle of the route

The route now eases a little, although the climbing is still relatively sustained, undulating over a number of false summits. The summit of **Monte Colac** (2715m) is reached in around 2hr and enjoys an airy position overlooking the Marmolada massif.

To descend, follow the waymarks and painted arrows down to the right to a gap in the rocks. From here follow intermittent cable protection steeply into a

Monte Colac (2715m)

Lift station

Ciampac cable car

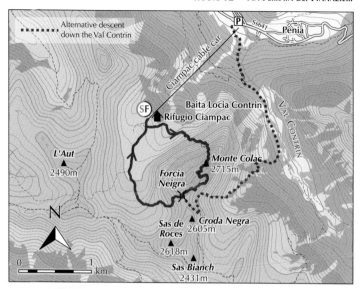

broad scree gully, then follow the path around to the right to reach **Forcia Neigra** (alternative descent possible – see below). Continue to descend more easily west down path 613 to return to the **cable car**.

Other possibilities

- For those wishing to avoid a lift descent it's possible to descend east from Forcia Neigra on path 646 that leads into Val Contrin. From here you can follow path 602 back to the bottom of the Ciampac cable car.
- When the cable car is closed or to avoid the cost of the fare, it's possible to ascend path 602 from the cable car station to join with the vehicle track leading to the plateau by the top lift station, adding around 2hr/5km of walking and 600m of ascent.
- It is also possible to reach the summit of Colac via the descent route, avoiding the more challenging ferrata and ascending steep scree and intermittent cable. From the top of the Ciampac cable car follow path 613 south to **Forcia Neigra**. Take the path traversing left around the hillside then follow waymarks and cables to the summit of **Monte Colac**, reached in around 2hr. To descend, reverse the route.

ROUTE 13
Via Ferrata Hans Seyffert

Start/Finish	Top of Pian del Fiacconi lift
Distance	6.5km
Total ascent/descent	850m
Grade	4C
Time	4–5hr
Wire length	400m
Map	Tabacco 06/07/15
Parking	Pian dei Fiacconi lift: 46.45859, 11.86354
Note	Ice axe, crampons, rope and experience in glacier crossing essential

Often referred to as the Marmolada West Ridge or Via Ferrata Punta Penia, this historic route provides access to the highest peak in the Dolomites at 3343m. It is the only true alpine via ferrata in the region and as such requires the appropriate equipment and expertise; less experienced groups may want to consider hiring a guide. As befits a route of such stature, the views are sublime and the climbing is interesting, with the final descent down the glacier completing a truly memorable alpine excursion. Due to the high altitude and aspect, the given grade is indicative only and may vary substantially depending on the snow, ice, glacier and weather conditions.

Driving approach

From Canazei in Val di Fassa, follow SS641 south-east towards the Passo Fedaia. On reaching Lago di Fedaia, continue to the east (far) side of the lake then turn right, crossing the dam and following the road up to the large parking area to the left of the Pian dei Fiacconi lift station. Take the Pian dei Fiacconi lift – open in high season and a unique experience in itself as the cabins are more reminiscent of shopping trollies than gondolas!

From the top of the lift descend right, following waymarks for the via ferrata and path 606. Follow the path as it descends west over slabs and glacial moraine before rounding a rock spur and ascending towards Forcella Marmolada.

Ascend the switchbacks towards the centre of a small glacier (crampons and axe recommended at this point) then bear right towards the rock walls and the start of the cable protection. Follow the wire as it leads diagonally leftwards to reach the prominent saddle of **Forcella Marmolada**, where stemples lead down towards Val Contrin (alternative approach route; see 'Other possibilities').

From the saddle follow a line of stemples leading up a leaning slab to exit onto a scree ledge. Follow the path up to the next set of cables and stemples then make an exposed traverse using the pegs as footholds. The next corner is climbed in a similar style on well-placed pegs before the stemples resume to ascend another leaning slab.

Exit onto easier ground, the cable now serving more as a handrail than anything else, to reach another long section of stemples up a rather polished wall.

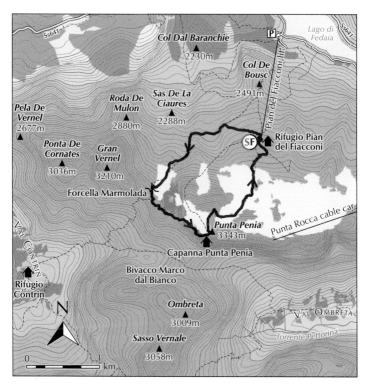

Exit onto another ledge and onto the next stemple ladder, then continue on similar terrain to reach a well-protected diagonal leftward traverse. Round the corner and climb an easy rocky buttress to gain the ridge.

Descend slightly then follow the cable up the obvious line in front, now with excellent views not only to the north but also south down to Val Contrin below. Follow the wire easily towards the snowy summit, either crossing the snowfield above direct or keeping right to follow the rock past the hut of **Capanna Punta Penia** and up to the cross on the summit of **Punta Penia**, rewarded with truly magnificent 360-degree views.

Crampons and an ice axe are required for the descent and it is essential to rope up for the lower section along the glacier. From the summit, descend the

Residual snow and ice can be found on the route early in the season

broad snow ridge (the Schiena del Mul), which curves down to the north to reach a marker post at the top of a rock wall. Downclimb the rock below to reach the glacier; although this section is well protected there is often snow or ice which makes the downclimbing feel considerably harder.

Reach the shattered rock at the base of the wall and follow a cable towards the glacier; it is essential to rope up from this point. Reach the edge of the glacier and cross the bergschrund with care, then follow the well-staked route down the glacier back onto the rocks above **Rifugio Pian dei Fiacconi**.

Other possibilities

It is possible to approach the route from **Rifugio Contrin**, ascending to the rifugio from Alba and spending the night there before ascending north-east to **Forcella Marmolada** on path 606, reached in around 2hr (5.5km, 500m ascent from Alba to Rifugio Contrin; 4km, 850m ascent from the rifugio to Forcella Marmolada).

MARMOLADA'S 'CITY OF ICE'

Remnants of the so-called 'City of Ice', once an 8-mile labyrinth of tunnels, are slowly emerging from the mountainsides surrounding the glacier as the ice retreats at some 7 metres per year. Most of the original structure dug by Austro-Hungarian soldiers remains intact, and Italian specialists have cleared away ice to reveal a network of communication tunnels, including sleeping space for 300 troops, an officers' mess and a hospital. During the excavations, several of the wooden huts built inside the glacier have been found, together with munitions, uniforms and the occasional body – perfectly preserved in sub-zero temperatures. From 1915 to 1917 Marmolada was a key military position along the Italian–Austrian front, which stretched from the Dolomites to the plains of north-eastern Italy. But in late 1917 the Austrians, aided by the Germans, broke through the Italian lines at the village of Caporetto, north of Trieste. The Italians retreated from their mountain-top positions to form a last line of defence on the River Piave, north of Venice. The Austrians abandoned the City of Ice to pursue the Italians south, and it was never used again.

Today the Italian authorities have ordered troops to start cleaning the honeycomb of tunnels surrounding the City of Ice for public visits. A museum has been opened at the second-stage station of the Marmolada cable car, so that young generations of Italians and Austrians can see the conditions in which their grandfathers and great-grandfathers fought in defence of their mother countries.

ROUTE 14
Via Ferrata Eterna Brigata Cadore

Start	Rifugio Fedaia
Finish	Top of Serauta cable car
Distance	8km
Total ascent/descent	1000m
Grade	4C
Time	6–7hr, plus return logistics
Wire length	1000m
Map	Tabacco 07/15
Parking	Rifugio Fedaia: 46.45362, 11.888099

Despite not reaching the summit like its western counterpart (Route 13), this is a long and satisfying route up the slabs of the eastern side of Marmolada, gaining the more modest summit of Punta Serauta before arriving at the upper midstation of the Serauta and Punta Rocca cable cars. A historic route, the cables were re-equipped in 2012/13 and the route is now superbly protected, enabling a thrilling yet secure ascent with some good exposure and tremendous views. Given the considerable ascent, the descent via cable car comes as a welcome treat, although this does require some forward planning to return to the car at the end of the day.

Driving approach
From Canazei in Val di Fassa, follow the SS641 leading south-east towards the Passo Fedaia. On reaching Lago di Fedaia, continue to the east (far) side of the lake and park in the roadside parking areas at the top of the pass by Rifugio Passo Fedaia.

From Passo Fedaia ascend the wide vehicle track leading up behind the rifugio, walking up to the third hairpin to reach a painted marker for 'F.E' on a rock slab. Leave the track here and begin to ascend vegetated rock slabs to the left, following sporadic red markers and cairns to reach the base of the scree slope below the ridgeline. Contour a more defined path leading towards a leftward-sloping traverse and a red information plaque marking the start of the route, reached in around 1hr from the pass.

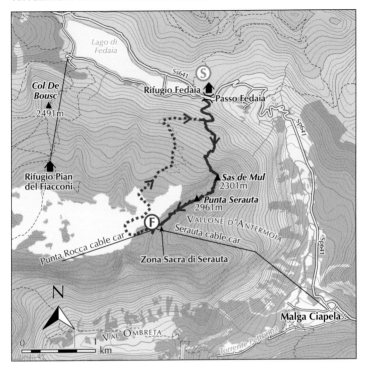

Follow the cables leading diagonally left on a leaning slab to reach more exposed terrain. Continue more vertically up a short series of stemples before another exposed traverse leads left. Ascend vertically for a short challenging section to reach easier ground. From this point the climbing is more straightforward on easy, well-featured rock.

Reach the shoulder of **Sas de Mul** (2301m) then begin an easy but somewhat arduous ascent of the slab above; this is superbly protected with a cable serving as a handrail and ascends for some 600 metres.

Eventually a short protected scramble leads onto the ridge, where the cable car station appears tantalisingly close; in fact the route continues at length across the ridgeline, now on more interesting terrain as the cable undulates over the articulated crest. Some sections of downclimbing may feel quite technical and exposed but the protection is always excellent and the cable well placed.

A fish-eye perspective on the undulating ridgeline towards the end of the route

After three distinct sections of downclimbing – the latter protected by a long series of stemples – a good ledge traverses easier terrain to reach the small **Zona Sacra di Serauta**, a memorial to those who died in the Great War. The total climbing time from the start of the wire to the cable car station is around 4–5hr.

Punta Serauta (2961m)

Cable car mid station

Possible descent

Rifugio Fedaia

The most common (and convenient) descent is to take the **Serauta cable car** down to **Malga Ciapela**. From here, either attempt to hitch a lift back to Passo Fedaia or in high season make use of the local bus service which runs infrequently (around four buses a day) from Malga Ciapela to **Pian di Fedaia**.

Other possibilities

- It is possible to descend the glacier to return directly to Passo Fedaia, negating the need for logistical arrangements at the end of the day. From the lift station follow a path down to the glacier below, keeping right, then join a vehicle track which marks the route of the winter ski piste. Follow this logically to reach **Passo Fedaia**. Crampons and an ice axe are required for this descent (1½–2hr).
- Some older maps may indicate a possible route down Vallone d'Antermoia along Ferrata B. Pontura; as neither the path nor the via ferrata has been maintained, this route is no longer viable and is strongly advised against.

2 SELVA

The beautiful and dramatic Odle ridgeline as seen from Val di Funes (Route 15)

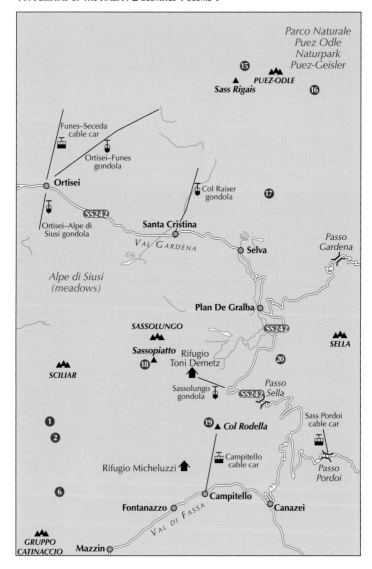

SELVA

Selva (Wolkenstein) is the main village in the classic V-shaped valley of Val Gardena. The village itself is sprawled along the main valley road and, although lacking a picturesque centre, is an excellent location for accessing the north-western Dolomites and is well served with amenities. The nearby villages of Santa Cristina and Ortisei also make excellent bases; all three villages offer a range of accommodation, shops, restaurants and bars, and in addition there are a number of cable cars and gondolas providing rapid access to the surrounding peaks and plateaus.

Routes 15 and 16 make use of the Col Raiser gondola out of Santa Cristina and explore the dramatic Odle group, while Routes 18, 19 and 20 are accessed by the Passo Sella road to the south.

ROUTE 15

Via Ferrata Sass Rigais Est/Sud

Start/Finish	Top of Col Raiser gondola
Distance	11km
Total ascent/descent	1000m
Grade	South (ascent) 1B; East (descent) 2B
Time	7–8hr
Wire length	800m
Map	Tabacco 05
Parking	Col Raiser gondola car park: 46.56487, 11.73643

Combining two via ferratas on the east and south sides of the mountain, the ascent of Sass Rigais is a long, committing but ultimately rewarding day in the scenic Odle group. Neither the ascent nor the descent route poses any real technical difficulties and the views are excellent, while the meadows surrounding Malga Pieralongia (shown on some maps as Regensburger) make for an idyllic setting. Even factoring in the Col Raiser gondola, the ascent is considerable and good timekeeping is essential to avoid missing the last lift down. The ferrata can be done in either direction and the choice is largely subjective; the route described here ascends the south side and descends the east.

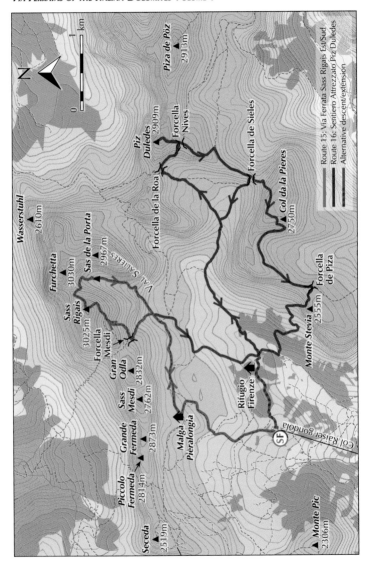

Piza de Pöiz 2913m

Wasserstuhl 2610m

Furchetta 3030m

Sas de la Porta 2967m

Piz Duledes 2909m

Forcella Nives

Forcella de Sieles

Forcella de la Roa

Col da la Pieres 2750m

VAL SALIÈRES

Sass Rigais 3025m

Forcella Mesdi

Gran Odla 2832m

Forcella de Piza 2555m

Monte Stevia

Sass Mesdi 2762m

Grande Fermeda 2873m

Piccolo Fermeda 2814m

Rifugio Firenze

Malga Pieralongia

Seceda 2519m

Col Raiser gondola

SF

Monte Pic 2306m

Route 15: Via Ferrata Sass Rigais Est/Sud
Route 16: Sentiero Attrezzato Piz Duledes
Alternative descent/extension

Driving approach
From Selva, follow the SS242 west along Val Gardena in the direction of Bolzano to reach a roundabout with the turn-off for Santa Cristina. Turn right here, following signs for the Col Raiser gondola and taking a small road through the village to the large car park at the bottom of the lift (parking charge applies). Take the gondola to the top station.

Exit the gondola station and head north on path 2 (often marked on maps as path 4A), following signs for Sass Rigais for 1km to reach a fork. Turn right and continue to the idyllic **Malga Pieralongia** and here turn right onto path 2B.

Follow the undulating track as it traverses east under the Odle peaks to reach the base of Sass Rigais and a sign for the 'Sud' and 'Est' variants of the via ferrata. Follow signs to Via Ferrata Sud and Forcella Mesdì, ascending a steep gully before bearing sharply right to the start of the ferrata.

Climb initially steeply to reach easier terrain on the broad shoulder of Sass Rigais. Follow waymarks and cairns to ascend more steeply, with sections of cable and a short but airy scramble leading to the **summit**.

To descend, head north-east from the summit, following cable to descend the eastern ferrata (Via Ferrata Est) down Val Salieres. At the end of the ferrata, follow the path south then west to rejoin path 2B, then retrace the approach route to return to the **Col Raiser gondola**.

Sass Rigais (3025m)

The Odle ridgeline with Sass Rigais visible at the back

Other possibilities

The route can equally be tackled in the opposite direction, ascending the harder of the two routes, the eastern route, to descend the easier southern variant.

On reaching the end of the ferrata, it is also possible to descend directly along path 13, crossing through the meadows to reach **Rifugio Firenze** and thus avoiding repetition of the approach route. From the rifugio, path 4 leads quickly and easily back to the **gondola station**.

ROUTE 16

Sentiero Attrezzato Piz Duledes

Start/Finish	Top of Col Raiser gondola
Distance	11km
Total ascent/descent	1020m
Grade	1A
Time	7–8hr
Wire length	150m
Map	Tabacco 05
Parking	Col Raiser gondola car park: 46.56487, 11.73643
Note	For route map see Route 15

Although not a via ferrata as such, this is nonetheless a good mountain walk with wire protection in the most exposed sections. The route follows a stretch of the long-distance Alta Via 2 and reaches the summit of Piz Duledes, an excellent viewpoint over the nearby Dolomites groups and the more distant Austrian Alps.

Driving approach

From Selva, follow the SS242 west along Val Gardena in the direction of Bolzano to reach a roundabout with the turn-off for Santa Cristina. Turn right here, following signs for the Col Raiser gondola and taking a small road through the village to the large car park at the bottom of the lift (parking charge applies). Take the gondola to the top station.

Exit the gondola station then follow a good path on the right slightly downhill to **Rifugio Firenze** (Regensburger Hütte). From here take path 2/3 towards Forcella de Sieles, crossing a wide glacial valley.

About 45–50min from Rifugio Firenze, branch left (north-east) onto path 3 and ascend steeply towards Forcella de la Roa. Just below the saddle itself, branch right onto a smaller path leading to the start of the wire protection.

Now following waymarks for Alta Via 2, follow the path up a series of broken gullies and ledges, with several short wired sections and a short ladder, to reach the ridge at **Forcella Nives**; this is straightforward and takes around 20min. Turn left at the ridge to follow an easy path to the summit of **Piz Duledes** in a further 20–30min. The summit is an excellent viewpoint and is reached in about 3hr from Rifugio Firenze.

To descend, retrace the route back to **Forcella Nives** then follow the well-waymarked path to the south along a high-level plateau. Continue down a ridge to the east before traversing to Forcella de Sieles (about 1hr from the summit of Piz Duledes). The traverse is protected by four short sections of wire but exposure is minimal and there is a good path all the way. From here, take path 2 and 2/3 back to **Rifugio Firenze**, then reverse the initial part of the route to return to the **gondola station**.

Other possibilities

For a longer and more challenging descent, from **Forcella de Sieles** continue south then west, ascending for around 200 metres with intermittent wire protection on path 17 to reach **Col de la Peires**. From here descend very steep terrain, again with some cabling, to reach **Forcella de Piza** just east of Monte Stevia. Turn right here and descend a steep scree slope to reach the meadow below, then at the junction with the more prominent path turn right to quickly return to **Rifugio Firenze**.

ROUTE 17
Via Ferrata Sandro Pertini (closed and wire removed)

Start	n/a

Mentioned in this guide for the sake of completeness and to avoid the possibility of error, this route was removed in 2015 due to a drawn-out dispute between the route's creators and the local council. Signs to the via ferrata have been taken down and the wire and stemples have been completely removed.

ROUTE 18
Via Ferrata Oskar Schuster

Start	Top of Sassolungo gondola
Finish	Hotel Passo Sella Dolomiti Resort
Distance	12km
Total ascent	800m
Total descent	1200m
Grade	3B
Time	5–6hr
Wire length	350m
Map	Tabacco 05
Parking	Hotel Passo Sella and Sassolungo gondola car park: 46.509410, 11.757045

Entering into the heart of the Sassolungo group, Via Ferrata Oskar Schuster provides a thrilling circular route with some enjoyable climbing. The cables were re-equipped and redirected in 2013/14 to take a more solid and logical line, although there are still some short sections of unprotected scrambling and the environment feels remote and rugged despite the gondola approach. By contrast, the Sassopiatto summit experience can feel rather crowded given the easy accessibility via the normal route along the west face.

Driving approach
From Selva, follow the SS242 east towards the Sella massif, reaching the junction with the Sella and Gardena passes. Keep right to follow the Passo Sella road for 9km to reach the lift station of the Cabinovia Sassolungo, characterised by rather archaic-looking white gondolas. There is ample parking at the lift station on the right side of the road (charge applies), although this can be busy in high season and as such an early start is advised. Take the gondola to reach Rifugio Toni Demetz in the prominent saddle in the centre of the Sassolungo group.

Behind the rifugio descend path 525, which leads down over scree and rock through the wide valley to reach **Rifugio Vicenza** in 45min. At this rifugio turn left to follow a well-signed and waymarked path up into the combe, crossing through

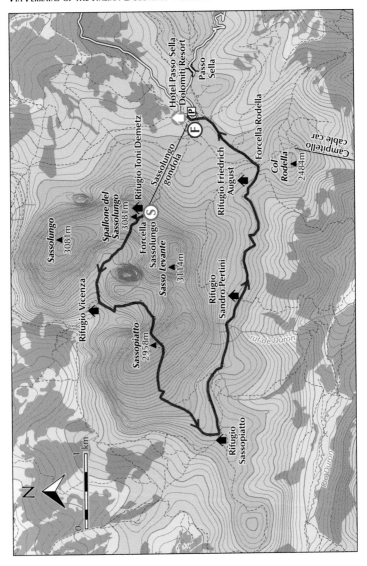

Traversing and ascending the many spires of Sassolungo

a boulder field and ascending scree to reach the base of the route in another 45min, marked by a red paint marker (snow possible late into the season).

Follow the cable right for a short way then continue up easier unprotected terrain. Carry on up a cabled gully to reach a saddle and the newly directed route, now following good rock to another saddle. Follow the markers across to a wall and ascend this via stemples and a ladder.

Continue to follow intermittent wire protection up a gully and some marginally more technical climbing before exiting onto a good ledge. This leads to the end of the wire and a short scramble up a small chimney to reach the summit ridge. Follow this easily right to the scenic summit of **Sassopiatto** (2958m) 2½–3hr from the base of the route.

To descend, follow path 527, which descends at length over the barren west face of Sassopiatto. Despite the route's popularity, the path is surprisingly difficult to follow at times as it crosses broken rock and scree, eventually reaching easier ground at **Rifugio Sassopiatto** after ¾–1hr.

Turn left onto path 557 towards Passo Sella, heading generally east along a very pleasant waymarked path, which follows contours and has little height loss or gain. Pass **Rifugio Sandro Pertini** and **Rifugio Friedrich August** and continue easily to reach **Forcella Rodella**, finally descending a wide track back towards the road and the parking area at **Hotel Passo Sella**.

Other possibilities
If the Sassolungo gondola is closed it's possible to walk up underneath the lift on path 525 to reach Forcella Sassolungo in just under 1hr (4km, 500m ascent).

Night time on the Sella Pass with views of Sassolungo

ROUTE 19
Via Ferrata Col Rodella

Start/Finish	Hotel Passo Sella Dolomiti Resort
Distance	5km
Total ascent/descent	350m (150m via alternative approach)
Grade	3A
Time	2–3hr
Wire length	175m
Map	Tabacco 05
Parking	Hotel Passo Sella Dolomiti Resort car park: 46.509410, 11.757045

A short but very pleasant and worthwhile route, with some excellent climbing and superb views despite its limited length. The cable protection and handholds are good but much of the footwork requires smearing on rather polished rock. The summit of Col Rodella is marred somewhat by the large radio mast that dominates the top, but Rifugio Des Alpes does feature an excellent terrace offering expansive views of Val di Fassa.

Driving approach

From Selva, follow the Val Gardena road east towards the Sella, reaching the junction with the Sella and Gardena passes. Keep right to follow the Passo Sella road for 4km to reach the parking area at Hotel Passo Sella Dolomiti Resort (fee applicable – there are some free parking spaces further up towards the pass, but these are liable to be very crowded in peak season). It is also possible to approach from Campitello using the cable car – see 'Other possibilities'.

From the parking area head south-west on path 557, following a broad vehicle track past a few rifugios. Although less distinctive from this side, the peak of Col Rodella can be clearly identified ahead by the large radio mast on the summit. Bear left onto path 529 to reach **Rifugio Des Alpes** and the top station of the **Campitello cable car** (alternative approach).

Turn left onto path 530 to descend slightly before branching right onto a path skirting the hillside and passing below the cable car. Follow this for 5min until a short series of switchbacks lead up to the wire.

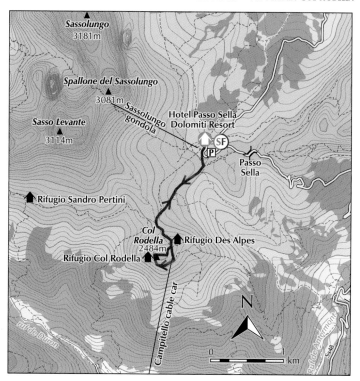

Follow the wire diagonally left then back right as it takes a logical and attractive line up the eastern end of the south face of Col Rodella. Climb a steeper wall then move left to a second steep wall protected with stemples. Scramble easily onto an enjoyable slab then ascend to reach a small pinnacle. Follow the wire left along the base of the pinnacle and onto easier ground, gaining a view of the radio mast on the summit.

A rightward traverse on a good ledge leads to a corner; climb this then reach a short buttress which is climbed easily but with good exposure to reach the summit of **Col Rodella** and **Rifugio Col Rodella**. The entire route from the start of the cable takes around 30–40min.

To descend, take path 529, which leads down from the rifugio to join with the wide track of path 557 taken on the approach, returning easily to the parking area at **Hotel Passo Sella**.

Other possibilities
It is possible to reach Rifugio Des Alpes via the Campitello cable car. From Canazei, follow SS48 west along Val di Fassa to reach the village of Campitello and follow signs left to the cable car. The lift runs in high season (June to September) and serves as a convenient (if expensive) approach for those without a car. There are regular buses up and down the Val di Fassa.

ROUTE 20
Via Ferrata Mesules (Pössnecker)

Start	Passo Sella
Finish	Pian Schiaveneis
Distance	12km
Total ascent/descent	800m
Grade	4C
Time	6–7hr
Wire length	500m
Map	Tabacco 05
Parking	Limited parking at the Passo Sella summit: 46.50854, 11.76632
Note	Short rope advised

Recognised as one of the oldest via ferrata routes in the Dolomites, Mesules (also known as Pössnecker after the Austrian Alpine Club branch which constructed it) is a superb mountain excursion, scaling the cold and shady west flank of the Sella to reach the lunar landscape of the plateau above. The climbing is technically straightforward for the most part but there are some long run-outs between anchors, sections of unprotected scrambling and some particularly exposed positions. There are a number of descent options but all are long and require some forward planning to avoid the trudge back to the car at the top of the pass. The recommended descent involves a car drop at Pian Schiaveneis for the most convenient return.

Driving approach

From Selva, follow the SS242 south-east for 5km to reach the junction with the Sella and Gardena passes. Keep right to follow the Passo Sella road for 6.5km to reach the top of the pass. There is ample parking on gravel laybys alongside the road but nonetheless spaces can be quite limited in high season.

From Passo Sella take path 649, which leads off to the left of Hotel Maria Flora, heading towards the distinctive Sella towers. Follow the path over scree and small boulders to contour more easily left below the imposing face of the Sella to the

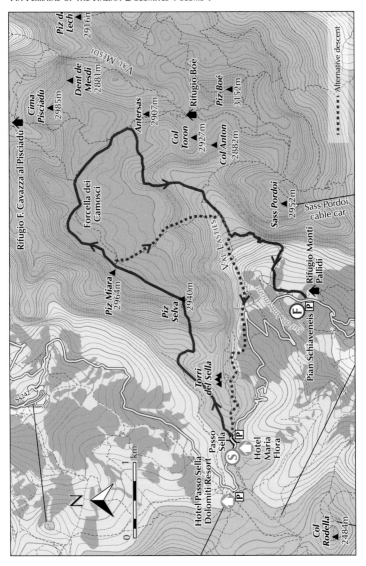

start of the route, marked by a long slack section of wire below a dark, water-streaked wall. The approach time from the top of the pass is around 20min.

Climb easily up good rock to reach an exposed ledge leading in to a smooth, polished and frequently damp chimney, ascended on widely spaced stemples with no cable protection. At the top of the chimney make an exposed move right onto an airy and unprotected detached pillar, without doubt one of the most characteristic parts of the route.

Continue up a short ladder then follow easy rocky ground protected by a fairly loose cable. The climbing becomes progressively easier but some unprotected movement is required on exposed sections. Exit onto the broad terrace and follow a well-marked path to a small lake below the rock face.

Continue to ascend a loose but well-protected slope to the final part of the route; climb shattered rock to reach a gully (late-lying snow possible) before exiting onto the summit plateau below Piz Selva, reached in around 1hr from the start of the second section of wire. A 25-metre scramble leads to the **summit** itself.

To descend, follow path 649 to the north-east, either cutting across the plateau or keeping high to the left to pass a series of summits. Just below the summit of Piz Miara, reach **Forcella dei Camosci** (well marked by a signpost and the junction with alternative descents – see 'Other possibilities') and turn right onto path 649, following the path south-east before bearing south-west onto path 647.

At the next junction, follow path 656 down the broad Val Lasties for 700 metres until the path forks. Turn left onto path 647 (if you want to walk back to the start, stay right on path 656 – see 'Other possibilities') signed posted towards 'Pian Schiaveneis' and descend to reach the road. Turn left and descend the road for 300 metres to arrive at **Pian Schiaveneis** and Rifugio Monti Pallidi where hopefully a second car awaits. The descent from the summit of Piz Selva takes about 3hr.

Other possibilities

There are a number of alternative descents possible for those wishing to return to a different valley or to shortcut the descent.

- To return more directly to Val Lasties, it is possible to take a shortcut down a poorly marked and poorly protected gully. From the end of the ferrata, follow the plateau towards Forcella dei Camosci as above until level with the summit cross of Piz Miara on the crest to the left. Here, turn right to follow a faint path towards a wide gully. Descend this on short rocky steps protected with loose cable to join the scree slope below, continuing more easily to rejoin the main descent route in **Val Lasties**. This descent route is, however, unpleasant and difficult to find, so good navigational skills and confidence on loose terrain are essential (1hr, 3km, 600m descent to rejoin the main route).
- To return to Val Gardena, from **Forcella dei Camosci** turn left onto path 676 to descend into Valun di Pisciadú, descending a short section of cable. Continue to reach **Rifugio Cavazza al Pisciadú** below, then bear north-west onto path 666, soon turning decidedly right to descend a loose cable down Val Setus (descent shared with Route 28), reaching the Tridentina car park below the Passo Gardena in around 3hr from the summit of Piz Selva (950m descent from Forcella dei Camosci).
- If you're without a second car, it's possible to return to the start by ascending path 656 from the fork in Val Lasties. Follow this for 45min to reach the road at a prominent hairpin, then follow the path right alongside the road, cutting off the hairpins and reaching Passo Sella in around 1hr (total 4km, 250m ascent).

3 BADIA/LA VILLA

Fanes as seen from Pralongia

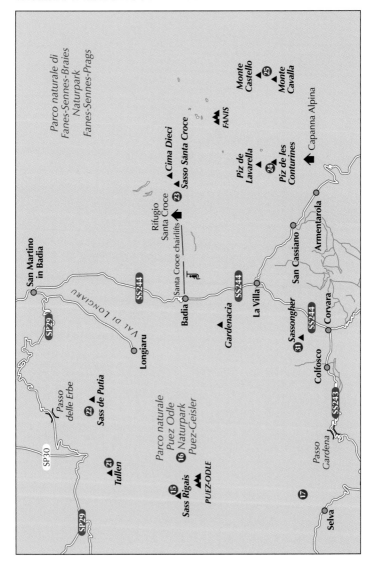

BADIA/LA VILLA

Perhaps one of the best known and loved areas of the Dolomites, Val Badia is scenically spectacular, dominated by the mountains of Puez-Odle Natural Park to the west and Fanes Natural Park to the east. The valley is one of the main access points to the Dolomites when coming from the north, with the road from Brunico forming a convenient route into the heart of the range.

Badia (formerly Pedraces) is one of several villages along the valley that make good bases for excursions into the surrounding mountains. Located a few kilometres further south, La Villa is an excellent base that has the advantage of sitting on the crossroads between the continuation of Val Badia up to Corvara and the road to the Passo Falzarego, in turn providing access to Cortina and Livinallongo.

There is accommodation to suit all budgets, with countless hotels and some more basic options such as the campervan 'Stellplatz' just outside La Villa. The nearby villages of San Cassiano, Corvara (covered in more detail in the next chapter) and Colfosco also afford easy access to this area, and there are campsites in the former and latter. The whole area is well served by public transport, with services connecting at La Villa.

The routes described in this section are not technically challenging but provide access to the heart of the two natural parks, offering excellent mountain days in an often very remote setting.

ROUTE 21
Sentiero Attrezzato Günther Messner

Start/Finish	Croce Russis
Distance	15km
Total ascent/descent	1000m
Grade	1B
Time	7–8hr
Wire length	200m
Map	Tabacco 05/07
Parking	Small car park at Croce Russis: 46.66056, 11.74913

A well-marked circular route providing a good mountain day with some limited sections of cable. The location in the northern Dolomites provides a good view towards the Austrian Alps while the route itself ventures into the wild and rarely frequented Puez Odle group. The brief optional extension to the summit of Tullen (2653m) is worthwhile.

Driving approach

From Corvara, follow the SS244 north for 18km to reach the village of San Martino in Badia located just off the road to the left. Turn left here, following signs for Passo delle Erbe and passing through the village to follow the road west for 15km to reach the top of the pass. Continue over the top of the pass and follow

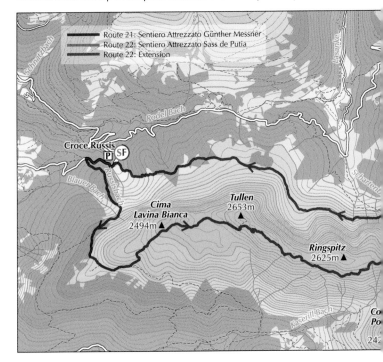

the road down for 8.5km to a junction; here keep left and continue for 500 metres to the car park at Croce Russis.

From the parking area at Croce Russis, walk back down the road to a path branching off to the south and signposted as path 32A and GM. Follow this steeply uphill through the forest for around 30min to then traverse right (west), with good views north across the lowlands between the Dolomites and the Austrian Alps.

Continue to ascend gradually to a shoulder at 2114m before bearing east then north-east, ascending a good path up a spectacular sunken valley to reach a signpost indicating the route to the summit of Tullen (see 'Other possibilities') about an hour after the shoulder.

To continue the route, follow the GM (Günther Messner) waymarks to make an easterly traverse for 5min to reach a section of cable in a stepped gully. Ascend this then follow switchbacks for a further 10min over an exposed ridge to descend

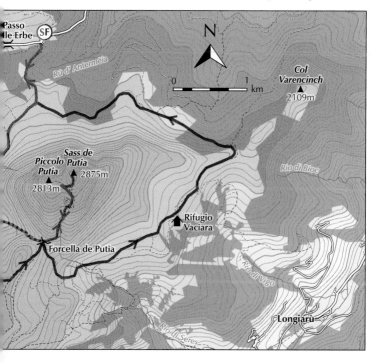

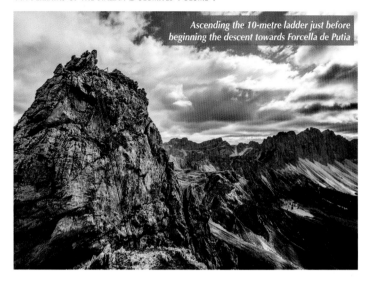
Ascending the 10-metre ladder just before beginning the descent towards Forcella de Putia

to a col. A short, easy, but exposed wired section now leads to a good viewpoint, marked by a small wooden cross.

The route now continues as a high-level traversing path (mostly on the south side of the mountain), protected intermittently in the most exposed sections. About 1hr from the viewpoint, reach and climb a 10-metre ladder then follow a short section of wire to descend and join with path 4 to **Forcella de Putia**. The total time from the start to here is about 5½hr.

From Forcella de Putia descend steeply to the north-west on path 4, ignoring path 8A branching off to the right (north-west). Continue to descend path 4 to reach another junction at around 2000m, where GM is signposted to the left (west), with path 4 continuing down to the right.

Keep left and make an undulating traverse on the north side of the ridge, passing below the summit of Tullen before descending through the forest and back to the road at **Croce Russis**. The time from Forcella de Putia to the road is around 2½hr.

Other possibilities
The ascent of Tullen (2653m) takes about 30min, with the total round trip completed in around 45min (0.5km, 100m ascent). Follow the signpost indicating the summit to reach the summit cross and the route book, with the additional effort rewarded by a commanding view. Reverse the ascent path to rejoin the main route.

ROUTE 22

Sentiero Attrezzato Sass de Putia

Start/Finish	Passo delle Erbe
Distance	10km
Total ascent/descent	1200m
Grade	1A
Time	5–6hr
Wire length	150m
Map	Tabacco 07
Parking	Paid parking at Passo delle Erbe: 46.67474, 11.81344
Note	For route map see Route 21

The commanding peak of Sass de Putia (Peitlerkofel) marks the northernmost point of the Dolomites. Although the ferrata grade is low, the route to the summit is a relatively serious undertaking given the exposed and unprotected nature of the scrambling, with cable only present on the final 100 metres to the summit.

Driving approach

From Corvara, follow the SS244 north for 18km to reach the village of San Martino in Badia located just off the road to the left. Turn left here, following signs for Passo delle Erbe and passing through the village to follow the road west for 15km to reach the top of the pass.

From the parking at the top of the pass, follow the vehicle track waymarked 8A for 20min to reach the junction between paths 8A and 8B. Keep right here, staying on path 8A and contouring at length below the base of Sass de Putia.

Continue past the junction on the right with paths 1 and 4 and keep left, now bearing south-east and ascending to reach **Forcella de Putia**, marked by signposts and a cross. Turn left here onto path 4B and ascend more steeply over increasingly rocky terrain to reach a scree plateau (optional out-and-back left turn to Piccolo Putia: a 30-minute round trip) and the start of the wire protection; this initially takes the form of a handrail before scaling a steeper but straightforward wall before a final section along the summit plateau leads to the cross on the summit of **Sass de Putia**.

The shortest descent is to reverse the route back around the west side of Sass de Putia to **Passo delle Erbe**; allow around 2hr. For a longer and more complete day encircling the entire mountain, see 'Other possibilities'.

Other possibilities

To complete the circuit of Sass de Putia, reverse the section of ascent from the summit to the **Forcella de Putia** then turn left onto path 4B to join with the main path 35 which leads around the east side of the mountain. This soon turns into a vehicle track and continues to reach **Rifugio Vaciara**; continue straight on to a junction and keep left, still on path 35, before meeting with path 8B. Follow this left at length to return to the junction with between paths 8A and 8B passed on the approach. Turn right to follow the vehicle track back to **Passo delle Erbe**. Allow around 3–4hr from the summit to complete the full circuit (9km from Forcella de Putia to Passo delle Erbe).

ROUTE 23

Via Ferrata Sasso Santa Croce

Start/Finish	Top of two-stage Santa Croce chairlift
Distance	15km
Total ascent/descent	900m
Grade	1B (2B with extension to Sasso delle Dieci)
Time	7–8hr
Wire length	150m
Map	Tabacco 07
Parking	Sasso Santa Croce lift car park: 46.60937, 11.89636

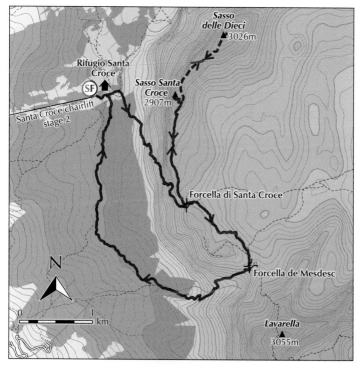

The striking west face of the Fanes massif looks steep and unassailable from a distance, yet is in fact home to an exposed yet technically straightforward protected route leading to the summit of Sasso Santa Croce (also known as Monte Cavallo, L'Ciaval, Sas dla Crusc and Helikreuzkofel). The lunar landscape of the plateau is particularly striking and the views are superb, while the ascent itself is unchallenging but very exposed in places.

Driving approach

From the village of Badia follow signs into the upper hamlet of San Leonardo to the Santa Croce chairlift and parking. Take the two-stage chairlift to the top station.

From the top chairlift follow the well-marked path up to the picturesque chapel alongside **Rifugio Santa Croce**. A large signpost behind the rifugio signs path 7 uphill; follow this through typical Dolomites vegetation to bear right below the imposing rock face above.

The path makes a rising traverse before encountering increasingly rocky terrain, equipped with intermittent wire protection in the most exposed sections. It is well waymarked and easy to follow, leading logically to the saddle of **Forcella di Santa Croce**.

The chapel and rifugio of Santa Croce with views over the Puez Odle

Now on the dramatic and barren plateau, turn left onto path 7B and follow this along the crest to the prominent summit of **Sasso Santa Croce** (2907m), from where it is also possible to continue along the crest to take in the summit of Sasso delle Dieci at 3026m (see 'Other possibilities').

To descend, reverse the route to the junction between paths 7 and 7B, reached in 45min, and turn left onto path 7, following this east for a short way before branching south-east onto the well-marked path 12B. Follow this to **Forcella de Mesdesc** then turn right to follow a broad scree slope, following waymarks for path 12. Where this splits just over the stream, keep right to follow path 12A until it meets with the well-trodden path 15; follow this right to undulate through the trees for around an hour and return to the top of the **Santa Croce lift station**.

Other possibilities
- For a longer day, it's possible to continue along the ridgeline from Sasso Santa Croce to reach the summit of Sasso delle Dieci, reached along path 7 and involving a short and rather steep scramble protected by cable to reach the summit. Around 45min/2km each way with an additional 150m of ascent, 2B.
- To avoid taking the chairlift in both directions, it's possible to descend on foot directly to La Villa, making using of the public transport network to return to Badia. Descend from Forcella de Mesdesc as described above, following path 12 to the junction just beyond the stream. Keep left here, now following path 12B to descend through the woodland into the village of La Villa (4km, 600m descent from the junction with path 12).

ROUTE 24
Sentiero Attrezzato Piz de les Conturines

Start/Finish	Capanna Alpina
Distance	17km
Total ascent/descent	1350m
Grade	1B
Time	7–8hr
Wire length	100m
Map	Tabacco 07
Parking	Paid car park at Capanna Alpina: 46.559687, 11.981256

This is a long mountain walking day with only a short section of ferrata to climb to gain the summit of Piz de les Conturines (Cunturinesspitze). Don't be put off by the prospect of returning along the same path; it's easy walking with spectacular views and the wooded section is particularly pleasant. The route could also be done just as a walk, excluding the via ferrata and ascending the slightly lower Lavarella (3055m) as an alternative summit.

Driving approach
From Corvara follow the SS244 north to reach the village of La Villa and the well-signed junction to the Valparola and Falzarego passes. Turn right here and follow the road for 7km, bypassing San Cassiano and reaching the hamlet of Armentarola. Just above the hamlet turn left towards Capanna Alpina, parking in the large parking area just below the bar (fee charged in high season).

From Capanna Alpina take path 11 and ascend steadily through attractive woodland to reach **Col de Locia** in around 1hr. From here continue through the broad glacial valley, following a fairly level path to reach a signpost at **Passo Tedega** in a further 30min. Keep left here, following a path up through a series of glacial bowls interspaced with easier walking.

Around 2hr after turning off, reach the ridgeline between Piz de les Conturines and Lavarella at 2885m, gaining an outstanding view of the villages below and across to the Sella massif.

Follow the waymarks left along the ridge to reach a large wooden ladder, the start of the protected section. Ascend this and the following intermittent

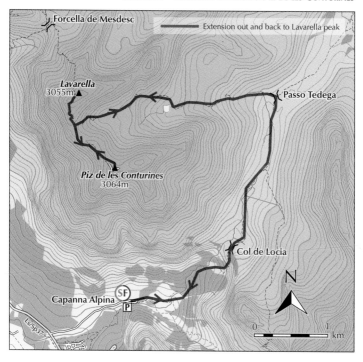

wires and wooden protection to climb a series of ledges to the summit of **Piz de les Conturines** (3064m). The ferrata is on the northern side of the mountain at 3000m, and in cold weather can be liable to icing.

To descend, reverse the route back to **Capanna Alpina**, reached in around 3hr from the summit.

Other possibilities

It's possible make an unprotected but very easy scramble to the summit of Lavarella (either as well as, or as an alternative to, Piz de les Conturines). On gaining the ridgeline between the two peaks at 2885m, take the path leading right and ascend a series of switchbacks steeply to reach a ledge. Follow this right with very easy scrambling to reach the summit of **Lavarella** (3055m) in around 30min, rewarding with a truly wonderful viewpoint in all directions. To descend, reverse the route.

ROUTE 25
Via Ferrata Furcia Rossa

Start/Finish	Capanna Alpina (alternative approaches possible; see 'Other possibilities')
Distance	19km
Total ascent/descent	1200m
Grade	2C
Time	7–8hr
Wire length	300m
Map	Tabacco 07
Parking	Paid car park at Capanna Alpina: 46.559687, 11.981256

The remoteness of this route makes it a fairly serious undertaking and it is not to be recommended in poor weather. The ferrata aspect of the route is anything but demanding but it is nonetheless a superb mountain day, crossing varied and fascinating terrain with significant geological and historical interest, while taking in stunning scenery in a remote setting.

Driving approach
From Corvara follow the SS244 north to reach the village of La Villa and the well-signed junction to the Valparola and Falzarego passes. Turn right here and follow the road for 7km, bypassing San Cassiano and reaching the hamlet of Armentarola. Just above the hamlet turn left towards Capanna Alpina, parking in the large parking area just below the bar (fee charged in high season).

From Capanna Alpina follow path 11 to ascend to **Col de Locia**, then cross a broad glacial plain to reach **Passo Tedega**. Descend slightly towards the junction with Valle di Fanes to meet a path on the right (south-east) signed VB-17, encountered some 5min before **Rifugio Malga Fanes Grande** and around 2hr from Capanna Alpina.
  Turn right onto path VB-17 and ascend steadily through an area of limestone pavement, reaching the junction with path 17 to Monte Castello in 30min. Keep left (east) and descend slightly before making a long rising traverse alongside an impressive cirque to the right.

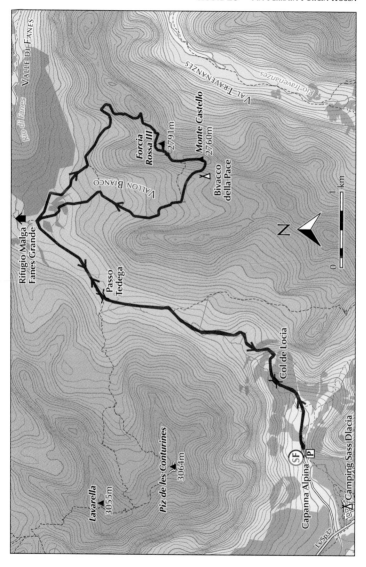

Reach a series of well-constructed switchbacks and ascend these steeply, passing a number of old wartime buildings on the left. Soon after look out for a large boulder to the left of the path; this bears a plaque reading 'ERBAUT COSTRUITO Nel 1915 ERNEUERT RIPRISTINATO Nel 1973'. This is in recognition of the reconstruction, in 1973, of the original First World War path now named Via della Pace (Friedensweg), or Path of Peace.

Faded paint markers on the boulder sign FR for Furcia Rossa to the right; leave the switchbacks here and follow the path along a shelf at the base of a rock wall. Follow the ledge, passing a number of natural caves on the left, and aim for the broad saddle at the head of the cirque. Follow the waymarks to reach a wide broken chimney protected with a section of cable, then descend to reach a series of three wooden ladders.

Continue up to the cirque to reach the saddle by a ruined wartime observation post offering a commanding view down into Val Travenanzes. Follow the path to traverse just below the saddle to reach the rock wall forming the upper south-west wall of the cirque. Ascend the cable up the zigzagging path to climb another set of ladders.

Continue up the scree slope above then traverse right along a ledge to reach a series of stemples; ascend these into a broad scree gully and exit easily to the right. Follow the path across the rocky summit plateau to a junction with painted markers on an old building; keep left, following signs for FR to reach the summit cross of **Furcia Rossa III**, where the views of the surrounding peaks and the lush green meadows of Pralongia to the west more than repay the 4–5hrs' worth of ascent made up to this point.

The Fanes, Lavarella and Piz de los Conturines as seen from Pralongia

To descend, return to the junction with painted markers below and take the path signed for 'CAST' towards **Monte Castello**. Descend a steep scree slope to reach a 10-metre wall; descend this using cable and ladders to reach another scree slope descending to a small saddle. Follow the well-waymarked path to contour southwards before descending a series of rather ramshackle ladders down a steep rock wall to reach the end of the ferrata.

To continue the descent, ignore the more obvious path towards Bivacco della Pace and instead continue for 10min to descend a scree slope direct to reach the floor of the valley (the route is visible from above).

Follow cairns along the base of **Vallon Bianco** to reach an unsigned junction; keep left here to traverse through sparse pines and limestone pavement, following faded yellow markers to rejoin path 11. From here reverse the approach route to return to **Capanna Alpina**, reached in around 3½hr from the summit of Furcia Rossa.

Other possibilities
There are two alternative approaches for this route; neither is as highly recommended as the option described above but both offer possibilities for those staying in areas other than the Alta Badia.
• Approach from Rifugio Pederu: from Corvara follow the SS244 north for 22km to the turn-off for San Vigilio. Turn right and follow the road beyond the village up Val Tamores to reach Rifugio Pederü, where a jeep taxi can be taken to **Rifugio Malga Fanes Grande**.
• Approach from Cortina: from Cortina follow the SS51 towards Fiames for 7km to reach the turn off for the Fanes-Sennes-Braies visitor centre car park at Sant'Umberto. From here, continue on foot, following path 10 along Valle di Fanes for 9km to join the route at **Rifugio Malga Fanes Grande**. This involves around 700m of ascent.

4 CORVARA

The long iron ladder provides the crux and focal point of Route 30

CORVARA

Corvara is the largest village in Val Badia and enjoys a scenically stunning setting, nestled below the modest yet striking profile of Sassongher to the north with the rather austere north face of the Sella massif to the south-west.

The village is best known as a winter destination; it forms the north-eastern cornerstone of the immensely popular Sella Ronda, the classic pisted ski tour around the Sella, while to the east the gentle slopes of the Pralongia plateau provide superb terrain for budding skiers.

In summer, the gentle meadows bring vibrant colour to the scene, complementing the pale tones of the mountains and making Corvara one of the most picturesquely located villages in the central Dolomites.

In terms of amenities, the village is well served with all the usual facilities such as banks, shops and cafés, and all standards of accommodation are in plentiful supply. The nearby village of Colfosco is just 3km away and offers additional

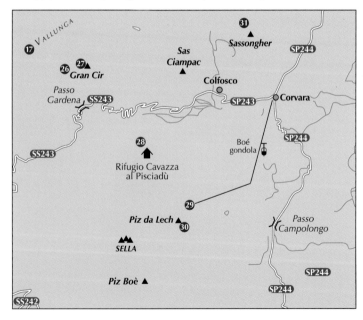

options, including a campsite ideally located between the two villages. There are regular buses down Val Badia and the Passo Falzarego, while a more sporadic service connects to Arabba.

Routes 26, 27, and 28 are accessed from the Passo Gardena road to the west, while Routes 29 and 30 make use of the Boè gondola, which departs from the centre of the village. Route 31 reaches the iconic summit of Sassongher and while the cabled section is very short, there is an undeniable satisfaction in looking back down towards the village from the prominent summit cross.

Many of the routes in this chapter benefit from short approaches and are in the lower to middle grades; consequently the via ferratas are very popular and it is rare to find solitude in this part of the region. Route 28 in particular has gained such classic status that it is arguably the most travelled via ferrata in the Dolomites, but its popularity is not unjustified and despite the queues it is a highly worthwhile excursion.

ROUTE 26
Via Ferrata Piz da Cir V

Start/Finish	Passo Gardena
Distance	3km
Total ascent/descent	450m
Grade	2A
Time	3–4hr
Wire length	100m
Map	Tabacco 07
Parking	Passo Gardena parking: 46.54994, 11.80666

Also known by its German name 'Tschierspitze', this short but excellent via ferrata scales the pinnacle of Piz da Cir V on the western edge of the Puez group. Given the reassuringly solid rock, the good protection and the ease of access, in addition to the surprising variety of the climbing on such a short length of wire, it is an ideal introduction to via ferrata. Unfortunately these attributes often make the route crowded and it is not uncommon to have to queue below the rather small summit – but the popularity is justified and the summit experience is worth the wait.

Driving approach

From Corvara follow the SS243 west, following signs for Selva and the Passo Gardena. Continue just beyond the pass to park on the right-hand side of the road alongside the Cir chairlift (fee charged in high season).

From the parking area take a path beside the chairlift station which ascends towards a small chapel before bearing north-west, following the line of a grassy crest towards the obvious building of **Rifugio Dantercepies** and the top station of the Dantercepies gondola, reached after 30min.

From the terrace at Rifugio Dantercepies follow waymarks to ascend the grassy rib that ascends directly north behind the ski station. When the grassy slope runs out, continue up the left-hand of the two narrow and loose scree gullies above to reach more solid rock just below the start of the route 30–45min after the rifugio.

An awkward move right leads to a good platform below the initial ladder; climb the ladder and continue on good rock to reach easier ground. Step over a cleft to join the main section of wire and ascend with enjoyable climbing, first with an easy leftward traverse and then a pleasant chimney before exiting onto a grassy plateau, reached in around an hour from the start of the climb.

Follow the path to reach a diagonal section of wire below the summit wall; follow this right then at the small col climb a short but rather vertical wall to reach

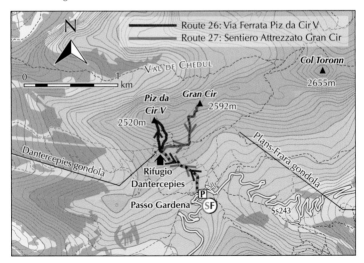

the small summit cross on **Piz da Cir V** (2520m), rewarded with excellent views of Sassolungo, the Sella massif, the wild Puez Odle group and the valleys below.

To descend, downclimb the summit wall then continue over the small col to reach a scree slope, initially protected with loose cable. Follow this down carefully on loose terrain to where the protection ends, then pick the best line to reach a more pronounced path on the grassy slope below, around 45min from the summit. (The route to Grand Cir (Route 27) turns left here; see 'Other possibilities'.)

To return to the pass, keep right and follow the path around the front of the peak to reverse the route back to **Rifugio Dantercepies** and down to the **Passo Gardena**.

Other possibilities
This route may be easily combined with an ascent of Gran Cir (Route 27).

The route may also be accessed using the **Dantercepies gondola** from Selva in Val Gardena (open mid June to late September).

Gran Cir provides spectacular views over Val Gardena

ROUTE 27
Sentiero Attrezzato Gran Cir

Start/Finish	Passo Gardena
Distance	3.5km
Total ascent/descent	450m
Grade	1A
Time	2–3hr
Wire length	100m
Map	Tabacco 07
Parking	Passo Gardena parking: 46.54994, 11.80666
Note	For route map see Route 27

More of an exposed walk than a via ferrata, this route accesses the summit of Gran Cir and is an enjoyable excursion for those with little scrambling experience, as well as providing an extension to an ascent of Piz da Cir V (Route 26). Despite the limited ascent, Gran Cir, or Grosse Tschierspitze, is the highest point in the chain of small peaks that form the ridgeline and thus has a slightly wider panorama than the nearby Piz da Cir V, rewarding with a splendid view north into the Puez National Park and south to the Sella and Sassolungo groups.

Driving approach
From Corvara follow the SS243 west, following signs for Selva and the Passo Gardena. Continue just beyond the pass to park on the right-hand side of the road alongside the Cir chairlift (fee charged in high season).

From the car park, take the vehicle track alongside Hotel Cir and ascend north-west, keeping left at a junction and continuing to the top station of the **Dantercepies gondola** (30min). Gran Cir is well signed off this track; at the sign-post turn right and follow a path initially over meadows to then ascend an eroded gully to the first section of cable.

Follow the cable up an easy-angled ramp for around 100 metres to reach a leaning corner. Ascend this easily to leave the wire protection and follow a narrow path up the hillside. A second section of wire equips an exposed but easy section before the protection ends again and the path leads up easily to the summit of **Gran Cir** (2592m), reached in around an hour from the start of the ascent. To descend, reverse the approach route.

Other possibilities
This route may be easily combined with an ascent of Piz da Cir V (Route 26).

The route may also be accessed using the **Dantercepies gondola** from Selva in Val Gardena (open mid June to late September).

ROUTE 28
Via Ferrata Brigata Tridentina

Start/Finish	Tridentina car park
Distance	5km
Total ascent/descent	750m
Grade	3B
Time	5–7hr
Wire length	400m
Map	Tabacco 07
Parking	Tridentina car park: 46.54695, 11.82062

Almost certainly the most popular via ferrata in the Dolomites, Via Ferrata Brigata Tridentina is perhaps best known for the suspension bridge between Mur de Pisciadú and Torre Exner. However, the true highlight is the sheer continuation of enjoyable climbing on consistently solid rock, with the descent down the impressive Val Setus completing a quintessential Dolomites experience. Unfortunately the route is a victim of its own success and in peak season the via ferrata can be incredibly busy, resulting in queues on the most challenging sections.

Driving approach
From Corvara follow the SS243 west, following signs for Selva and the Passo Gardena. After 7km at a prominent hairpin to the right, turn left into the well-signed CAI car park – the surface is rather coarse gravel and is quite broken in places, while spaces can be limited in high season.

From the south-east corner of the car park, follow the sign for 'Pisciadú via ferrata', taking the upper of the two paths. This leads easily below the walls of Mur de Pisciadú to reach the start of the route in less than 10min.

The first section of the route is short and leads easily up a series of stemples to a leaning slab, exiting onto a good grassy plateau. Follow the well-walked path to the left, passing between two boulders and undulating for 15–20min to reach a spectacular view of the Pisciadú waterfall to the left of the second section of wire.

Follow the wire on excellent rock alongside the waterfall. The route ascends steadily up the featured rock before traversing left towards a scree bowl below the upper plateau. (There is a path leading left here which avoids the final – and arguably most challenging – part of the ferrata to access Rifugio Cavazza al Pisciadú direct.)

To continue the route, stay on the wire to climb more vertically, the most difficult sections aided by stemples. Climb a ladder to easier ground then traverse left to reach the iconic suspension bridge between Torre Exner and Mur de Pisciadú. Cross the bridge to the end of the wire and follow the well-worn path up and generally left for 15min to reach **Rifugio Cavazza al Pisciadú**. (An optional ascent of Cima Pisciadú can be made from here; see 'Other possibilities.)

To descend, from the rifugio follow the well-marked path 666 initially north-west before bearing north and dropping steeply into the dramatic **Val Setus**. The initial part of the gully is protected with wire and is marked to indicate two ways;

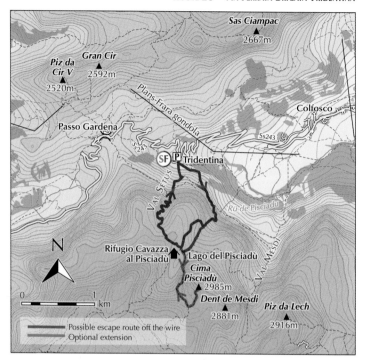

follow the downward arrows to descend the natural line of the slope, eventually meeting and joining path 666A. Follow this, signed for 'Parcheggio', to descend the final section through shrubs to return to the **car park**.

Other possibilities

The route can be extended up to the summit of Cima Pisciadú following path 666 south from Rifugio Cavazza al Pisciadú. Follow the path for 800 metres before a well-signposted left turn leads with some scrambling and wire to the summit of **Cima Pisciadú**. To descend, retrace your steps back to **Rifugio Cavazza al Pisciadú** and follow as above. (This extension involves an additional 2–3hr, 2km and 400m of ascent.)

It's also possible to descend the quieter **Val Mesdi** on path 676, which descends further east of the more common Val Setus descent to arrive at the

Superb rock and climbing with views of Colfosco and Corvara

village of **Colfosco** (9km, 900m descent to the main road). This would be the logical option for those accessing the via ferrata by bus from Corvara.

BRIGATA TRIDENTINA

Constructed in 1960 by the Italian army with help from Germano Kostner, the then custodian of Rifugio Pisciadù, Brigata Tridentina is the most famous and well travelled via ferrata in the Dolomites. The route owes much of its fame to the dramatic suspension bridge, which was added during 1967 to span the gap between Torre Exner and the Mur de Pisciadù. The via ferrata was completed in 1968 and named Brigata Tridentina al Pisciadù, in honour of the troops who helped to construct it.

ROUTE 29
Via Ferrata Vallon

Start/Finish	Top of Vallon chairlift
Distance	8km
Total ascent/descent	600m
Grade	2B
Time	5–6hr
Wire length	200m
Map	Tabacco 07
Parking	Boè gondola station car park: 46.54894, 11.87141
Note	For topo see Route 30

Despite being situated close to the hugely popular Via Ferrata Piz da Lech (Route 30), this route receives very little attention and indeed many don't even realise it exists. While this may be in part due to the less than obvious signposting, despite its brevity the route is enjoyable and provides an excellent 'off the beaten track' approach to Piz Boè.

Driving approach
Park in the well-signed pay and display car park at the Boè gondola station in the centre of Corvara in Badia. Take the gondola and the subsequent Vallon chairlift to the top station just north of Rifugio Kostner.

From the top of the Vallon chairlift, head south towards Rifugio Kostner to join path 638. Here turn right onto a smaller path that skirts the left-hand side of the Vallon Corrie, aiming for the lowest part of Sasso delle Nove just left of the summit.

Around 45min after leaving the chairlift, reach the start of the wire at the bottom of the face, to the left of the waterfall that provides the characteristic suspension bridge crossing. The lower half is comprised of straightforward climbing up a series of ledges with some loose rock before reaching the waterfall after around 15min of climbing.

Cross the superbly situated metal suspension bridge (prepare for an icy shower in windy conditions!) and ascend to the right of the fall, now on steeper ground leading with interest to the top, exiting at a col between Sasso delle Nove and Cima del Vallon about an hour from the start of the wire.

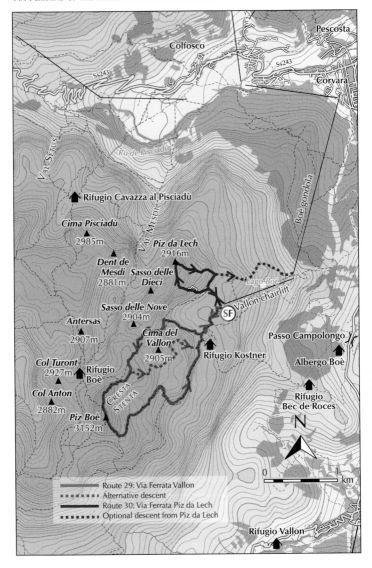

Route 29: Via Ferrata Vallon
Alternative descent
Route 30: Via Ferrata Piz da Lech
Optional descent from Piz da Lech

Continue upwards, now following rather faint red waymarks south and then west along the lunar landscape of the **Cresta Strenta**, crossing to the south face of Cima del Vallon where the path forks. Continue straight ahead along the north-east ridge to the summit of **Piz Boè**. (Turning left begins a descent towards Rifugio Kostner along path 672, descending down an impressive gully protected by wire to the east of Cima del Vallon.)

From the summit of Piz Boè, the recommended return route is via path 638, which descends south and then north-east back to **Rifugio Kostner** in around 1–1½hr. From here a short walk leads back to the **Vallon lift system**.

Other possibilities

For those wanting to approach on foot, it's best to follow path 638 from **Albergo Boè** on the Campolongo pass. The walk will take around 2hr (4km, 700m ascent) and is something of an arduous affair. From the top of the pass, follow path 636 south then west, following a good vehicle track to **Rifugio Bec de Roces**. Continue on the same path to reach the junction with path 637 and here turn left, following the path through characteristic pinnacles before turning right towards **Rifugio Kostner**. Continue on path 638 for 200 metres until a small path branches off left and behind the traverse to the start of the wire.

The suspension bridge crossing the waterfall provides one of the highlights of the route

ROUTE 30
Via Ferrata Piz da Lech

Start/Finish	Top of Vallon chairlift
Distance	4km
Total ascent/descent	400m
Grade	3B
Time	3–4hr
Wire length	200m
Map	Tabacco 07
Parking	Boè gondola station car park: 46.54894, 11.87141
Map	For route map see Route 29

A relatively short but enjoyable route, offering varied climbing on solid rock, two rather steep ladders and a wonderful view from the summit of Piz da Lech (Boeseekofel). The access by gondola and chairlift is convenient and the route was redirected in 2013 to take a more logical line.

Piz da Lech (2916m)
Sasso delle Dieci (2908m)
Sasso delle Nove (2904m)
Cima del Vallon (2905m)

29: Via Ferrata Vallon 2B
30: Via Ferrata Piz da Lech 3B

Ascending good rock towards the summit of Piz da Lech

Driving approach
Park in the well-signed pay and display car park at the Boè gondola station in the centre of Corvara in Badia. Take the gondola and the subsequent Vallon chairlift to the top station just north of Rifugio Kostner (alternative start avoiding the lift possible from Passo Campolongo – see 'Other possibilities').

From the top of the Vallon chairlift, follow the signpost indicating 'Vie Ferrate/ Klettersteige Piz da Lech & Vallon' to the right. At the next junction continue straight on then bear left below the rock walls to the start of the wire.

Climb direct alongside a chimney to reach a terrace, then move left to a leaning corner. Climb this to continue up more vertical but well-featured rock, moving right. A series of short but enjoyable chimney-gullies lead to a well-protected ledge. Continue to traverse right then climb vertical rock on good holds, making an awkward exit left.

Exit onto a good ledge and follow the path towards two successive metal ladders equipping a steep wall. Climb these, the second exited by a strenuous move, then continue more easily on rock before reaching the end of the wire protection. Follow the path over the summit plateau to reach the **Piz da Lech** summit cross 15min after exiting the wire.

To descend, follow waymarks east along path 646, the normal route to the summit. This goes over scree before making a steep downclimb protected by stemples to reach the grassy slope below. At the junction just beyond, turn right to follow path 646B south-west across scree, descending a rather unpleasant and loose gully protected with cable before arriving at the signed junction just before the start of the route. Turn left here to retrace the approach route back to the **Vallon lift station**.

Other possibilities

- The route may also be accessed from the Campolongo pass, avoiding the cost of the lift and opening up the route out of season (4km, 700m ascent). From the top of the pass, follow path 636 south then west, following a good vehicle track to **Rifugio Bec de Roces**. Continue on the same path to reach the junction with path 637 and here turn left, following the path through characteristic pinnacles before turning right towards **Rifugio Kostner**. From here continue easily to the top of the **Vallon lift station**.

- It's also possible to descend to the top of the Boè gondola (1.5km, 360m descent), making a small saving on the lift fare and completing a slightly longer route. At the junction with path 646B, keep left and continue straight on over the grassy crest to reach a ladder. Descend this then follow the well-waymarked path 646 down past **Lago Boè** to reach the gondola station.

ROUTE 31
Sentiero Attrezzato Sassongher

Start/Finish	Top of Col Pradat gondola
Distance	7km
Total ascent/descent	700m
Grade	1A
Time	3–4hr
Wire length	100m
Map	Tabacco 07
Parking	Col Pradat gondola car park: 46.557503, 11.854806

Despite its rather modest height, Sassongher (2665m) is undoubtedly one of Corvara's iconic peaks and is a satisfying destination for a mountain day. The cabled section is limited to the final scramble below the summit and as such this is much more of an exposed walk than a via ferrata; nonetheless it is a worthy excursion and the panorama is well worth the effort.

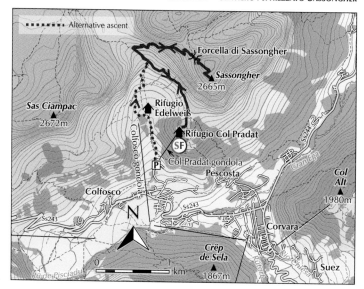

Driving approach

From Corvara take the SS243 west towards the Passo Gardena for 2km to reach the village of Colfosco. Shortly after passing the Raffeisen bank on the left, turn right onto Strada Col Pradat and follow this to just after the church. Turn left and drive through the residential housing and apartments to reach the car park below the Col Pradat lift. Take the lift to reach the rather luxurious Rifugio Col Pradat above.

From the top of the Col Pradat gondola, descend slightly on the wide track to quickly reach waymarks for path 4A. Branch right onto this and follow it north then north-west for 15min to join with path 4, then shortly after reach a prominent junction where Forcella de Ciampei is signed left. Turn right here, following the signs for Sassongher and descending down a number of switchbacks.

Reach and follow a rising ledge towards the obvious peak ahead then ascend vegetated terrain to reach the saddle of **Forcella di Sassongher**. Turn right to ascend steeply up the broad shoulder which descends from the peak itself, following switchbacks reinforced with wooden beams. After 10min a short section of wire is encountered by a rocky buttress; ascend the wire with easy scrambling to reach a good path and follow this up the steep slope above for 15min to reach the summit

of **Sassongher**, where you are rewarded with an expansive panorama of the Fanes group, the Marmolada, the Sella, Sassolungo and the Puez Odle range.

To descend, reverse the route to **Col Pradat** and the gondola station.

Other possibilities

Sassongher can be accessed via several different routes for a longer day or to avoid using the lift.

- The shortest and simplest ascent is to begin from the bottom of the Col Pradat lift station and follow the wide vehicle track of path 4 north to **Rifugio Edelweiß**. Continue straight on from the refuge up the grassy valley to cross another vehicle track; here turn left then almost immediately right onto path 4 and continue to join with the junction with path 4A, continuing to the summit of **Sassongher** as above. The total ascent via this route is 1000m.

- A longer and more interesting itinerary is to ascend from Funtanacia or La Villa via paths 7 or 11, reaching **Forcella di Sassongher** from the east (10km, 1000m ascent). For this option it can be interesting to descend via the normal route given above (with or without the lift) before descending into Colfosco or Corvara and making use of the local bus service to return to your car.

5 ARABBA

Afternoon light on Monte Civetta and Col di Lana (Route 35)

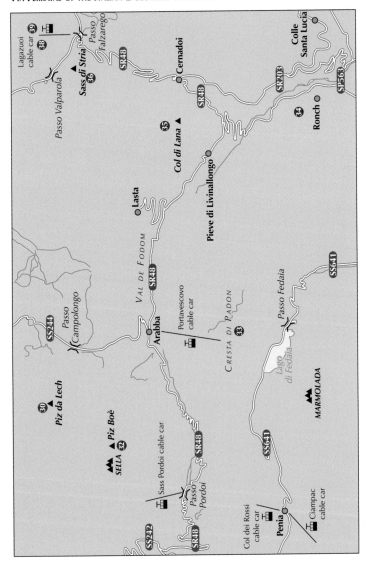

ARABBA

Located at the foot of Passo Pordoi and Passo Campolongo, Arabba sits at the south-eastern corner of the Sella massif. To the east, the Livinallongo valley provides access north to Passo Falzarego or south to Caprile, making Arabba an ideal location for accessing many of the areas described in this book.

This small, friendly village is noticeably less commercialised than many of its neighbouring counterparts, and in spite of the thriving winter tourist industry the village has retained a certain amount of local authenticity. Naturally the consequence of this is that there are significantly fewer amenities than in some Dolomites villages, but nonetheless Arabba still boasts the necessary range of facilities such as banks, bars, a small selection of shops and a modest yet adequate range of accommodation. There is also a basic campervan park in the village itself.

Public transport to and from the village is unfortunately rather limited, but the Porta Vescovo cable car does provide easy access straight from the village to the Padon ridge to the south, making light work of the approach to the highly popular Route 33. The other routes in this chapter are located a short distance from the village – Route 32 departs from the top of Passo Pordoi while Routes 34 and 35 are accessed from the Livinallongo valley.

ROUTE 32
Via Ferrata Cesare Piazzetta

Start/Finish	Passo Pordoi
Distance	9km
Total ascent/descent	900m
Grade	5C
Time	5–6hr
Wire length	500m
Map	Tabacco 07
Parking	Pordoi cable car parking: 46.488025, 11.810759

A superb but challenging route that lives up to its difficult and strenuous reputation. For a long time considered the hardest via ferrata in the Dolomites, its grade has since been surpassed by some of the more modern routes, yet the technicality of the climbing and the overall physicality of the moves – particularly in the first 100 metres – still earn this a place as one of the most committing routes in the area. A further challenge is brought by a particularly narrow chimney; smaller rucksacks are an asset here. The route given here reaches the summit of Piz Boè, at 3152m the highest point on the Sella.

Driving approach
From Arabba, follow the SS48 west for 9km to the top of the Passo Pordoi. There is ample free parking just opposite the cable car station on the left.

From the car park, walk back along the road towards Arabba for a couple of minutes then turn left just before Hotel Maria to follow an access road to the **Ossario del Pordoi mausoleum**. From the mausoleum, follow the well-waymarked path uphill towards the rock walls of the Sella, traversing right at a rock spur then continuing to ascend the gully above on a good path. Reach and skirt the rock walls

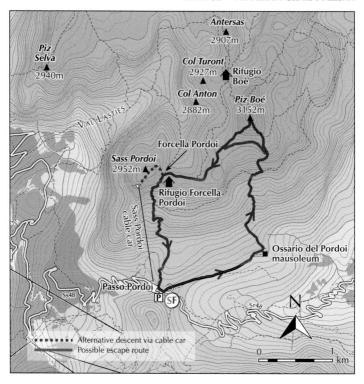

for 250 metres to the right to reach the start of the route; the approach from the mausoleum takes just over 1hr.

The route is immediately steep, scaling a vertical and rather featureless wall. Move left then continue vertically, climbing a series of old metal stemples to reach a good ledge. Follow the ledge then make an awkward move through a very narrow chimney, continuing to reach a suspension bridge above. Cross this with good exposure to reach a large ledge and the end of the most challenging sections.

The route now continues more easily up off-vertical and well-featured rock. Climb a final technical wall to reach the top of a buttress then continue with intermittent wire protection on technically straightforward terrain to reach a junction. (See 'Other possibilities' for a continuation of the route avoiding Piz Boè.)

157

The enjoyable suspension bridge provides a welcome relief from the steep terrain

To continue to the summit of Piz Boè, head right and ascend rock and scree for 30min to reach the final (and very popular) ascent to the **summit**.

To descend, take path 638 south before joining with path 627 and following this to **Forcella Pordoi**. (An ascent towards Sass Pordoi and subsequent descent to Passo Pordoi via cable car is possible from here; see below.) From the forcella, descend the scree gully south-west – this is initially steep and protected with wire (fixed rather too high to be any use); pick the best line down the scree then reach a more pronounced path. Follow this off the scree and across a grassy plateau to descend directly to **Passo Pordoi**. Allow about 1½hr for the descent from the forcella.

Other possibilities
- To avoid the summit of Piz Boè, turn left at the junction at the end of the ferrata and follow waymarks to traverse a large scree bowl, reaching and joining paths 638 and 627 leading to the saddle of **Forcella Pordoi**. Continue on the route described above.
- To return to Passo Pordoi via cable car, ascend path 627A behind Rifugio Forcella Pordoi for 15min to reach the cable car station (100m ascent).

ROUTE 33
Via Ferrata delle Trincee

Start/Finish	Top of Porto Vescovo cable car
Distance	7km
Total ascent/descent	500m
Grade	4B
Time	6–7hr
Wire length	300m
Map	Tabacco 07
Parking	Porta Vescovo cable car parking: 46.4959, 11.87442
Note	A new 'pinnacle' extension was added in 2018. Headtorch required for tunnels.

Developing on the volcanic rock of the dramatic Padon ridgeline above Arabba, this via ferrata has an entirely different character to the limestone routes that predominate in the Dolomites. It is a true ridge route and as such is airy and exposed in places, requiring downclimbing moves between sections and crossing an iconic suspension bridge. It is, however, a route of two halves, with the first section being particularly steep and technical before the difficulties ease in the latter part. There are a number of escape routes to exit the ridge if weather conditions change.

Driving approach

In the centre of Arabba, at the roundabout turn downhill, passing Ristorante Pizzeria El Table on the left. Cross the bridge and turn right to follow the short one-way system to the large car park below the Porta Vescovo cable car. Take the cable car to the top station.

Exit the cable car station and follow a path waymarked with the traditional red and white markers, keeping to the left of the prominent path 680 leading towards Rifugio Padon. Ascend the grassy slope to reach the distinctive conglomerate rock of the Padon ridgeline and the start of the wire protection.

The first few moves are some of the hardest on the route, requiring confident footwork and some use of the cable. The initial technical slab is followed by a rather featureless corner and a rightward traverse before climbing a leaning corner. Reach easier ground and cross a spectacular suspension bridge.

Now on the ridge proper, follow the wire protection to descend to a col, the end of the first section and the first escape point down the gully to the right. At this point there is also short but worthwhile extension equipped in 2018. Follow the sign for 'Sasso dell'eremita' to reach the taut wires of the new section. The variant gains the summit of a small tower and offers excellent views and some exposed, vertical climbing. A separate descent route leads back to the main route. Continue following the ridgeline, now with a section of unprotected walking uphill past a number of wartime ruins. (The second, easier escape leads right from here along a good path.)

The ridge continues to undulate across ledges, passing more wartime buildings and descending a rather awkward and exposed series of stemples. Continue

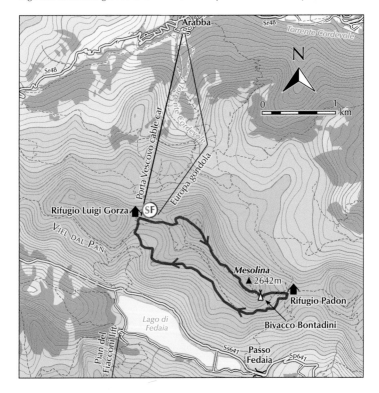

around the next corner to make another awkward downclimb onto a good path. Follow this across a steep grassy slope to another cluster of wartime ruins. This is often considered the end of the route and a path leads down the south side of the ridge to bear back towards the cable car. Instead, continue towards Padon along the airy crest ahead to reach another section of cable. Descend this and follow the waymarks past a walled-up tunnel and a cave.

Ascend back to the ridgeline then descend over to the north side to enter the first short tunnel, keeping left at the fork (headtorch essential for this section). The tunnels are well waymarked but have a number of junctions and side galleries, so care must be taken to follow the indications in the gloom.

Exit the first tunnel and continue into a second before following a series of trenches. Reach the final section of cable and follow this uphill to enter a long ascending tunnel, offering excellent views of the Marmolada through the old lookout points.

Exit the tunnel at **Bivacco Bontadini** then follow the obvious path down to **Rifugio Padon**. The route to this point takes around 5hr.

From the rifugio follow the well-signed Sentiero Geologico di Arabba (path 680) to contour the hillside back towards the cable car. Keep right at the forks to stay high, reaching the top of the **Porta Vescovo cable car** in around 1hr.

Other possibilities

If accessing the route out of season or to avoid the cable car, there are a number of alternative approaches.

- The most direct is to ascend path 698, which departs from behind the cable car station in Arabba and leads steeply through trees to join the winter ski pistes up to the top of the cable car (3.5km, 700m ascent). This is, however, a rather arduous and uninteresting ascent and is not recommended.
- A long but considerably more scenic approach is to begin from the Passo Pordoi, located 9km west of Arabba, and to walk in along the panoramic **Viel dal Pan** on path 601, which traverses a terrace east to reach the top of the cable car in around 3hr (8km, 400m ascent).

ROUTE 34
Via Ferrata Sass de Rocia

Start/Finish	Ronch
Distance	1km
Total ascent/descent	100m
Grade	1A
Time	1–2hr
Wire length	30m
Map	Tabacco 15
Parking	Ronch car park: 46.447690, 11.976600

A rather remote spot off the beaten track for most visitors to the Dolomites, Sass de Rocia is a great little route for a rest day. Although hardly qualifying as a via ferrata, it visits an interesting little summit and is in an idyllic location, while the route itself, although very short, is surprisingly engaging.

Driving approach

From Arabba, follow the SS48 south-east for 9km to reach a well-signed junction just after Hotel Excelsior. Make a sharp right turn here onto the SP563, descending the winding road for 5km to Digonera. Here follow signs for Laste, turning right onto a narrow road to reach the hamlet, then continue to the next hamlet of Val. Soon after turn left, signed for Ronch, and ascend an even narrower road to a good parking area at the end of the road.

From the parking area walk back along the road towards Laste for 100 metres then turn left onto a path leading up through the trees to the wooded glen of Sass de Rocia. The via ferrata is accessed through a distinctive cleft in the rocks with bolted sport climbing lines alongside.

To begin the route, enter into a small but impressive gorge with a bridge overhead. Turn left to walk past the Madonna perched on a rock on the left, then climb the stemples up the left-hand wall. This leads to a small footbridge; cross this to follow a cable to a good track, first over the footbridge viewed from below, then through pines and finally over a third footbridge.

Follow the track through more pines to Bivacco Pian delle Stelle, with its veranda equipped with benches and picnic tables. The route from the car park to this point takes around 45min. Continue along the track behind the bivouac for a few minutes to reach the small summit of Sass de Rocia, taking care when stepping over the deep, narrow cleft.

Return to the gorge by the same route and now go downhill. The slope is at a relatively easy angle, but a cable is attached to the left wall for security. At the end of the cable descend a set of fairly steep stemples to reach a path and follow this easily back to the road and the car park.

ROUTE 35
Sentiero Attrezzato Col di Lana

Start/Finish	Lasta
Distance	11km
Total ascent/descent	850m
Grade	1A
Time	4–5hr
Wire length	100m
Map	Tabacco 07
Parking	Corte/Lasta: 46.49867, 11.92853

A technically undemanding route and more of an exposed walk than a true via ferrata, Col di Lana is nonetheless a worthwhile excursion. Not only are the panoramic views from the summit truly excellent, but the route is particularly interesting for its historical and geological significance (headtorch recommended for exploration of tunnels).

163

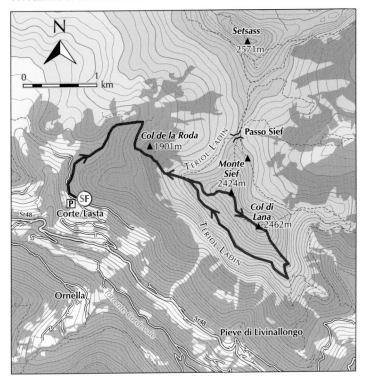

Driving approach

From Arabba follow the SS48 east for 5km to reach a sharp turning on the right, signed towards Corte, Contrin and Lasta. Follow the narrow road up three hairpins to reach the hamlets of Corte and Lasta, leaving the car on the grass verge.

From Lasta, follow the road north towards Contrin for a short distance to where a track branches right, waymarked as path 21C for Monte Sief and Col de la Roda. Follow this to **Col de la Roda**, passing below its rounded summit and continuing first through woodland then more open grassy terrain past wartime trenches to reach the junction with the Teriol Ladin – a path dedicated to the soldiers who fell in the Great War. (Walking time to this point is around 1hr.)

Continue to ascend the western spur of **Monte Sief**, reached in around 30min, then bear right to reach its summit cross (2424m) in another 25min. The ridge between Monte Sief and Col di Lana begins here, formed by the crater caused by a huge mine exploded by the Austrian troops in the autumn of 1917. Follow the loose cable that protects the ridge, ascending the next peak along the ridge via a vertical wall protected with stemples.

Continue to undulate along the ridgeline, keeping just to the side of the arête on a protected path. The ridge is featured with various tunnel entrances dating back to the war, some of which can be explored with a headtorch. Finally enter into a trench and ascend easy rocky terrain to reach the summit of **Col di Lana** (2462m). Below the large summit cross there is a small chapel and a shelter.

To complete the circuit, continue south-east on path 21, descending a broad grassy shoulder before entering into sparse trees. Keep right at the junction with the forestry track and continue to reach another junction with the Teriol Ladin. Follow this north then north-west, entering back onto the open hillside and

BLOOD MOUNTAIN

Infamously known as Col di Sangue ('Blood Mountain') by the Italian infantry during the First World War, Col di Lana was the scene of much trench and mine warfare between 1915 and 1916. Throughout the war the Italian forces repeatedly tried to storm the peak, which was defended by German Alpenkorps and Austro-Hungarian regiments. On 8 November 1915 the Italians, led by Lieutenant Colonel Giuseppe Garibaldi II, managed to briefly capture the summit before being driven off by well-coordinated enemy forces the next morning.

What followed was a period of intense mine warfare as the two armies went to ground. Employing silent hand drills and using chisels, the Italian 12th infantry and 14th Alpini brigades slowly dug a series of mined tunnels under the Austrian positions. The Italian scheme was eventually spotted by Austro-Hungarian artillery observers on the Passo Pordoi, leading to the detonation of an Austrian counter mine on the 6 April 1916. The mine was ineffective, however, allowing the Italians to finally detonate 5 tonnes of explosive at midnight on 17 April. Stunned by the large ordinance, the Austrians surrendered the summit and retreated to the adjacent peak of Monte Sief, where the stalemate would begin again. Reports indicate that in the first year of conflict alone there were some 1050 Italians killed, 5100 wounded and 435 missing in the battle for Col di Lana. The twin craters created by the mine blasts can still be seen to this day.

contouring the slope, following sporadic waymarks to rejoin the junction below Monte Sief. Keep left and retrace the approach route back below Col de la Roda and back to **Lasta**. (Total return time 2–2½hr.)

Other possibilities

- For a shorter route, reverse the route from the summit of Col di Lana back across the ridge.
- Col di Lana can also be accessed from Pieve di Livinallongo via the forestry track of path 21 (6km, 750m ascent to the summit), or alternatively from Passo Valparola on path 23, which contours below Settsass before veering south to **Passo Sief** (7km, 650m ascent).

6 FALZAREGO

Wild alpenrose (Rhododendron) at Cinque Torri

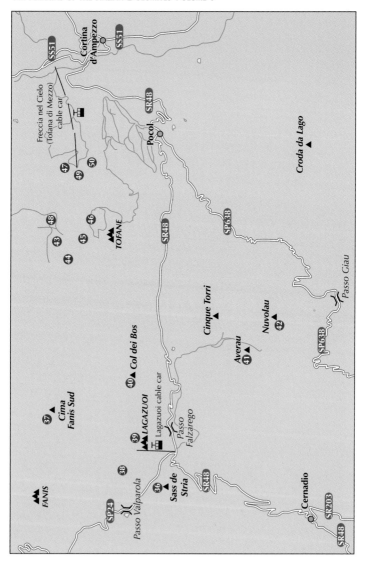

FALZAREGO

Passo Falzarego is located equidistant between Corvara in Val Badia to the west and Cortina d'Ampezzo to the east. The starting point for many excellent via ferratas and walks, it is perhaps one of the most scenic passes in the central Dolomites, taking in expansive views of the Tofana, Cristallo and Sorapiss groups. It is also the site of the Lagazuoi cable car, a characteristic suspended lift that ascends sharply for 650 metres to reach Piccolo Lagazuoi and Rifugio Lagazuoi – whose terrace view is arguably one of the most breathtaking in the Dolomites.

There is very little in terms of facilities at the top of the pass itself; Bar Bazar Passo Falzarego is more of a souvenir shop serving drinks and snacks, and helmets and torches can be hired from a small kiosk by the car park. For overnight accommodation, Rifugio Lagazuoi at the top of the cable car and Rifugio Col Gallina located a kilometre down the pass towards Cortina offer dormitory-style rooms with half-board options, although thanks to the easy road access from Val Badia, Cortina and Livinallongo, it can be just as convenient to stay in one of the many surrounding villages such as San Cassiano, La Villa and Cortina. In high season there are public buses between Val Badia and the pass, while the Cortina Express bus service (www.cortinaexpress.it) provides connections to Cortina.

The mountains around Passo Falzarego offer one of the most varied selections of via ferratas: Route 37 is a challenging and exposed route deep in the Fanis group, while Route 39 is technically straightforward but explores an extensive and fascinating network of wartime tunnels. To the south-east, Routes 41 and 42 make use of the Cinque Torri chairlift at Bai de Dones 3km down the pass, venturing into the breathtaking environment above the iconic five towers of Cinque Torri.

ROUTE 36
Sentiero Attrezzato Sass de Stria

Start/Finish	Passo Valparola
Distance	2.5km
Total ascent/descent	300m
Grade	1A
Time	1–2hr
Wire length	20m
Map	Tabacco 07
Parking	Forte Tre Sassi car park: 46.52735, 11.99262

A short protected path which, although not really constituting a via ferrata, is well worth exploring for the historic interest and superb views. The route follows a series of wartime trenches which hold snow late into the season. There is minimal cable and the route is not exposed at any time, but the rock can be icy early and late in the season.

Sunrise on the summit of Sass di Stria

Driving approach

Reach the top of the Passo Valparola from La Villa in Val Badia (SP37) or via the Passo Falzarego road from Cortina or Livinallongo (SR48). Park in the large gravel car park just south-west of the Forte Tre Sassi war museum.

From the north-western side of the car park take a small path marked by a sign for 'Sentiero Attrezzato Sass de Stria'. This takes a meandering route up the north-western slope of the mountain, following a mini-labyrinth of trenches and short wooden ladders. There are numerous possible deviations and it is worth simply taking the time to explore the various branches before making your way to the prominent summit cross on **Sass de Stria** (2477m).

To descend, reverse the route.

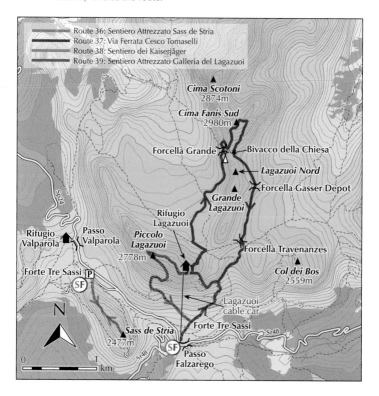

ROUTE 37
Via Ferrata Cesco Tomaselli

Start	Top of Lagazuoi cable car
Finish	Passo Falzarego
Distance	7.5km
Total ascent	450m
Total descent	1000m
Grade	5C (ascent)/3C (descent)
Time	6–7hr
Wire length	600m
Map	Tabacco 07
Parking	Lagazuoi cable car parking: 46.51959, 12.00832
Note	Torch required for extension to Cima Scotoni. For route map see Route 36

An excellent route which is technically hard in places and fairly sustained. Some of the route is north-facing and so can be prone to icing, especially if an early start is made. The strenuous yet delicate initial traverse and the exposed final arête are particular highlights, while the descent route down the north-east side of Cima Fanis Sud (Südliche Fanisspitze) is a via ferrata in its own right.

Driving approach

Reach the top of the Passo Falzarego via the Passo Valparola road from La Villa in Val Badia (SP37) or the Passo Falzarego road from Cortina or Livinallongo (SR48). Park in the large car park alongside the Lagazuoi cable car at the top of the pass and take the cable car to arrive below Rifugio Lagazuoi.

From the top of the Lagazuoi cable car, descend the wide track below (the site of the winter ski piste) on path 401, bearing right to reach **Forcella Lagazuoi** in a few minutes. Turn left here onto path 20 and continue to the next junction, here keeping right and following path 20B towards Bivacco della Chiesa. This undulates below the north-west ridge of Grande Lagazuoi before ascending to **Forcella Grande** and the shelter, reached in around 1½hr from the cable car. Ascend the slope just beyond for a few minutes to reach the start of the wire.

The route begins with the famous leftward traverse, a delicate yet strenuous section that moves awkwardly around a bulge with good exposure. Continue vertically but on more featured terrain past a number of old ladders before reaching a broken scree slope.

Continue to ascend an unprotected gully, which is easy-angled but rather dirty, to reach a path above. Follow this through the slabs across a number of exposed ledges crossing steep scree slopes to reach the base of a huge detached pillar. Continue to the left, rejoining the cable as the exposure increases.

Follow the ledge to reach a steeper wall with good holds, climbing this to reach easy-angled terrain. After about an hour from the start of the wire, at a prominent junction, keep right to continue the route (left leads to Cengia Veronesi and the Alta Via di Fanis; see 'Other possibilities'), continuing over broken rock to the base of a rock wall.

Move right to rejoin the cable protection and ascend an easy-angled buttress interrupted by a steep groove. Continue to reach a short yet quite strenuous corner to exit into a sloping corner crack. Bridge up this to exit onto a splendid, very airy and steep slab, climbing this with superb exposure. Reach the series of easy ledges above and continue to the summit of **Cima Fanis Sud** (2980m), gained after 2hr from the start of the wire.

The ferrata descent departs directly from the summit platform to the right (north-east). The protection is good throughout but the grade is still reasonably

Immaculate rock on the upper section of Cesco Tomaselli

high for a downclimb (3C) and the descent can be complicated by people coming the other way, therefore timings will vary.

Descend over a series of ledges, short gullies and rock walls, the hardest passage being a short, slightly bulging chimney which is overcome thanks to small but positive holds just below the lip. The end of the cabled descent is reached in around 45min from the summit.

The route now continues down a loose and unpleasant scree gully to join the more prominent path 20B just east of Forcella Grande. Keep left here and follow the path to reach **Forcella Gasser Depot** then remain on the well-marked path 20B to reach **Forcella Travenanzes**. From here, rather than ascending the 250 metres to the top lift station, keep left and descend the wide track of path 402 all the way down to the **Passo Falzarego**.

Other possibilities

- **Diversion to Cima Scotoni via Cengia Veronesi and Alta Via di Fanis**: a short yet worthwhile diversion to Cima Scotoni can be accessed from the junction midway up the ferrata (torch required for exploration of the galleries). Where the cable splits and the main route keeps right, follow the cable left to make a gently rising traverse along a scree ledge. After 100 metres cross a dirty gully then move left to the obvious shoulder and a number of wartime ruins. Follow the ledge along the base of a steep slab with moderate exposure in places to reach a wider area below the entrance to two tunnels. Don't enter the tunnels just yet and instead keep traversing the ledge, following a metal sign for 'Alta Via Fanis – Luigi Veronesi'. Follow the waymarks along the path, with cable protecting the most exposed parts, to reach a col just below the summit. A 15-minute scramble up easy but loose terrain leads to the top of **Cima Scotoni** (2874m), offering wonderful views into the heart of the Fanes group. Reverse the route to return to the entrance to the tunnels; the lower tunnel is blocked but the upper can be explored as it curves down for just over 100 metres to emerge on a ledge overlooking Ciadin di Fanes, a rugged cirque above Val Travenanzes. Follow a ledge to the right for 100 metres, partly protected with cable, before descending a short wall to the floor of the cirque. At this point there is often a steep snowfield and the surrounding rock is loose, so it is recommended to retrace the route back through the tunnels to rejoin the main route.

- **Via the descent route:** it is also possible to climb Cima Fanis Sud via the descent route described in the main route above, ascending a 3C via ferrata then descending the same way. However, given that there are a number of preferable routes at the grade in the area, not to mention the complication of encountering descending climbers, this is not generally recommended.

ROUTE 38
Sentiero dei Kaiserjäger

Start	Top of Lagazuoi cable car
Finish	Passo Falzarego
Distance	3km
Total ascent	Cable car or Route 39 (700m)
Total descent	700m
Grade	1B
Time	2–3hr
Wire length	100m
Map	Tabacco 07
Parking	Lagazuoi cable car parking: 46.51959, 12.00832
Note	For route map see Route 36

Created by the Austrian troops during the siege warfare of the Great War, this path traverses and descends the south-west side of Piccolo Lagazuoi, crossing a characteristic suspension bridge. Although there is little wire protection, the path is quite exposed and descends steeply in places. It forms an interesting alternative descent from the Gallerie del Lagazuoi (Route 39) but is also a worthwhile ascent in its own right, beginning from the Passo Valparola (see 'Other possibilities').

Driving approach

Reach the top of the Passo Falzarego via the Passo Valparola road from La Villa in Val Badia (SP37) or the Passo Falzarego road from Cortina (SR48). Park in the large car park alongside the Lagazuoi cable car at the top of the pass. Take the cable car to the spectacular viewpoint at the top.

Exit the cable car station and follow the path left up steps to **Rifugio Lagazuoi**. Just beyond the rifugio a good path leads to the nearby summit of **Piccolo Lagazuoi**, offering a superb panorama of the three Tofana peaks, Civetta, Pelmo, the Sella and the Fanes group, among many others.

Follow signs for 'Sentiero dei Kaiserjäger', beginning the descent protected with intermittent wire. After a kilometre, the characteristic suspension bridge

From left to right: Rifugio Lagazuoi, Croda da Lago, Monte Pelmo and Averau, Monte Civetta and Col di Lana

38: Sentiero dei Kaiserjäger   1B
39: Sentiero Attrezzato Galleria del Lagazuoi   1A

is reached, a replica of the original. Cross the deep gorge and continue to descend, keeping left to follow a section of the Cengia di Martini, a key strategic position during the war.

Follow the ledge to a junction and keep left, taking a path that cuts across the mountain to join the large track of path 402. Turn right onto this and descend easily to the car park at **Passo Falzarego**.

Other possibilities

If choosing to ascend the route rather than using it as a descent, the path is best accessed from the Passo Valparola, located north-west of the Passo Falzarego:

- From **Rifugio Valparola**, cross the road to take a path leading east towards the rock walls. Follow this as it bears right and contours the hillside, following signs for Sentiero dei Kaiserjäger. Continue ascending to reach the wire protection and follow this over the bridge and on to the summit of **Piccolo Lagazuoi** (total 3–4hr).

ROUTE 39

Sentiero Attrezzato Galleria del Lagazuoi

Start/Finish	Passo Falzarego
Distance	3km
Total ascent	700m
Total descent	By cable car (alternative descent possible; see Route 38)
Grade	1A
Time	2–3hr
Wire length	200m
Map	Tabacco 07
Parking	Lagazuoi cable car parking: 46.51959, 12.00832
Note	Headtorch and helmet essential. For route map see Route 36

An atmospheric alternative to a traditional via ferrata, this route explores the wartime tunnels excavated into Monte Lagazuoi by the Italian troops in 1917. Free to access and well maintained, the tunnels are not lit and as such a torch is essential, with the damp and gloom adding to the poignancy of the experience. The route is never overly steep but the ascent over the damp rock and wooden steps is tiring. The tunnels offer numerous opportunities for exploration, while the diversion along the Martini ledge and the alternative descent via Sentiero dei Kaiserjäger (Route 38) are well worthwhile.

Driving approach

Reach the top of the Passo Falzarego via the Passo Valparola road from La Villa in Val Badia (SP37) or the Passo Falzarego road from Cortina (SR48). Park in the large car park alongside the Lagazuoi cable car at the top of the pass.

From the top of the Passo Falzarego, follow the wide vehicle track ascending behind and right of the cable car station, signed for Monte Lagazuoi and the Gallerie along path 402. The entrance to the tunnels is well signed, branching off the main track which continues to Forcella Travenanzes around 30min after leaving the car park.

A short section of wire leads to the start of the tunnels. Enter into the tunnel and follow the slope to quickly exit on a ledge. Descend slightly then ascend the rising ledge ahead, equipped with cable, to reach the true start of the tunnels.

The following network is a labyrinth of passageways, ledges and caverns, with numerous diversions to viewpoints and gun emplacements. It is best to simply spend some time exploring; the route to the subsidiary summit below the top cable car station is well signed as 'Anticima Lagazuoi', so there is little chance of getting truly lost. (See 'Other possibilities' for details of an optional extension to the Martini ledge.)

Continue to reach an obvious junction, where both the spiral gallery and the main tunnel eventually rejoin to exit the tunnels definitively. Follow the signs and

Rifugio Lagazuoi

38

Martini ledge

Lagazuoi cable car

39

38: Sentiero dei Kaiserjäger   1B
39: Sentiero Attrezzato Galleria del Lagazuoi   1A

waymarks to ascend easily to the cable car station and **Rifugio Lagazuoi**, offering a stunning view of the Passo Falzarego, Marmolada, Monte Pelmo, Tofana and Cristallo, to name but a few.

The easiest and most popular descent is to make use of the Lagazuoi cable car to return effortlessly to the **Passo Falzarego** below, although there are several possible descent options (see below).

Other possibilities

A worthwhile extension is the well-signposted route to the Cengia Martini, the Martini ledge. This was a key position during the siege and goes along the south and south-west buttress of Piccolo Lagazuoi, reaching a restored wooden barracks and the remains of original buildings. From this point the route is reversed to return to the main tunnels; the diversion there and back takes 1–2hr.

There are a number of descent options for Route 39:

*   The easiest descent by foot is to descend path 401 east to reach **Forcella Travenanzes**. From here keep right and descend the wide track of path 402 all the way down to the **Passo Falzarego** (1–1½hr, 3.5km).
*   The most satisfying descent for a complete circuit of historical interest is to descend via Sentiero dei Kaiserjäger – see Route 38.
*   It is of course possible to ascend via the cable car and descend through the tunnels, removing any ascent from the route. The descent through the tunnels takes around 1–1½hr.

PICCOLO LAGAZUOI

Piccolo Lagazuoi above Passo Falzarego was the site of fierce combat during the First World War. For two years the Austrians defended the top of the mountain while the Italians attacked from their position on the Cengia di Martini (Martini ledge) below. On 20 June 1917, after six months of tunnelling 1100 metres into the mountain, the Italians detonated 33,000kg of blasting gelatin in order to dislodge the Austrians. However, the Austrians, hearing the constructions work, abandoned their position before the explosion, and all the efforts of the Italians were wasted.

ROUTE 40
Via Ferrata degli Alpini al Col dei Bos

Start/Finish	Magistrato alla Acque
Distance	5.5km
Total ascent/descent	470m
Grade	3B
Time	3–4hr
Wire length	350m
Map	Tabacco 03
Parking	Bar Magistrato alla Acque parking: 46.51980, 12.02805

Constructed between 2007 and 2008 by the Bolzano brigade of the Italian Alpini military, this is an excellent route combining an easy approach, enjoyable climbing, far-reaching views, historical interest and an amenable descent. The route scales the south face of Col dei Bos and develops over a number of sections interrupted with unprotected walking. The first 100 metres are fairly stiff for the grade but the difficulties relent as you get higher. It should be noted that the route is occasionally closed to public access at certain times in July, when it is used for military training; army vehicles parked in the vicinity are a good indication of this.

Driving approach
Bar Magistrato alla Acque is located 2km to the east of the Passo Falzarego (the Cortina side), accessed via the SR48 from Cortina or Livinallongo or the SP24 via the Passo Valparola from Val Badia. From the top of the Passo Falzarego descend SR48 east for 2km, passing Bar Strobel (a popular alternative start point) to reach the ruined red remains of Bar Magistrato alla Acque on the left side of the road. There is ample parking adjacent to the building.

Take the path leading off from behind the bar, signed towards Torri del Falzarego and Col dei Bos. Ascend through vegetation to reach the old military road in around 15min and turn left onto this, continuing for another 10min to reach the ruins of a number of wartime buildings, the most striking of which is the old **field hospital** excavated into the rock on the left. The pyramidal buttress of Col dei

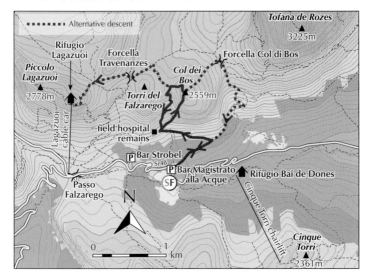

Bos is located to the right of the broad and broken gully just right of the hospital. Follow the path leading up over the grassy slope for 5min to reach the left (south-west) corner of the pyramid and the start of the cable protection.

The climbing is immediately challenging, encountering the hardest passage of the route in the first 100 metres. Climb a steep wall, make a short traverse right then enter into a steep corner. The wire protection is excellent but the traverse feels delicate and exposed while the corner is quite strenuous.

Exit the corner onto easier ground and continue along the path above to move left to a steep wall. A strenuous move up and right leads onto easier scrambling. Cross a grassy slope to the next wall, making a pleasant rightward traverse around a bulge to reach steep but well-featured rock. Climb this with enjoyable moves to exit the cable on a grassy shoulder, continuing along the path with some sections of easy scrambling.

Continue to ascend a further two sections of good, steep rock before arriving at a large shoulder. The cable initially takes a rising traverse line up the left-hand side of the pyramid, before turning back to ascend a final steep and rather technical black wall. The terrain eases soon after, followed by an easy scramble to reach a broad grassy plateau and the end of the wire protection. Ascend north over easy ground for a couple of hundred metres to reach the summit of **Col dei Bos** (2559m).

Making a winter ascent of Col dei Bos

Col dei Bos
(2559m)

The most direct descent from the summit takes the gully to the north-west of Col dei Bos. From the end of the wire, follow an unmarked path leading left over meadows and scree to reach a saddle. Descend into the rather unpleasant scree gully below and pick the best line to return quickly to the ruins of the **military hospital**. From here reverse the approach route to **Bar Magistrato alla Acque**.

Other possibilities
- For a longer but more pleasant descent, from the summit of Col dei Bos, follow sporadic cairns north east on a small, ill-defined path to reach **Forcella Col dei Bos**. From here descend path 402 to join with the access track that encircles the east side of Col dei Bos, passing through a tunnel and shortly after branching left onto path 412 leading down to **Bar Magistrato alla Acque** (2hr, 5km, 600m descent).
- It is also possible to traverse west along path 401/402 to reach the summit of **Piccolo Lagazuoi** (3km, 300m ascent, 100m descent) and then descend either Sentiero dei Kaiserjäger (Route 38) or Sentiero Attrezzato Galleria del Lagazuoi (Route 39).

ROUTE 41
Via Ferrata Averau

Start/Finish	Top of Cinque Torri chairlift
Distance	4km
Total ascent/descent	400m
Grade	2A
Time	2–3hr
Wire length	75m
Map	Tabacco 03
Parking	Rifugio Bai de Dones parking: 46.51897, 12.03799

A very short and technically straightforward route, not without interest. The plateau above the iconic Cinque Torri is well worth a visit in itself, affording excellent views of the surrounding mountains and an enjoyable destination for an easier day. Unfortunately the route must be downclimbed, which can result in queues on good weather days, but the panorama from the summit of Averau makes the wait worthwhile. There are a number of alternative approaches to the route, but access via the Cinque Torri chairlift is the most convenient from the bases suggested in this guide.

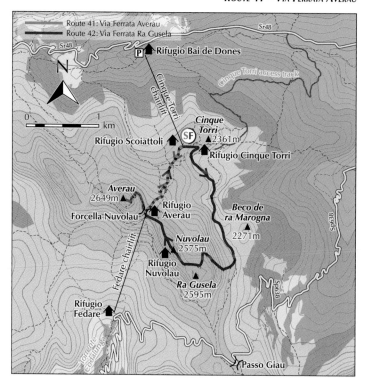

Driving approach

The large car park by the Cinque Torri chairlift and Rifugio Bai de Dones is located 3.5km below and east of the Passo Falzarego and is easily accessed from Cortina via the SR48, from Val Badia via the Passo Valparola and Passo Falzarego on the SP24, or from Livinallongo via the Passo Falzarego on the SR48. Take the chairlift to reach Rifugio Scoiattoli and a wonderful view of the iconic towers of the Cinque Torri below.

From Rifugio Scoiattoli follow the wide vehicle track ascending south-west for 30min to reach **Rifugio Averau**, nestled in Forcella Nuvolau to the right of the mountain of the same name. (Rifugio Nuvolau, one of the oldest rifugios in the Dolomites, can be seen perched on the summit to the left.) From Rifugio Averau

Admiring the views of Cinque Torri after the initial section of wire

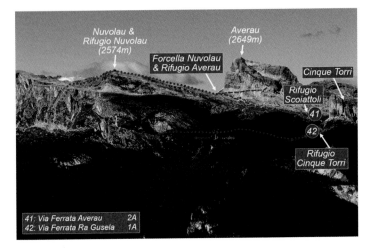

Nuvolau &
Rifugio Nuvolau
(2574m)

Forcella Nuvolau
& Rifugio Averau

Averau
(2649m)

Cinque Torri

Rifugio
Scoiattoli

41

42

Rifugio
Cinque Torri

| 41: Via Ferrata Averau | 2A |
| 42: Via Ferrata Ra Gusela | 1A |

follow the path signed for Ferrata Averau, skirting the scree on the east side of the mountain for 15min to reach the start of the wire.

The route initially ascends diagonally left up a pale face before climbing vertically alongside a cleft. After a few metres there is a junction in the wire; the damp chimney to the left is more commonly used on the descent in an attempt to ease the two-way traffic. Keep right here and climb a slightly bulging wall before following easier terrain to reach the end of the short ferrata. Follow cairns to ascend the featureless scree combe above, switchbacking up rugged terrain for 20min to reach the summit of **Averau** (2649m) and a superb viewpoint.

To descend, reverse the route, keeping right at the junction to descend the narrow chimney mentioned above on stemples, returning to the base of the face and retracing the path back to **Rifugio Averau**. From here either descend direct to the Cinque Torri chairlift or spend some time exploring the surrounding plateau (see below).

Other possibilities
A number of alternative approaches to Averau are possible:
- Perhaps the quickest and most convenient access to Rifugio Averau is using the Fedare chairlift, located 2.5km below and west of the Passo Giau. The chairlift leads directly to **Forcella Nuvolau**.
- The route can also be combined with Route 42, ideally combined with the first of the alternative approaches in 'Other possibilities', ascending from

Passo Giau to reach the summit of **Nuvolau** before descending to Forcella Nuvolau and continuing as per the route above.

• Finally it is possible to reach Rifugio Cinque Torri to the south-east of the towers via an access road located 5.5km east of the Passo Falzarego on the SR48 road. In low season the steep and narrow road is open to private vehicles, with limited roadside parking available just before the private car park of Rifugio Cinque Torri. However, during the day in high season (from 8:30am–4pm in July and August) the road is closed and is instead served by a taxi shuttle service.

There are a number of interesting options to extend the day, two suggestions of which are:

• the straightforward ascent of Nuvolau along path 439
• a tour of the Cinque Torri, exploring the Open-Air War Museum on paths 439 and 425.

ROUTE 42
Via Ferrata Ra Gusela

Start/Finish	Top of Cinque Torri chairlift
Distance	7km
Total ascent/descent	500m
Grade	1A
Time	3–4hr
Wire length	125m
Map	Tabacco 03
Parking	Rifugio Bai de Dones parking: 46.51897, 12.03799
Note	For route map see Route 41

This beautiful walk along a series of exposed gullies and ledges is sometimes referred to as 'Ferrata Nuvolau', named after the broad peak to the north west of Ra Gusela. The approach is through stunning surroundings and the route itself is a satisfying and enjoyable excursion in a typically Dolomitic setting. The short vertical section is well protected with stemples and a short ladder, while most of the route involves very straightforward scrambling. The ferrata finishes at the iconic Rifugio Nuvolau, one of the oldest refuges in the area.

Driving approach

The large car park by the Cinque Torri chairlift and Rifugio Bai de Dones is located 3.5km below and east of the Passo Falzarego and is easily accessed from Cortina via the SR48, from Val Badia via the Passo Valparola and Passo Falzarego on the SP24, or from Livinallongo via the Passo Falzarego on the SR48. Take the chairlift to reach Rifugio Scoiattoli and a wonderful view of the iconic towers of the Cinque Torri below.

From Rifugio Scoiattoli, begin to walk east on the large track skirting the right side of the towers to quickly reach a path cutting off to the right, soon joining with the well-waymarked path 443. Follow this as it leads across meadows with beautiful views towards the striking ridgeline of Croda da Lago. Descend steeply through

Cinque Torri panorama with views of Tofana di Rozes

a particularly attractive landscape of huge boulders and tiny outcrops to reach a path leading right (west), signed to Rifugio Nuvolau and the via ferrata (reached roughly 1hr from the chairlift).

Follow the path to reach the first section of cable, protecting a series of good ledges with only limited exposure. These are followed by a rather dirty red gully, ascended initially on the rock before a short ladder leads onto easier rocky scrambling, again protected by wire as it leads easily onto the rocky plateau above and the end of the first section. The route to Rifugio Nuvolau is less clear from this point as the terrain is very rocky and barren, but the waymarking is good. It is well worth making a short diversion to the summit of **Ra Gusela** (2595m), with several unsigned paths leading to and from the summit.

To continue to Rifugio Nuvolau, follow the waymarks for path 438 for 30min to reach the final section of cable, involving a short climb and a metal ladder. Reach the plateau above and walk easily to the **rifugio**. To descend, follow the broad track waymarked 439 to return in 30min to Rifugio Scoiattoli and the chairlift.

Other possibilities
A couple of alternative approaches to Ra Gusela are possible:

- From the Passo Giau to the south via path 443 (2hr, 3km, 300m ascent); if opting for this route, don't be misled by a distinct footpath climbing towards a broken gully, marked by a metal plaque at the base – this is the line of a long-abandoned route and the plaque is a sign indicating that it is now closed.
- From Rifugio Cinque Torri to the south-east of the towers, accessed via an access road located 5.5km east of the Passo Falzarego on the SR48 road. In low season the steep and narrow road is open to private vehicles, with limited roadside parking available just before the private car park of Rifugio Cinque Torri. However, during the day in high season (from 8:30am–4pm in July and August) the road is closed and is instead served by a taxi shuttle service.

This route may also be enjoyably combined with Route 41 for a longer day.

7 CORTINA

Lago del Sorapiss and the distinctive tower of Dito di Dio ('Finger of God') (Route 59)

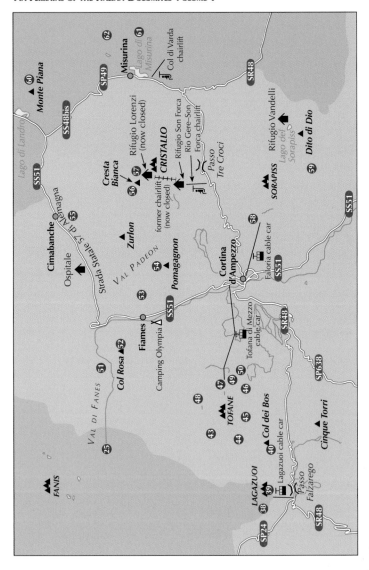

CORTINA

Cortina d'Ampezzo is internationally famous as a winter sports venue having hosted the 1956 Winter Olympics, and as such it is a very popular holiday destination during the winter months. In summer the streets are noticeably quieter (although August is still very busy) but the town nonetheless retains much of its trendy and glamorous nature, while the atmosphere is significantly more Italian than in other areas in the Dolomites. With a long history of independence, Cortina is unique in the Dolomites in still having its own legislative system, the *Regole D'Ampezzo*, and Ampezzano Ladin, the local dialect, is still widely spoken.

Something of a ghost town out of season, in summer the town provides everything the visitor could possibly want, with numerous cafés, pizzerias, sports shops, hotels and supermarkets. The Cooperativa on the main street is more of a classy department store than anything else and sells everything from groceries, maps and books to clothing and climbing equipment. For a true Italian experience, visit Cortina in the evening to enjoy a leisurely stroll (the Italian *passeggiata*), have a drink in one of the many outside bars and people-watch.

Inevitably, the glamour and popularity comes at a price, with accommodation in particular being much costlier than in other, smaller villages. However, there are several campsites just outside the town if your budget doesn't stretch to Cortina's prices, and there's a large car park by the bus station if travelling in from elsewhere. The centre of Cortina is pedestrianised and there's a rather complicated one-way system around the town.

If using public transport, there are numerous bus services connecting the outlying villages and passes, while there are various lift systems providing access to the surrounding mountains: the three-stage Freccia nel Cielo (literally 'Arrow in the Sky') cable car serves the Tofane group, the Faloria cable car leads to the Sorapiss group, while to the east the Rio Gere chairlift shaves 500m off the ascent to the Cristallo group.

There is a wide geographic distribution of routes accessible from Cortina. The **Tofane group** is formed of three main peaks: Tofana di Rozes, Tofana di Dentro and Tofana di Mezzo. The latter is the third highest mountain in the Dolomites and all three are over 3000m; consequently, all of the routes in the group should be considered fairly serious undertakings and good weather conditions are highly advisable, regardless of the relatively easy technical standard of some of the routes. In addition to some excellent via ferrata days, these mountains offer wonderful rugged walking, with Routes 43, 45, 46, 48, 49 and 50 offering interesting yet technically straightforward excursions. By contrast, Route 44 to the summit of Tofana di Rozes and Route 47 to the summit of Tofana di Mezzo are both long, strenuous and challenging routes.

There are four routes in **Cortina North**, all of which are at relatively low levels and therefore may be in condition when other high-level routes are still covered in residual winter snow. Route 51 is an excellent wet-weather option, exploring the dramatic Cascate di Fanes waterfalls, while Routes 52 and 53 are classic mid-grade via ferratas offering enjoyable climbing on solid rock. These routes are accessed from the SS51 Cortina to Dobbiaco road.

The **Cristallo group** hosts a handful of routes with very varied characteristics: Routes 56 and 57 are technically straightforward but long and committing ridge routes, while Route 58 is a high-grade modern route scaling the steep western buttress of Monte Faloria. The latter benefits from easy access via the Faloria cable car that departs from the centre of Cortina, whereas Routes 56 and 57 in particular require some inventive planning in terms of logistics.

Sorapiss is an imposing mountain located south-east of Cortina and is best known for the vivid turquoise waters of its eponymous lake nestled in the heart of the group below the melodramatically named Dito di Dio ('Finger of God'). There are three via ferratas in the area – Francesco Berti, Sentiero Carlo Minazio and Alfonso Vandelli – which, due to their remote locations from the road yet close proximity to one another, are best combined into a two-day circular route (Route 59). Access is from Passo Tre Croci to the east of Cortina.

Information on route conditions can be checked with the Cortina Guides office (tel + 39 0436 868505, email info@guidecortina.com, visit www.guidecortina.com).

Fleeing a fast approaching storm on Via Ferrata Francesco Berti (Route 59)

ROUTE 43
Via Ferrata Scala del Menighel

Start/Finish	Rifugio Dibona
Distance	11.5km
Total ascent/descent	850m
Grade	1C
Time	5–6hr
Wire length	70m
Map	Tabacco 03
Parking	Rifugio Dibona car park: 46.53269, 12.07032

Although the ferrata section of this route is only very short, the excursion as described here makes a complete clockwise circuit of Tofana di Rozes and ascends the characteristic stemples of the 'Scala'. The route was originally equipped in 1907 by the then warden of Rifugio Wolf von Glanvell; subsequently the iron was either removed or bent out of use during the war and the rifugio itself was destroyed by the Italian artillery in 1915. The stemples in their current state were reinstated in 1958.

Driving approach
Rifugio Dibona is accessed from the SR48, either ascending for 10km from Cortina or descending 7.5km from the Passo Falzarego, accessed via the SR48 from Livinallongo or the SP43 via the Passo Valparola from Val Badia. A few hundred metres west of the small chapel of Vervei, turn off the main road, passing under a wooden height barrier signed 'Parco Naturale d'Ampezzo'. Follow signs for Rifugio Dibona and Rifugio Duca d'Aosta then at the fork keep left, continuing for a further 2km to reach the ample parking area at Rifugio Dibona.

From Rifugio Dibona, follow the track uphill on path 403 to reach a junction by the old goods cableway station. Turn left here onto path 442 and continue to reach 404, a well-marked path which traverses below the south face of Tofana di Rozes, continuing past the turn-offs for the Gallerie del Castelletto and Giovanni Lipella to ascend to **Forcella Col dei Bos**, surrounded by remnants of the First World War.

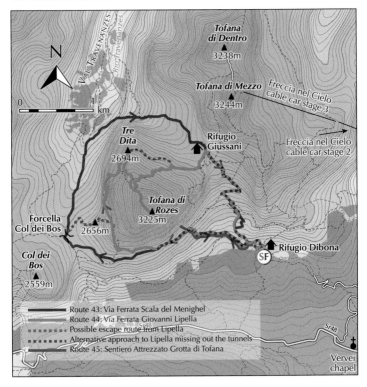

Tofana
di Dentro
▲
3238m

Tofana di Mezzo   Freccia nel Cielo
▲   cable car stage 3
3244m

VAL TRAVENANZES

Rio Travenanzes

N

0   1
——————————————— km

Tre
Dita   Rifugio
▲   Giussani
2694m
                           ← Freccia nel Cielo
                              cable car stage 2

Tofana di
Rozes
▲
3225m

Forcella
Col dei Bos   ▲   ▲ Rifugio Dibona
              2656m   SF

Col dei
Bos
▲
2559m

——————— Route 43: Via Ferrata Scala del Menighel
——————— Route 44: Via Ferrata Giovanni Lipella
••••••••• Possible escape route from Lipella
▬▬▬▬▬ Alternative approach to Lipella missing out the tunnels   Sr48
——————— Route 45: Sentiero Attrezzato Grotta di Tofana

Sr48

✝
Vervei
chapel

Continue north on path 404, now rounding the west side of the mountain and entering into the dramatic Val Travenanzes. At the next junction, branch right following signs for the Scala del Menighel. Continue for a few minutes to reach the start of the characteristic and steep set of stemples in about 2hr from Rifugio Dibona.

Although the Scala is technically straightforward, effectively presenting a long ladder of single-bar stemples, the ascent is very exposed. At the end of the ladder (15min of climbing), follow path 403 right for about an hour to make the final ascent to **Rifugio Giussani** in the heart of the dramatic landscape between Tofana di Rozes and Tofana di Mezzo.

From the rifugio, descend initially rocky terrain past old wartime ruins, following the well-marked path 403 to join the old military road ascending from the valley below, returning easily to **Rifugio Dibona** in 1½–2hr.

Other possibilities
If time permits, this route can be combined with Sentiero Attrezzato Grotta di Tofana (Route 45).

Topping out on the stemples of Via Ferrata Scala del Menighel

ROUTE 44
Via Ferrata Giovanni Lipella

Start/Finish	Rifugio Dibona
Distance	12km
Total ascent/descent	1250m
Grade	4C
Time	7–8hr
Wire length	600m
Map	Tabacco 03
Parking	Rifugio Dibona car park: 46.53269, 12.07032
Note	Torch required for the tunnel section. For route map see Route 41

A true classic of the Cortina region, Via Ferrata Giovanni Lipella reaches the commanding summit of Tofana di Rozes, offering a sustained and demanding mountain excursion with long sections of climbing. The rock is generally excellent and the initial part of the route traverses a set of First World War tunnels at the base of the mountain. Given the northerly aspect and the significant altitude, icing and snow are possible at any time of year.

Driving approach
Rifugio Dibona is accessed from the SR48, either ascending for 10km from Cortina or descending 7.5km from the Passo Falzarego, accessed via the SR48 from Livinallongo or the SP43 via the Passo Valparola from Val Badia. A few hundred metres west of the small chapel of Vervei, turn off the main road, passing under a wooden height barrier signed 'Parco Naturale d'Ampezzo'. Follow signs for Rifugio Dibona and Rifugio Duca d'Aosta then at the fork keep left, continuing for a further 2km to reach the ample parking area at Rifugio Dibona.

From Rifugio Dibona, follow the track uphill on path 403 to reach a junction by the old goods cableway station. Turn left here onto path 442 and continue to reach path 404, a well-marked path traversing below the south face of Tofana di Rozes. Follow this for around 1hr to reach a sign for Ferrata Giovanni Lipella and Gallerie di Castelletto; turn right here and ascend to reach the entrance to a series of wartime tunnels below a set of stemples.

Climb the stemples and enter into the steep and often damp tunnels. Follow these for around 500 metres then at the fork keep right, ascending for a few more metres and exiting the tunnels to descend a short section of wire to a path below. Now follow the unprotected path across the scree slope for 10min to reach the true start of the ferrata.

The route now continues with intermittent wire protection along a series of ledges, walls and horizontal traverses. Around 2½hr from entering the tunnels, reach a large ledge marked with arrows and painted signs. (Left here leads west around the buttress towards Tre Dita and a shorter descent to Rifugio Giussani, forming a convenient escape route if required.) To continue the route, turn right, signed for 'CIMA', following a long scree ledge to reach a dramatic red bowl and the second part of the ferrata.

This section takes some drainage in places and so can be iced up even in dry weather; climb steeply for around 300 metres to reach the shoulder of Tofana di Rozes, marked by a memorial plaque to Giovanni Lipella. A short ascent leads to the broad saddle to the north-west of the summit, where the ascent joins on to the normal walking route. Turn right onto this and follow the cairns and waymarks for around 30min, ascending the final 200 metres to reach the large summit cross on **Tofana di Rozes** (3225m).

To descend, retrace the upper walking section to the saddle, then descend to the north-east. Route-finding is not completely straightforward as there are

Ascending the huge amphitheatre on the north-west side of Tofana di Rozes

numerous possible lines, but generally the descent is well travelled and there are sporadic cairns and paint markers to indicate the way.

Continue to reach **Rifugio Giussani** then join onto the old military road, waymarked as path 403. Descend this easily to return to **Rifugio Dibona**, with the total descent from the summit taking around 2hr.

Other possibilities

For parties without a head torch the start of the wire can be accessed from further west, skipping the initial tunnels. Continue traversing around the base of Tofana di Rozes following path 404 to **Forcella Col di Bos**. Here follow signposting towards Giovanni Lipella as a small path leads to a ladder. Climb this to rejoin the route after the tunnels. This is not recommended, however, as you miss one of the most interesting and historical sections.

ROUTE 45
Sentiero Attrezzato Grotta di Tofana

Start/Finish	Rifugio Dibona
Distance	3km
Total ascent/descent	350m
Grade	1A
Time	2–3hr
Wire length	100m
Map	Tabacco 03
Parking	Rifugio Dibona car park: 46.53269, 12.07032
Note	Headtorch essential. For route map see Route 43

Something of a hidden gem, the Grotta di Tofana is not so much a via ferrata as an excursion into a subterranean world. The cave is particularly worth a visit in late spring, when the meltwater seepage causes stunning stalactites to form.

Entering the Grotta di Tofana

Grotta
di Tofana

Driving approach

Rifugio Dibona is accessed from the SR48, either ascending for 10km from Cortina or descending 7.5km from the Passo Falzarego, accessed via the SR48 from Livinallongo or the SP43 via the Passo Valparola from Val Badia. A few hundred metres west of the small chapel of Vervei, turn off the main road, passing under a wooden height barrier signed 'Parco Naturale d'Ampezzo'. Follow signs for Rifugio Dibona and Rifugio Duca d'Aosta then at the fork keep left, continuing for a further 2km to reach the ample parking area at Rifugio Dibona.

From Rifugio Dibona, follow the track uphill on path 403 to reach a junction by the old goods cableway station. Turn left here onto path 442 and continue to reach path 404, a well-marked path traversing below the south face of Tofana di Rozes. Here, a painted sign on a boulder indicates the path to the Grotta di Tofana; turn right onto this and ascend the scree slope above to reach the start of the short cabled section on the left.

Traverse an exposed ledge for 10–15min to reach the entrance to the cave, then follow the cables and short metal ladders to complete a short circular route inside the cavern. On returning to the entrance of the cave, reverse the route back to **Rifugio Dibona**.

Other possibilities

If time permits, this route can be combined with Via Ferrata Scala del Menighel (Route 43).

ROUTE 46
Sentiero Astaldi

Start/Finish	Rifugio Dibona
Distance	3km
Total ascent/descent	300m
Grade	1A
Time	2hr
Wire length	400m
Map	Tabacco 03
Parking	Rifugio Dibona car park: 46.53269, 12.07032
Note	For route map see Route 47

This is a wonderfully airy and exposed walk through unique rocky terrain. The route is particularly interesting from a geological point of view, passing alongside the exposed strata of limestone interwoven with layers of pale green and red clay-like material of the 'Raibl' series, which glow startlingly in sunlight. The path traverses from Rifugio Dibona to Rifugio Pomedes and forms a useful approach to Punta Anna (Route 47), but despite the low grade the route is nonetheless worth exploring in its own right.

Driving approach
Rifugio Dibona is accessed from the SR48, either ascending for 10km from Cortina or descending 7.5km from the Passo Falzarego, accessed via the SR48 from Livinallongo or the SP43 via the Passo Valparola from Val Badia. A few hundred metres west of the small chapel of Vervei, turn off the main road, passing under a wooden height barrier signed 'Parco Naturale d'Ampezzo'. Follow signs for Rifugio Dibona and Rifugio Duca d'Aosta then at the fork keep left, continuing for a further 2km to reach the ample parking area at Rifugio Dibona.

From Rifugio Dibona, walk uphill on path 403, following the old military road towards Rifugio Giussani. When drawing level with the top of the steep rock band that runs directly above Rifugio Dibona, take a less well-defined path leading off to the right (east) up to the crest of a grassy ridge. The ferrata begins at the point where this ridge meets the curiously stratified rock wall above.

Tofana di Mezzo
(3244m)

Freccia nel Cielo
cable car top station

Bus de Tofana
(3026)

Punta Anna
(2731m)

1A
5C
1B

46: Sentiero Astaldi
47: Via Ferrata Punta Anna & Gianni Aglio
49: Sentiero Giuseppe Olivieri

Rifugio
Pomedes

49

47

Rifugio Dibona

46

Possible escape
route through the
Bus de Tofana

path 403

path 412

Passing underneath one of the many overhangs on the traverse

Follow intermittent cable as the path makes an undulating traverse, with some quite exposed passages, to reach a junction towards the end of the ledge. A path up a shallow, broken gully leads up towards Rifugio Pomedes here; to complete the circuit back to Rifugio Dibona, continue straight on to reach path 421 and descend this easily right to return to the **parking area**.

Other possibilities
This route can be used to approach the considerably more challenging Punta Anna (Route 47), keeping left at the junction towards the end of the ledge to ascend to **Rifugio Pomedes**.

ROUTE 47
Via Ferrata Punta Anna and Gianni Aglio

Start/Finish	Rifugio Pomedes, top of two-stage Duca d'Aosta chairlift
Distance	10km
Total ascent/descent	1200m
Grade	5C
Time	7–8hr
Wire length	800m
Map	Tabacco 03
Parking	Ristorante Pietofana: 46.54066, 12.09868
Note	For topo see Route 46

Without doubt one of the classics of the Cortina area and the Dolomites, Punta Anna is a long, airy and technical route that culminates at the summit of Tofana di Mezzo (3244m). The length and difficulty, not to mention the altitude, require good stamina and commitment, while ice and snow are possible at any time of year. In high season the chairlift approach and cable car descent shorten the day somewhat, but the route is still a sustained and demanding affair. The route given here combines Via Ferrata Giuseppe Olivieri and Via Ferrata Gianni Aglio.

Driving approach

From the centre of Cortina d'Ampezzo, take the SR48 west towards the Passo Falzarego. After 2km turn right, signed for Gildardon and Ristorante Pietofana, and follow the narrow road for 3.5km to reach Ristorante Pietofana and the base of the Duca d'Aosta-Pomedes chairlift. Take the chairlift to Rifugio Pomedes.

From Rifugio Pomedes, follow a steep path which switchbacks up behind the chairlift, signed for Via Ferrata Punta Anna. The start of the cable protection is reached in around 15min. Follow the wire up and left to reach an airy traverse; this leads into a steep ridge and gives an immediate feeling of exposure. An hour of excellent, technical and sustained climbing leads to the indistinct rocky plateau of **Punta Anna** (2731m) which makes for a logical rest point.

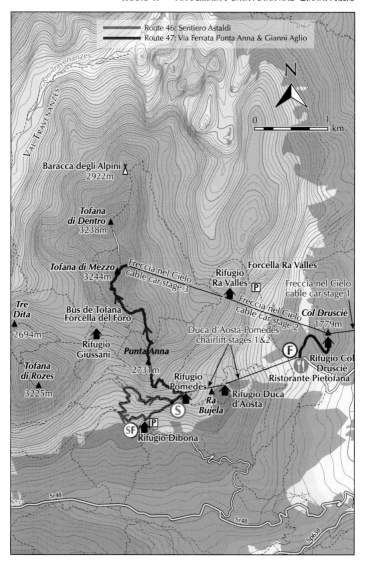

Continue to follow a narrow path with intermittent protection along the crest of the ridge to a notch (be sure to follow the waymarks as false tracks appear to lead down ledges and the route may be less obvious in poor weather). In around 20min come to a painted sign marked 'Cima'; at this point there is also a way-marked escape route to Rifugio Giussani down to the left.

To continue the ferrata, keep right to reach a sloping ledge. Follow this right to join another exposed rightward ledge and continue to reach another junction. Here 'Cima' is indicated up diagonally to the left, while paint on a separate rock on the other side of the track indicates 'Pomedes' and 'Sent. Olivieri' straight ahead to the north-east (another possible escape route; see Route 49). Follow the arrow for 'Cima', following sporadic waymarks leading up a series of scree slopes. Reach the next ridge and follow intermittent cable to reach a ladder, overcoming a short and steep rock wall.

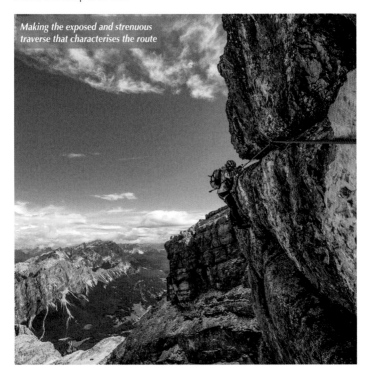

Making the exposed and strenuous traverse that characterises the route

Follow the ridge before descending a sloping ledge on the west side to a notch. Cross this on dirty rock and loose earth, with gullies falling away on both sides, after which a strenuous pitch leads from the notch onto the base of the tower above, where the protection branches uphill for an optional out-and-back ascent of the tower itself.

To continue the route, move right along a ledge to a strenuous, exposed move around a corner, which is very airy but well protected. Continue behind a rock pillar to reach **Bus de Tofana**, having now been on the route for around 4hr and with at least a further 1½hr to go.

Before continuing the route to the summit it is worth following the wire that leads downhill on the left to the giant rock window of **Forcella del Foro** (2910m) to gain a view through the rock archway. (At the time of writing there are plans to add new wire adjacent to the rock window thus bypassing the avalanche barriers and continuing direct along the ridge.) Reverse this then continue straight on (north) across broken ground to reach a series of avalanche barriers, where it is not uncommon to find a snowfield.

Continue through the barriers to reach two successive ladders; climb these then follow exposed ledges to the final short ladder and the end of the cable protection. Follow waymarks to reach the summit of **Tofana di Mezzo** (3244m), taking in outstanding views not only of the nearby Dolomites but also the Stubai, Zillertal and Glockner ranges in Austria.

The most convenient descent is to take the Freccia nel Cielo cable car from the summit of Tofana di Mezzo to Col Druscié (the second stop on the way down), to then follow an obvious track back to the parking area at **Ristorante Pietofana**.

Other possibilities

- It is also possible to descend on foot to Rifugio Dibona by reversing the ascent route to Bus de Tofana. On reaching **Forcella del Foro**, pass through the window to the west side and follow a steep path down through the scree to join path 403 below **Rifugio Giussani** to return to **Rifugio Dibona**. Allow around 2½hr for the descent from the summit to Rifugio Dibona.
- An alternative descent can be made via Route 49, returning to Rifugio Pomedes and the top of the chairlift; however, this is more commonly used as an escape route or to avoid the final ascent to the summit.
- Alternatively it's possible to start the route from Rifugio Dibona, ascending Sentiero Astaldi (Route 46) to Rifugio Pomedes. This makes for a nice combination but does complicate the return to the car without a second vehicle or taxi journey.

ROUTE 48
Via Ferrata Lamon and Formenton

Start	Top of Freccia nel Cielo cable car
Finish	Rifugio Ra Valles, cable car midstation
Distance	5.5km
Total ascent	200m
Total descent	950m
Grade	2B
Time	3–4hr
Wire length	200m
Map	Tabacco 03
Parking	Freccia nel Cielo cable car parking, Cortina: 46.54528, 12.13152

A combination of two routes, Ferrata Lamon and Ferrata Formenton, the route given here departs from Tofana di Mezzo and reaches the summit of the nearby Tofana di Dentro before descending the north ridge to reach Rifugio Ra Valles.

Driving approach

It's possible to take the cable car directly from the centre of Cortina for two stages to reach the Ra Valles midstation, or alternatively to park at Ristorante Pietofana and walk up the track to Col Druscìè and the lower midstation, taking the cable car for one stage to Ra Valles.

To reach the Freccia nel Cielo cable car in the centre of Cortina, follow good signposting towards the 'Stadio Olimpico del ghiaccio' (Olympic ice rink) in the northern part of town. The Freccia nel Cielo cable car is located just behind the ice rink and has ample parking.

To access Rifugio Pietofana, take the SR48 west from Cortina towards the Passo Falzarego. After 2km turn right, signed for Gildardon and Ristorante Pietofana, and follow the narrow road for 3.5km to reach Ristorante Pietofana and a large car park.

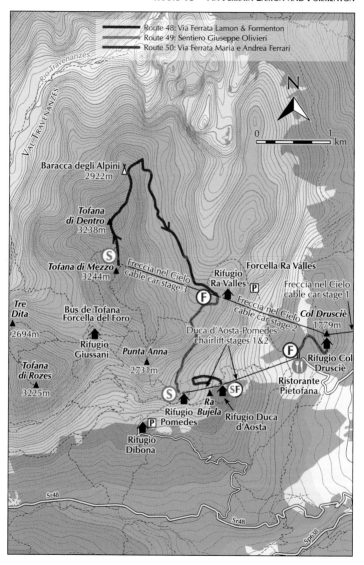

Route 48: Via Ferrata Lamon & Formenton
Route 49: Sentiero Giuseppe Olivieri
Route 50: Via Ferrata Maria e Andrea Ferrari

N

0   1
km

Baracca degli Alpini
2922m

Rio Travenanzes

Val Travenanzes

Tofana
di Dentro
3238m

Tofana di Mezzo
3244m

Freccia nel Cielo
cable car stage 3

Forcella Ra Valles

Rifugio
Ra Valles   P

Freccia nel Cielo
cable car stage 1

Freccia nel Cielo
cable car stage 2

Col Druscè
1779m

Tre
Dita
2694m

Bus de Tofana
Forcella del Foro

Duca d'Aosta-Pomedes
chairlift stages 1&2

Rifugio
Giussani

Punta Anna
2731m

Rifugio Col
Druscè

Ristorante
Pietofana

Tofana
di Rozes
3225m

Rifugio
Dibona   P

Ra
Bujela

Rifugio
Pomedes

Rifugio Duca
d'Aosta

Sr48

Sr48

Sp638

213

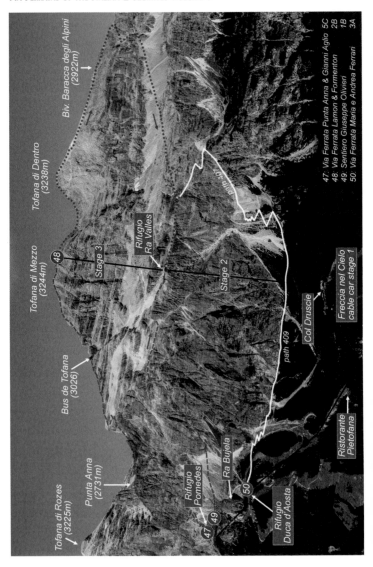

47: Via Ferrata Punta Anna & Gianni Aglio   5C
48: Via Ferrata Lamon & Formenton   2B
49: Sentiero Giuseppe Olivieri   1B
50: Via Ferrata Maria e Andrea Ferrari   3A

Biv. Baracca degli Alpini (2922m)

Tofana di Dentro (3238m)

Tofana di Mezzo (3244m)

Bus de Tofana (3026)

Tofana di Rozes (3225m)

Punta Anna (2731m)

Rifugio Ra Valles

Stage 3

Stage 2

path 401

path 409

Col Druscie

Freccia nel Cielo cable car stage 1

Ristorante Pietofana

Rifugio Pomedes

Ra Bujela

Rifugio Duca d'Aosta

47 49 50

From the top station of the cable car a short walk leads to the summit of **Tofana di Mezzo** (3244m). Return from here towards the cable car station and follow red waymarks down a ramp on the left (west) side of the ridge, protected by somewhat loose cables.

Continue down to the saddle between Tofana di Mezzo and Tofana di Dentro and then ascend the ridge towards Tofana di Dentro. The cable protection is reasonable as the route works its way up the ridge, passing a number of First World War fortifications. Time from summit to summit (which involves a descent and ascent of 140m) is around 1–1½hr. While the route is technically very straightforward, the terrain can be subject to snow and icing even in the middle of the summer.

From the top of **Tofana di Dentro** (3238m), continue north-east down the wide ridge, passing a wartime fortification and following a waymarked path to reach a very broken ridge with some unstable rock. After passing Biv. **Baracca degli Alpini**, the ridge descends on more discontinuous wires and drops down broken ground to the right.

After an exposed traverse along a ledge to the right, follow switchbacks down a broken gully with some exposed, unprotected scrambling before passing through a window in the rock and out onto an open path below some more wartime buildings. The path descends into a rocky gully to reach a traverse leading around the left-hand wall of some rocks to avoid some unnecessary descent.

A final section of ascent leads up to **Rifugio Ra Valles** and the second intermediate station of the Tofana cable car. Descend in the cable car to return to the car.

Other possibilities
- For a much shorter day it is possible to climb Ferrata Lamon in isolation, ascending to the summit of Tofana di Dentro and returning to the top cable car station the same way.
- Alternatively, for a slightly longer day (4½–5½hr), the via ferratas can be travelled in the opposite direction to the route described here, beginning from Rifugio Ra Valles (easily accessed by cable car or via a short walk from Ristorante Pietofana) and ascending the routes to finish at the top station of the cable car.

ROUTE 49
Sentiero Giuseppe Olivieri

Start	Rifugio Pomedes, top of two-stage Duca d'Aosta chairlift
Finish	Ristorante Pietofana
Distance	3km
Total ascent/descent	280m
Grade	1B
Time	2–3hr
Wire length	300m
Map	Tabacco 03
Parking	Ristorante Pietofana: 46.54066, 12.09868
Note	For route map and topo see Route 48

Not to be confused with Via Ferrata Giuseppe Oliveri (part of Route 47 and the ascent of Punta Anna and Tofana di Mezzo), this is a rarely travelled but panoramic route linking Rifugio Pomedes to Rifugio Ra Valles. The path follows a series of exposed ledges and offers superb views over Cortina d'Ampezzo. The route can be joined midway through Route 47 but as a standalone excursion it is accessed from Rifugio Pomedes.

Driving approach
From the centre of Cortina d'Ampezzo, take the SR48 west towards the Passo Falzarego. After 2km turn right, signed for Gildardon and Ristorante Pietofana, and follow the narrow road for 3.5km to reach Ristorante Pietofana and the base of the Duca d'Aosta-Pomedes chairlift. Take the two-stage chairlift to Rifugio Pomedes.

From Rifugio Pomedes, head right across the scree to reach the start of the route, where Via Ferrata Punta Anna (Route 47) is signed left. Keep right, following signs for Sentiero Attrezzato Giuseppe Olivieri.
   The route develops over moderately exposed scree ledges, interrupted by steeper rocky walls equipped with ladders. The wire is intermittent but the airiest

sections are well protected. Midway through the route, above a wide scree bowl by the top of a chairlift station, the alternative access to the route for those who have climbed the initial part of Route 47 joins. The route ends at **Rifugio Ra Valles** and the upper midstation of the Freccia nel Cielo cable car.

The most convenient descent from this point is to take the cable car down one stage to **Col Druscié**, then follow the broad vehicle track below easily to reach **Ristorante Pietofana**.

Other possibilities

- This route may be used as a shorter alternative to Route 47, keeping right at the junction marked 'Cima' to join the route midway through.
- To avoid descending by cable car, from Rifugio Ra Valles it is possible to descend north-east along path 407 to **Forcella Ra Valles**. From the saddle descend the steep scree slope to the south-east to a prominent junction; keep left here to descend steeply to **Ristorante Pietofana** below (2–3hr, 7.5km, 900m descent from Rifugio Ra Valles).
- Rifugio Pomedes may also be accessed a number of ways on foot; the most interesting of these is to ascend Sentiero Astaldi (Route 46), accessed from Rifugio Dibona, or Via Ferrata Maria e Andrea Ferrari (Route 50) from Rifugio Duca d'Aosta.

ROUTE 50
Via Ferrata Maria e Andrea Ferrari

Start/Finish	Rifugio Duca d'Aosta, top of first Duca d'Aosta chairlift
Distance	1km
Total ascent/descent	150m
Grade	3A
Time	1–2hr
Wire length	380m
Map	Tabacco 03
Parking	Ristorante Pietofana: 46.54066, 12.09868
Note	For route map see Route 48

Inaugurated in 2015, this is one of the most recently constructed via ferratas in the Dolomites. It was designed to provide an alternative to the more challenging, higher-altitude routes of the surrounding area while offering more technical interest than the many lower-grade protected paths. The route scales the small tower of Ra Bujela and although short, offers excellent views and enjoyable climbing. When climbed in conjunction with the chairlift it makes for a very short day, but the route may also be conveniently combined with Sentiero Giuseppe Oliveri (Route 49) or Punta Anna (Route 47).

Driving approach

From the centre of Cortina d'Ampezzo, drive the SR48 west towards the Passo Falzarego. After 2km turn right, signed for Gildardon and Ristorante Pietofana, and follow the narrow road for 3.5km to reach Ristorante Pietofana and the base of the Duca d'Aosta-Pomedes chairlift. Take the first chairlift to reach Rifugio Duca d'Aosta.

The start of the via ferrata is located a mere 200 metres away from Rifugio Duca d'Aosta. Follow good signposting towards 'Ferrata Maria e Andrea Ferrari', aiming for the right-hand side of the tower. Pass through scrub and dwarf pines to arrive at the start of the wire, which is clearly denoted with a plaque.

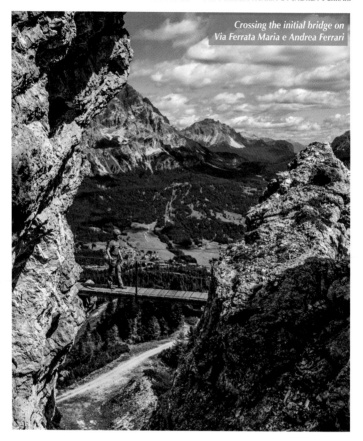

Crossing the initial bridge on Via Ferrata Maria e Andrea Ferrari

The route is immediately steep with varied and interesting climbing on good, well-protected rock. After the initial vertical section the route veers left, crossing over the first of two suspension bridges which provide excellent views back towards Cortina.

A further section of rightward-trending scrambling leads to the second bridge; here cross back over onto the right-hand side of the tower. One final exposed traverse right and an ascent of an excellent arête marks the end of the difficulties, followed by easy scrambling up to a fork in the wire just below the summit.

Turn right to reach the small summit (with only room for about four people) and then reverse the wire back to the fork and turn left to descend to a grassy knoll. From here descend either of the two ski pistes encircling the tower to return back to **Rifugio Duca d'Aosta**.

Other possibilities
- This route can be combined with Sentiero Giuseppe Olivieri (Route 49) to create an excellent excursion. From the top of Maria e Andrea Ferrari, continue up to **Rifugio Pomedes** before ascending Sentiero Giuseppe Olivieri as far as **Rifugio Ra Valles** and the Freccia nel Cielo lift midstation. Take the cable car down to **Col Drusciè** and from here return on foot to Ristorante Pietofana and the car park in 15min.
- The route can also be used as an effective and interesting approach to Punta Anna (Route 47) by continuing up to **Rifugio Pomedes** after completing Maria e Andrea Ferrari.

ROUTE 51
Sentiero Attrezzato Giovanni Barbara/Lucio Dalaiti/Cengia de Mattia

Start/Finish	Ponte Felizon car park, Valle di Fanes
Distance	12km
Total ascent/descent	200m
Grade	2B
Time	4–5hr
Wire length	100m
Map	Tabacco 03
Parking	Ponte Felizon car park: 46.59349, 12.11325

A combination of two or even three short via ferratas, the route described here offers a spectacular exploration of the Cascate de Fanes waterfalls. Traversing a series of ledges interrupted with short rocky steps above a dramatic gorge, the route passes behind the waterfall itself and presents some excellent photographic opportunities. Given the low altitude and the fact the route is wet by nature, it's a good option on rainy days – although the views and setting are naturally best appreciated in good weather.

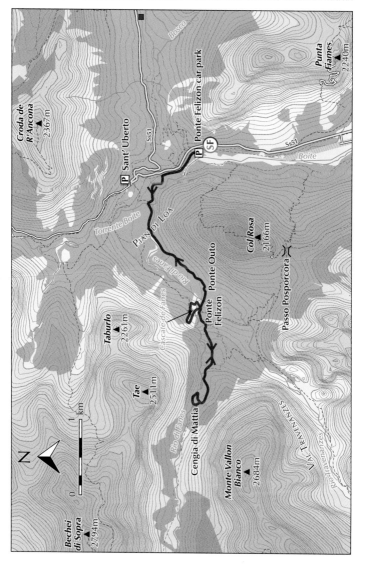

Crossing behind Cascate di Fanes

Driving approach

From Cortina d'Ampezzo, follow the SS51 north, passing International Camping Olympia and Hotel Fiames on the left. Shortly after Hotel Fiames and 5.5km from Cortina, turn left down a narrow road with a wooden archway overhead reading 'Parco Naturale delle Dolomiti Ampezzane'. Follow the road down for 1km and park in the large clearing at the end of the road.

From the car park follow path 10 along the paved road, signed for Cascate di Fanes and Ponte Outo. In 20min reach a fork at **Pian de Loa** and keep left, continuing on path 10 to undulate through the trees. After a further 25min reach **Ponte Outo** – a bridge over a narrow gorge over which, according to local legend, a knight once leapt on his horse in order to visit his beloved in Cortina.

Cross the bridge and continue for 150 metres to a small picnic site in a copse just beyond on the right; the via ferrata begins here. Head to the back right of the copse to reach a metal plaque marking the start of the first ferrata. Follow this down a sloping ledge, soon reaching a view of the spectacular waterfall.

Follow the route behind the waterfall itself then continue through a notch before descending to the bottom of the gorge. (There is a path leading left at this point that takes a series of steep reinforced wooden switchbacks to exit onto the north side of the gorge. A path descends to the east from here to join up with path 10 just short of the car park.) To continue the route, cross a metal bridge over the river and walk up to an obvious ramp, again marked with a metal plaque. Ascend the ramp then overcome two slightly steeper rock steps to reach a ledge. Continue more easily to the end of the wire, exiting the ledge system just below the picnic site.

It's possible to end the route here and return to Ponte Felizon via the approach route; however for a full exploration of the falls, follow the track by the picnic site west for a short way to where a smaller path leads back into the trees to the right. Take this, ascending through woodland to reach another junction; keep right again, crossing a bridge and following the course of the river upstream.

Cross back over the river a number of times, eventually reaching more level ground and a view of the fall in front, Cascata di Sopra. Follow the path to the left side of the fall to reach the **Cengia di Mattia** ledge, again marked by a metal plaque. Metal cable protects the route as it traverses behind the fall before climbing a short wall. Follow the path across the top of the crest and curve back left to rejoin the main path.

Turn left to descend east back towards Ponte Outo, eventually joining a gravel track (there is shortcut on a steep woodland path here; either route will lead back to Ponte Outo). On reaching **Ponte Outo**, cross back over the bridge and retrace the approach route back to the **car park**.

Other possibilities

- The route given here combines three via ferratas; for a shorter day, it is possible to avoid continuing to the upper fall and the Cengia di Mattia and instead return directly to the car park after completing the first two routes.

ROUTE 52
Via Ferrata Ettore Bovero

Start/Finish	International Camping Olympia
Distance	10.5km
Total ascent/descent	900m
Grade	3B
Time	5–6hr
Wire length	300m
Map	Tabacco 03
Parking	Fiames tourist information parking: 46.57226, 12.11727

This excellent route ascends Col Rosa on solid rock, offering superb positions and interesting, albeit occasionally strenuous, climbing. Although rather low in altitude, Col Rosa enjoys a privileged and isolated position, standing alone from the surrounding higher peaks, and as such the views from the summit are excellent. The somewhat long approach is more than compensated by the time on the wire, while the woodland descent is straightforward and pleasant.

Driving approach
From Cortina d'Ampezzo, follow the SS51 north for 5km to International Camping Olympia. There is limited parking at the campsite but generally the spaces are reserved for residents, however there is ample parking just beyond the campsite turn-off at the tourist information centre on the left.

From the tourist information centre, take the path through the woods adjoining the river to the bridge over the River Boite to reach the entrance of **International Camping Olympia**. Follow the track to the left of the entrance to skirt alongside the campsite perimeter on path 417.

After undulating along the track for 1.5km, turn left onto path 408, signed for the via ferrata. This ascends steeply through the trees for around 1½hr to reach **Passo Posporcora**.

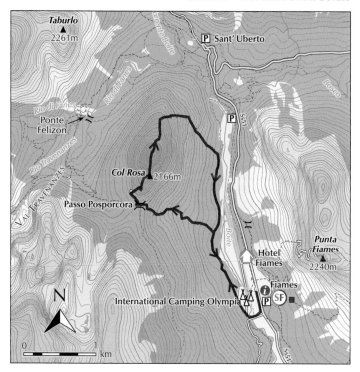

Just beyond the pass, turn right onto a smaller path, still following signs for the via ferrata. The path climbs steeply through shrubs and onto scree, negotiating a series of short ledges to reach a plaque marking the start of the route in 30min.

Follow the first section of wire past dwarf pines clinging to the steep rock wall. A short but airy unprotected section follows before the cable resumes to ascend a superb arête. Continue to make an exposed traverse to the left then onto easier rocky ground, with interesting climbing leading to the end of the main part of the route.

Follow the well-trodden path towards the final summit rocks then scale a gully equipped with stemples to arrive just below the summit. Walk easily up to the summit cross on **Col Rosa** (2166m); as well as superb views of Cortina and the surrounding peaks, there is a network of wartime tunnels and chambers. The

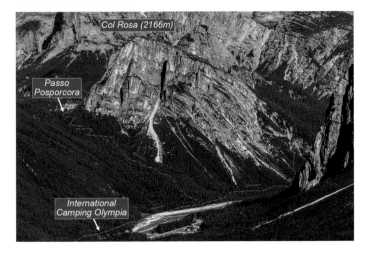

entrance to these is not obvious but is located in the trench running across the summit plateau, about 25 metres from the cross.

The descent follows path 447, descending the rocky plateau below the summit along the north ridge before bending right (south-east) to wind through pleasant pine forests towards the valley floor. The final few hundred metres of descent is steeper, following a series of reinforced steps before rejoining the forestry track of path 417 taken on the approach. Follow this right alongside the river to return to the campsite and **car park**.

Other possibilities
This route may be enjoyably combined with Route 51, beginning from the Ponte Felizon car park and exploring the Cascate de Fanes before ascending to **Passo Posporcora** from the west on path 408. After the ascent of **Col Rosa**, descend as per the description above then on joining the forestry trail turn left to return quickly to the car park at Ponte Felizon.

ROUTE 53

Via Ferrata Michielli Strobel

Start/Finish	Hotel Fiames
Distance	8km
Total ascent/descent	950m
Grade	3B
Time	5–6hr
Wire length	600m
Map	Tabacco 03
Parking	Hotel Fiames parking: 46.57571, 12.11613

A discontinuous but satisfying route that reaches the summit of Punta Fiames, enjoying a commanding position on the Pomagagnon ridge to the north of Cortina. The route travels a series of ledges and short walls interrupted by stretches of walking through dwarf pines to reach the small summit cross. The descent is made via a broad and steep scree slope, where confidence in scree running is a distinct advantage.

Driving approach

From Cortina d'Ampezzo, follow the SS51 north for 5.5km, passing International Camping Olympia to reach Hotel Fiames shortly after on the left. There are some public parking spaces to the left of the hotel, otherwise there is ample parking just before by the tourist information centre.

Cross the road to join a path directly opposite the hotel that leads up into the woods. After a few minutes this exits onto a gravel path; turn right onto this and continue for 100 metres to a signpost on the left. Follow this up through sparse pine trees and dwarf pines, crossing the broad track of the old railway line (now a popular cycle route) on the way. Continue to ascend upwards over scree towards an obvious deep corner in the rock face. A ledge runs at the base of the rock face and forms a good place to gear up.

Follow the broad ledge right for 400 metres to reach the first section of wire, protecting a short and rather greasy wall. The route is discontinuous, with short walls and arêtes broken with sections of unprotected walking. A couple

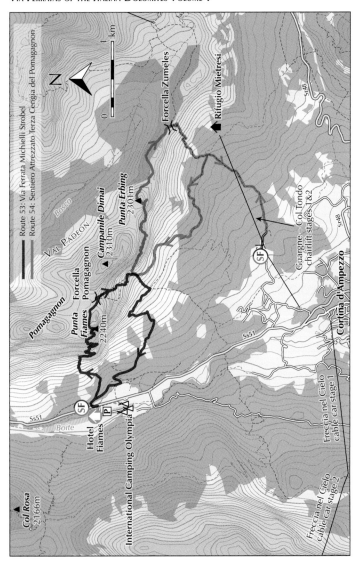

Route 53: Via Ferrata Michielli Strobel
Route 54: Sentiero Attrezzato Terza Cengia del Pomagagnon

Punta Fiames
(2240m)

Campanile
Dimai (2310m)

| 53: Via Ferrata Michielli Strobel | 3B |
| 54: Sentiero Attrezzato Terza Cengia del Pomagagnon | 2C |

of stemples protect an awkward move up shattered rock before a short walk to
the right leads to a long ladder. Climb the ladder and the stemples above, then
continue on discontinuous rocky terrain to exit onto the vegetated summit slope.
Follow a path right through the dwarf pines to reach the summit of **Punta Fiames**
(2240m).

To descend, reverse the final 100 metres below the summit then turn right
(east), following a waymarked path down to **Forcella Pomagagnon**; a short and
rather exposed traverse just above the saddle is protected with loose cable.

From the saddle, drop carefully into the large scree slope below, descending
this for 300 metres with numerous possible lines. At the end of the slope, take a
small path branching right, traversing and descending rugged and vegetated rocky
terrain to rejoin the track of the old railway line. Turn right and follow this easily
to reverse the approach to **Hotel Fiames**.

Other possibilities
The route can be extended into a much longer day by linking the descent into the
start of Sentiero Attrezzato Terza Cengia del Pomagagnon – see Route 54.

ROUTE 54

Sentiero Attrezzato Terza Cengia del Pomagagnon

Start/Finish	Col Tondo
Distance	11km
Total ascent/descent	650m
Grade	2C
Time	5–6hr
Wire length	250m
Map	Tabacco 03
Parking	Col Tondo: 46.55392, 12.14705
Note	Many parties choose to carry a short rope for the exposed sections. For route map see Route 53

Although technically straightforward, this is an exposed and rather remote route traversing the ledge system of the Pomagagnon ridgeline. There is only intermittent protection interspersed with long unprotected stretches on airy and narrow ledges. Although possible in either direction, west to east as described here is recommended.

Driving approach

From the centre of Cortina d'Ampezzo follow the SS51 north for 1km then immediately before Hotel Menardi, turn right towards Chiave and continue for 2km to reach Bar Col Tondo, at the midstation of the two Guargne – Col Tondo chairlifts. The chairlift forms the most convenient access but unfortunately this only runs in August.

From Bar Col Tondo, ascend the vehicle track waymarked 204 underneath the lift for just over 1km, then before reaching Rifugio Mietres and the top of the chairlift turn left onto a path. Continue to intersect path 211 and turn left onto this, following the undulating path for 1.5km to a signed junction with path 202. Turn right, following signs for the Terza Cengia and ascending towards Forcella Pomagagnon. Ascend the final scree slope on rather difficult and steep terrain to reach the rock walls. Continue to reach more solid rock and the start of the ledge.

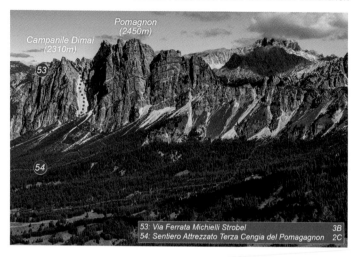

53: Via Ferrata Michielli Strobel   3B
54: Sentiero Attrezzato Terza Cengia del Pomagagnon   2C

Follow the first short section of wire before continuing along unprotected ledges for around 20min with superb exposure. Reach a longer section of cable and continue to climb a steep ramp. At its top, continue with intermittent protection along the continuation ledge to reach a small col offering excellent views across to Cristallo. The summit of **Punta Erbing** (2301m) is located just above; this small peak can be reached in a few minutes and is well worth the detour.

Return to the col and continue east, descending initially steeply and then more steadily down a gully and into sparse trees to reach **Forcella Zumeles** in around 45min.

From the saddle, descend switchbacks down path 204 then follow an open gully to reach path 211 below. Cross over this to reverse the approach route down path 204 to rejoin the vehicle track and return easily to **Col Tondo**.

Other possibilities

This route can be added on to Route 53, beginning directly from the end of the scree slope descent.

ROUTE 55
Sentiero Attrezzato Renè de Pol

Start/Finish	Cimabanche
Distance	11.5km
Total ascent/descent	2000m
Grade	2B
Time	6–7hr
Wire length	500m
Map	Tabacco 03
Parking	Cimabanche: 46.62018, 12.18322

A technically straightforward but long day out, this route is characterised by its wartime remains, which bring considerable historical interest to the day. The via ferrata traverses the north and north-east side of the Forame group and leads to an ascent of Punta Ovest del Forame (2385m) and Forame di Fuori (2413m). While the climbing itself does not pose any real difficulties, the considerable ascent and descent should not be underestimated.

Driving approach
From Cortina d'Ampezzo follow the SS51 north then north-east to Cimabanche, where there is ample parking.

From Cimabanche follow path 208 south-west, skirting the road and following the line of the disued railway. After 3km cross a wooden bridge to reach a junction, where Renè de Pol is signed to the left. Turn left and follow the waymarks up a steep woodland path, continuing for 45min to reach more open terrain and a sign left for the via ferrata.

Follow the traversing path, crossing a wide gully and then following way-marks past a number of wartime caves and trenches. Ascend a final scree slope to reach a cave housing the route book, then continue left to the start of the cable, reached in around 2hr from leaving Cimabanche.

Follow the first short section of cable around to the right then continue with intermittent wire to reach and ascend a loose gully. Reach and climb a short lad-der then scramble easily to reach a broad scree ledge. Traverse the ledge, passing

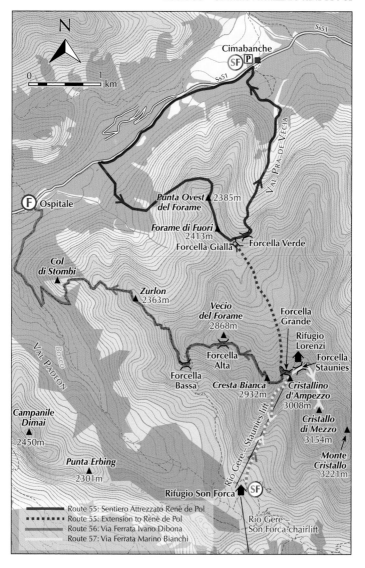

Route 55: Sentiero Attrezzato Renè de Pol
Route 55: Extension to Renè de Pol
Route 56: Via Ferrata Ivano Dibona
Route 57: Via Ferrata Marino Bianchi

233

numerous wartime trenches and caves, to reach a narrow gully. Climb this on the left side then ascend a short series of stemples and a section of more vertical wire. Above, the remains of an old walkway can be seen crossing a vertical wall on the right; this doesn't form part of the ferrata but must have been quite a feat of engineering in its time.

Continue up a short gully to exit onto more open ground and the end of the ferrata, with views to the Tofanas and the north side of Ivano Dibona (Route 56) with its long suspension bridge to Cresta Bianca. A 15-minute walk leads to the summit of **Punta Ovest del Forame**, reached in a total of around 1½–2hr from the start of the wire.

From here descend the path on the west side of Il Forame, dropping to around 2200m before ascending to the summit of **Forame di Fuori**, with more wartime fortifications continuing along the ridge.

Continue to descend to reach **Forcella Gialla**, marked with a sign. Various faint paths lead east here, descending steep scree and shortening the descent slightly, however it is preferable to continue on the waymarked path to the next saddle of **Forcella Verde**.

At the saddle turn left to descend path 233 down the wild **Val Pra de Vecia**, initially down a steep scree gully and then a good path through the valley to continue all the way back to **Cimabanche**.

Other possibilities

This route can be extended with an out-and-back ascent of **Cresta Bianca** (2932m) from Forcella Verde before descending down Val Pra de Vecia (3km each way, 550m ascent/descent).

The route could also be approached from Rifugio Lorenzi (see Route 56), beginning as for Ivano Dibona before turning north at **Forcella Grande**. However, the ferrata section of Renè de Pol is on the north side of Punta Ovest del Forame, with direct access from the Cortina to Dobbiaco road (SS51), and as such climbing this route in a single day from that point is recommended.

ROUTE 56
Via Ferrata Ivano Dibona

Start	Rifugio Son Forca
Finish	Ospitale
Distance	13km
Total ascent	850m
Total descent	1600m
Grade	2B
Time	7–8hr
Wire length	500m
Map	Tabacco 03
Parking	Rio Gere car park: 46.5512, 12.18966
Note	At the time of writing the Rio Gere–Staunies lift system was closed, adding 700m of scree ascent to the once classic route. Alternatives approaches and circuits are offered in 'Other possibilities'. For route map see Route 55

Undoubtedly a classic of the Cortina area, Via Ferrata Ivano Dibona traverses the prominent Cristallo ridgeline, beginning with the iconic suspension bridge made famous by the film *Cliffhanger*. Once easily accessed from the Rio Gere–Staunies lift system, access to the route is currently restricted by the closure of the upper section of the lifts (previously served by characteristic yet admittedly very aged oblong gondolas), resulting in 700m of additional ascent. As the start and end points are a substantial distance apart, some thought must also be given to return transport.

Driving approach
From Cortina d'Ampezzo, follow the SS48 east for 6km, following signs for the Passo Tre Croci. Reach the Rio Gere lift station and the rifugio of the same name and park in the ample gravel car park on the right. Take the Rio Gere chairlift to reach Rifugio Son Forca.

From the rifugio, ascend the prominent, steep scree gully to the north, aiming for (the now closed) Rifugio Lorenzi in the saddle above. This rather laborious ascent takes around 2½hr. From the top station of the former lift, follow the path to the left to reach a ladder. Climb this and continue with easy protected scrambling to pass through a short tunnel. This is soon followed by the spectacular suspension bridge, offering superb views and photographic opportunities.

Continue to reach a ladder and ascend this to gain the airy ridge of **Cresta Bianca**. There is an optional diversion here to Cristallino d'Ampezzo – a 3008m summit, clearly waymarked at the end of the ridge (30-minute detour in total). The main route continues down a ladder and a series of downclimbs to **Forcella Grande**, where Sentiero Attrezzato Renè de Pol (Route 55) is north-west. Keep left, continuing along the well-waymarked route.

Around 2hr beyond Forcella Grande, reach **Forcella Alta**, taking care to descend the reddish scree gully to the left for 200 metres. At a warning sign, turn right (north-west) towards **Forcella Bassa** and continue along the ridge to **Zurlon** and eventually the small summit of **Col di Stombi**. From here descend a good path which switchbacks down for half an hour to join path 203; an easy walk right for 45min along a gravel road leads to **Ospitale**.

A group crossing the famous bridge on Via Ferrata Ivano Dibona, used in the film Cliffhanger

56: Via Ferrata Ivano Dibona   2B
57: Via Ferrata Marino Bianchi   2B

Rifugio Lorenzi

Other possibilities

To avoid the logistical difficulties, at the intersection with path 203 it is possible to turn left to ascend **Val Padeon**, returning to **Rifugio Son Forca** and the top station of the chairlift. This adds around 6km and 500m of ascent, so timekeeping is important to avoid missing the last lift down (in this case, allow another hour for the descent on foot down path 206 to Rio Gere).

Alternatively it is possible to complete a long circular route, starting from Ospitale on the SS51 and ascending Via Ferrata Ivano Dibona up to the summit of **Cresta Bianca** before turning north and descending Sentiero Attrezzato Renè de Pol (Route 55) to return to Ospitale. This is an excellent itinerary but requires a suitably fit party (9–10hr at a good pace).

ROUTE 57
Via Ferrata Marino Bianchi

Start/Finish	Rifugio Son Forca
Distance	6.5km
Total ascent/descent	950m
Grade	2B
Time	5–6hr
Wire length	200m
Map	Tabacco 03
Parking	Rio Gere car park: 46.5512, 12.18966
Note	At the time of writing the Rio Gere–Staunies lift system was closed, adding 700m of scree ascent to the classic itinerary. For route map see Route 55

Another classic of the Cortina and Cristallo area, Via Ferrata Marino Bianchi is a linear route to the lofty summit of Cristallo di Mezzo. It follows the ridgeline to the south-east of Forcella Staunies, crossing a series of ledges and airy crests. The low grade rather belies the exposure, which is superb, but the protection is always good and the climbing very straightforward. Unfortunately, the ascent has been lengthened by the recent closure of the Staunies lift system, necessitating an additional 700m of ascent to reach the traditional departure point of Rifugio Lorenzi.

Driving approach
From Cortina d'Ampezzo, follow the SS48 east for 6km, following signs for the Passo Tre Croci. Reach the Rio Gere lift station and the rifugio of the same name and park in the ample gravel car park on the right. Take the Rio Gere chairlift to reach Rifugio Son Forca.

From the rifugio, ascend the prominent, steep and unpleasant scree gully to the north, aiming for Rifugio Lorenzi in the saddle above. Reach the (now closed) **rifugio** and walk around the front of the building; the route begins directly from the back right corner of the wooden terrace.

Follow the first section of cable to traverse easily along a ledge. Move left around a corner to gain the airy ridge; the route now undulates along the

articulated crest, with sections of downclimbing interspersed with more vertical terrain overcome by ladders. The summit of **Cristallo di Mezzo** (3154m) is reached in around 2hr, traffic dependent.

The return is made by reversing the ascent route, although the first section from the summit is now equipped with an alternative route. Just below the summit cross, a waymarked route leads left (looking back towards Rifugio Lorenzi); follow a cable along a descending ledge, keeping left at the next junction to follow more scree ledges before rejoining the ascent route by a large red tower. Continue back to **Rifugio Son Forca**.

Other possibilities

With a suitably fit party and if the logistics of returning can be overcome, this route can be combined with a descent of Via Ferrata Ivano Dibona (Route 56).

ROUTE 58
Via Ferrata Sci Club 18

Start/Finish	Mandres, midstation of the Faloria cable car
Distance	3km
Total ascent	650m
Total descent	By cable car
Grade	5C
Time	3–4hr
Wire length	400m
Map	Tabacco 03
Parking	Faloria cable car parking: 46.53843, 12.13946

Constructed in 2009, this is a demanding via ferrata that scales the steep walls of Crepe di Faloria, the western buttress of Monte Faloria. As is typical of the more modern via ferratas, the route is largely on artificial protection and while the ascent is undoubtedly steep and strenuous, the rock is liberally scatted with stemples and ladders in the most exposed sections. It is a good option when the weather is due to worsen in the afternoon, as the route itself is relatively short and descent is made by cable car.

Driving approach

From the centre of Cortina d'Ampezzo, follow the one-way system around to park in the large car park by the bus station and the Faloria cable car. Take the cable car for one stage to reach the midstation at Mandres.

Exit the cable car station and follow new signs for 'Ferrata Sci Club 18' along path 206. This ascends gently through the trees before exiting into more open terrain and leading more steeply up a final scree slope to reach the base of the face in around 45min from Mandres.

The route is immediately vertical, ascending cracked rock to reach a steep series of stemples up a blank wall. This is followed by a corner, again equipped with stemples, to reach a ledge. Continue on easier terrain then make an awkward diagonal traverse right to reach another ledge. Ascend vertical rock before making another traverse right to exit onto a grassy terrace.

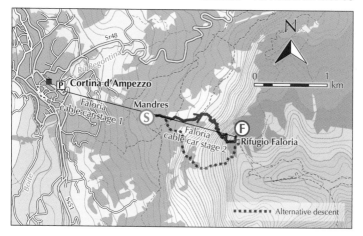

The route continues much in the same vein, with less strenuous climbing interspersed with more vertical and bulging terrain aided by metal stemples and ladders. Continue to exit at a pronounced saddle by a squat tower.

Follow the wire as it runs along a rather broad ridge. A ledge leads to the final vertical section; climb stemples then make a leftward traverse to exit the route on

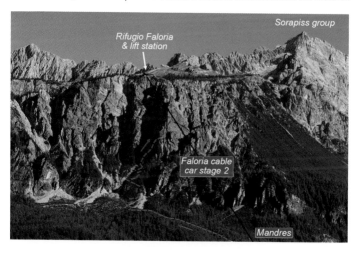

One of the several overhanging sections on Via Ferrata Sci Club 18

the grassy slopes below the Faloria cable car. From here, descend easily by cable car to **Mandres** and Cortina.

Other possibilities
- Out of season or to avoid using the lift, it is possible to walk up to the start of the route. The shortest approach in this case is from Ristorante Lago Scin on the SS48 Passo Tre Croci road, following path 210 south-west to **Mandres** (45min, 2km, 150m ascent). Alternatively, from the outskirts of Cortina path 210 can be ascended to the east.
- To descend on foot, path 212 leads steeply west from the top cable car station back to **Mandres**; from here continue on path 210 north-east or west to return to Ristorante Lago Scin or Cortina respectively (1½hr, 4km, 900m descent).

ROUTE 59
Via Ferrata Giro del Sorapiss

Start/Finish	Passo Tre Croci
Distance	26km
Total ascent/descent	2220m
Grade	3C/1C/3C
Time	12–16hr (overnight stay recommended)
Wire length	700m
Map	Tabacco 03
Parking	Passo Tre Croci: 46.55614, 12.20431

Although never technically challenging, the combination of the three via ferrata routes that form the Sorapiss circuit – Francesco Berti, Sentiero Carlo Minazio and Alfonso Vandelli – makes for a thrilling and scenically stunning mountain excursion, crossing rugged and wild terrain often in complete solitude. The circuit can be completed in a day, but it is recommended to factor in an overnight stay either at Rifugio Vandelli, Bivacco Slataper or Bivacco Comici; the latter two are unmanned shelters equipped with bunks and blankets.

The details of the individual via ferratas are given in the route description below, while the data given above refers to the route as a whole. The route is described in an anti-clockwise direction here, although either way is possible. While the routes can be confronted individually, this generally entails a very long approach and return by the same route, and consequently the combination described here is recommended.

Driving approach
From Cortina d'Ampezzo follow the SS48 east for 10km to reach roadside parking at the top of the Passo Tre Croci.

From the top of the pass, walk east along the road towards Misurina for 200 metres to reach a well-signed path on the right (south), signed for Rifugio Vandelli along path 215. Follow this at length, entering into the trees and following the well-waymarked route for around 2hr to reach the **rifugio** by the stunningly coloured **Lago del Sorapiss**, from where you should be able to see – among other things – the distinctive tower of Dito di Dio ('Finger of God').

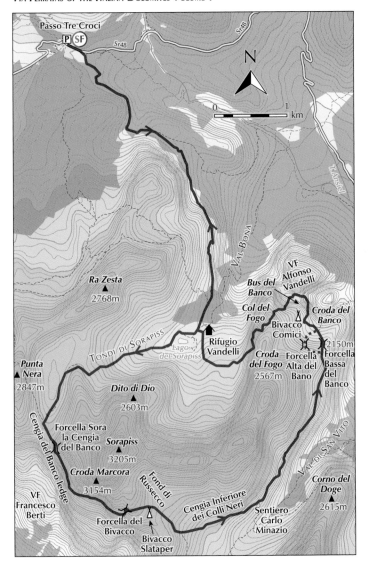

Francesco Berti

Sorapiss
(3205m)

Sentiero
Carlo Minazio

59

Rifugio Vandelli

path 217

Alfonso
Vandelli

59: Via Ferrata Giro del Sorapiss
(broken down as follows)
Francesco Berti   3C
Sentiero Carlo Minazio 1C
Alfonso Vandelli   3C

Superb views and situations on Alfonso Vandelli, part of the Giro del Sorapiss

Francesco Berti

From Rifugio Vandelli follow path 215 west, passing along the right side of the lake before ascending the scree slope above. After 1hr reach the glacial valley of **Tondi di Sorapiss** and continue to reach the junction between paths 215 and 242. Turn left onto path 242, crossing through scree to reach the **Cengia del Banco ledge**.

Follow the undulating ledge with some steep sections of scrambling, reaching the first cables in around 1hr, then continue with intermittent protection, descending a series of ladders to reach a junction. Keep right, following signs for Francesco Berti and Bivacco Slataper, ascending to another series of ladders.

A rightward traverse leads to **Forcella del Bivacco** and the end of the first ferrata; continue easily across the limestone pavement to reach **Bivacco Slataper**.

Sentiero Carlo Minazio

From Bivacco Slataper, follow the faint waymarks for path 247 to cross the large scree bowl of Fond di Russecco. Descend across the scree before following a series of ledges and grassy slopes to join paths 226/243 coming up from Val di San Vito. Keep left here to begin Sentiero Carlo Minazio, traversing north-east easily to reach **Cengia Inferiore dei Colli Neri**.

Continue along the ledge with infrequent cable protection, with excellent views across to Corno del Doge. After 1–1½hr, reach a large scree bowl and a junction, where left leads to **Forcella Alta del Banco** before descending to **Forcella Bassa del Banco**, and right offers a slightly harder but shorter alternative across an exposed slope to rejoin at the lower saddle. Descend easily from the saddle for 15min to reach **Bivacco Comici**.

Alfonso Vandelli

From Bivacco Comici, follow path 243 (with some faded waymarks for path 280) north across **Bus del Banco**. A short climb leads to a ledge, which soon bears west; descend slightly then ascend at a steady gradient to reach **Col del Fogo** around 1½hr after leaving Bivacco Comici.

Descend steadily across ledges and steep gullies, with intermittent protection, for around 1hr. Continue following the wire, downclimbing the western flank of Croda del Fogo. The lower half of the route is better protected; cable equips much of the steeper downclimb, ending with the descent of a series of ladders. Reach the scree below and follow waymarks for path 243 to trend west across scree and limestone slabs, returning to **Rifugio Vandelli** in around 30min.

To return to Passo Tre Croci, reverse the approach route along path 215, reaching the **pass** in around 1hr.

8 MISURINA

MISURINA

Located just south-west of the iconic Tre Cime di Lavaredo and easily accessible from Cortina d'Ampezzo and Dobbiaco, Misurina is best known for the glistening waters of Lago di Misurina. Although the village itself is rather nondescript with only limited facilities, its location makes it a very popular destination in the summer months.

There are a number of hotels scattered along the banks of the lake; Grand Hotel Misurina offers 4-star accommodation and apartments, while slightly more affordable options are available in smaller hotels and B&Bs. There is also a campsite just north of the lake as well as a campervan overnight parking area. Below Grand Hotel Misurina there is a Spar shop selling groceries and souvenirs with a couple of small sports shops alongside and public toilets are located just off the Spar car park.

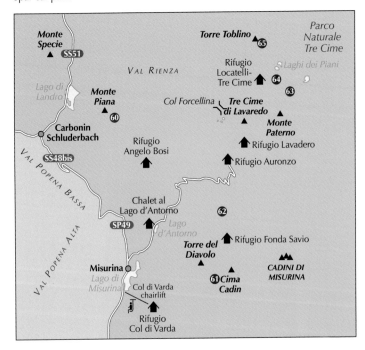

The routes in this chapter are all in the low to mid grades but are nonetheless interesting excursions, crossing rugged and beautiful terrain while taking in stunning views of the famous Tre Cime peaks. This area is also particularly rich in wartime history, with Routes 60, 63, 64 and 65 being of particular interest to history enthusiasts.

ROUTE 60
Sentiero Attrezzato Capitano Bilgeri/Monte Piana/Monte Piano

Start/Finish	Rifugio Angelo Bosi (accessed by jeep taxi from the area sosta)
Distance	2km
Total ascent/descent	250m
Grade	1B
Time	2–3hr
Wire length	250m
Map	Tabacco 10
Parking	At the area sosta: 46.58849, 12.25661
Note	Headtorch recommended

The site of intense siege warfare during the Great War, a visit to Monte Piana is highly recommended for a better appreciation of the conditions and circumstances of early 20th-century mountain warfare. There are several sections of path protected by cable, stemples and ladders, although the excursion itself is not so much a via ferrata route as an opportunity to explore the open-air war museum that occupies much of the summit plateau. Access to the route is facilitated by a jeep taxi service from the *area sosta* to Rifugio Bosi.

Driving approach
From Cortina d'Ampezzo, follow the SS48 east, passing over the Passo Tre Croci and continuing down to a rather blind junction. Turn left here, following the road uphill to reach Lago di Misurina. Continue to the north end of the lake then shortly after turn right, signed towards Rifugio Auronzo and Tre Cime. Park almost

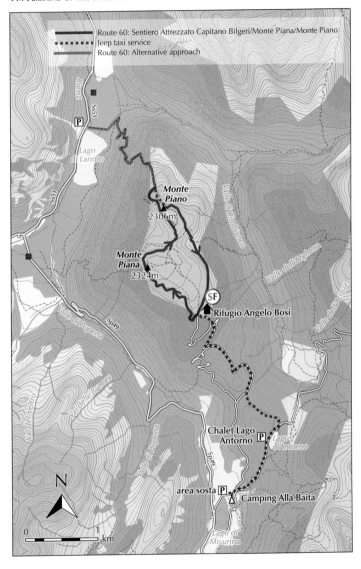

immediately after the junction in the large car park on the left. From here in high season a jeep taxi goes to Rifugio Angelo Bosi.

From Rifugio Angelo Bosi, follow signs for the 'Sentiero Storico'; this winds around the most historically interesting areas of the two summits, visiting remains of many fortifications, galleries, dugouts and a number of memorials. Some of the major galleries are several hundred metres long, so a torch is essential. Just before the summit of Monte Piano it is possible to branch right onto Ferrata Bilgeri – see below.

Return via jeep taxi from **Rifugio Angelo Bosi** to the parking area at the **area sosta**.

Other possibilities

- If you don't plan on using the jeep taxi or if you simply want a longer itinerary, Monte Piana is best accessed from Lago di Landro to the north-west. From the ample parking on the lake edge, head north and just past the lake join path 6 to ascend the north-west flank of Monte Piano. Follow this past wartime ruins to pass over the north summit of the mountain and keep left to join onto Ferrata Bilgeri, named after an Austrian general who directed the construction of the original route in 1916. This follows a series of ledges with intermittent cabling, climbing a short and rather awkward chimney to reach

One of the many war memorials scattered around the site

the summit cross of **Monte Piana**. To complete the circuit, follow the 'Sentiero Storico' paths across the plateau before descending path 6A west towards the valley. Reach the junction with path 6B and turn right to return easily to **Lago di Landro** (1000m of ascent/descent, 6–8hr).

- If you want to approach on foot from the south, while it's possible to walk up the jeep track used by the taxi service it's nicer to park at **Lago d'Antorno** and then ascend path 122 to join up with the jeep track three-quarters of the way up it.

Whichever ascent option is chosen, it's worth allowing the whole day to explore the war trenches and tunnels of the twin-summited Monte Piana and Monte Piano.

ROUTE 61
Via Ferrata Merlone

Start/Finish	Lago d'Antorno
Distance	9km
Total ascent/descent	920m
Grade	3B
Time	4–5hr
Wire length	300m
Map	Tabacco 10
Parking	Rifugio Fonda Savio parking: 46.59091, 12.26325

This route is characterised by the series of ladders scaling the steep west face of Cima del Cadin NE, with only limited climbing on the rock. The views from the summit are outstanding, offering a superb outlook to the Tre Cime south faces, the rugged spires of Torre Wundt and Torre del Diavolo and the grassy plateau of Monte Piano and Monte Piana.

Driving approach
From Cortina d'Ampezzo, follow the SS48 east, passing over the Passo Tre Croci and continuing down to a rather blind junction. Turn left here, following the road uphill to reach Lago di Misurina. Continue to the north end of the lake then shortly

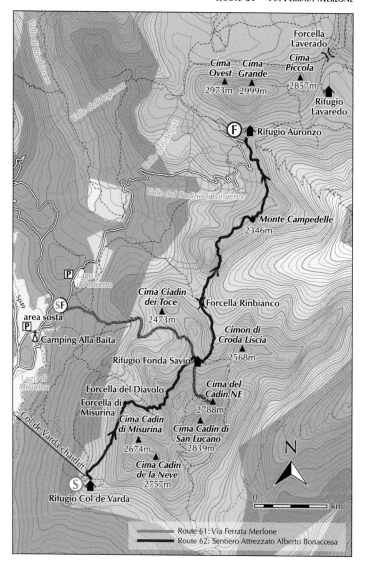

Route 61: Via Ferrata Merlone
Route 62: Sentiero Attrezzato Alberto Bonacossa

after turn right, signed towards Rifugio Auronzo and the Tre Cime. Continue past a campsite on the right and follow the road up a short series of hairpins until a small road branches off to the right, signposted towards Rifugio Fonda Savio, some 350 metres short of Lago d'Antorno. Take this and park in the small parking area provided (if there are no spaces then you can continue up to Lago d'Antorno, which has a bigger car park).

Walk to the back of the parking area and follow good signposting along path 115 to Rifugio Fonda Savio. Follow the steadily ascending track to reach the superbly situated **rifugio** in around 1½hr.

From the rifugio, follow waymarks for Alta Via 4 due south, signed for Via Ferrata Merlone and ascending a broad boulder-strewn slope towards the steep faces above; the approach is not obvious but the unlikely ladders can be seen clinging to the rock. The route begins just below and left of these.

Make an easy-angled rightward scramble to reach the start of the ladders; these ascend reasonably steeply but without presenting any great difficulties, although the exposure is significant. A short but airy traverse interrupts the vertical ascent, before more ladders and an unprotected scramble up the final scree slope lead to the summit of **Cima del Cadin NE** (2788m).

The descent reverses the route; given that it is impossible to pass ascending climbers on the ladders, this may involve some waiting.

Cima del Cadin NE (2788m)

The south faces of the Tre Cime di Lavaredo reflected in Lago d'Antorno

Other possibilities

For a longer approach, it's possible to begin the route at **Col de Varda**, following the southern section of Sentiero Attrezzato Alberto Bonacossa (Route 62) to traverse below the west face of the Cadini (10km, 700m ascent, 3hr without using the chairlift to Rifugio Fonda Savio).

Ascending one of the many iron ladders on Via Ferrata Merlone

ROUTE 62
Sentiero Attrezzato Alberto Bonacossa

Start	Top of Col de Varda chairlift
Finish	Rifugio Auronzo
Distance	10km
Total ascent	400m
Total descent	200m
Grade	1A
Time	5–6hr
Wire length	400m
Map	Tabacco 10
Parking	Col de Varda: 46.57796, 12.25313
Note	For route map see Route 61

More of a protected walk than a via ferrata, this route has the great merit of dramatic and strikingly contrasting scenery, the final stretch being dominated by outstanding views of the Tre Cime. It makes for an enjoyable mountain traverse and offers good protection on the relatively short stretches that negotiate difficult ground. The route can be done either way around, making use of the bus service to return to the start.

Driving approach
From Cortina d'Ampezzo, follow the SS48 east, passing over the Passo Tre Croci and continuing down to a rather blind junction. Turn right here, following the road uphill to reach Lago di Misurina. The Col de Varda chairlift is located at the south (near) side of the lake; take the lift to reach Rifugio Col de Varda above (the chairlift is quite short and it is equally possible to walk up path 120 below, reaching the rifugio in under an hour).

From Rifugio Col de Varda, follow path 117 north to climb diagonally up the scree-covered hillside beneath the impressive west wall of Cima Cadin di Misurina. Scramble up the ridge with intermittent protection to reach **Forcella di Misurina**, then descend a broad gully below to intersect with path 118. Continue

straight on (north-east), ascending a series of switchbacks and heading for the next ridge. Reach **Forcella del Diavolo**, the highest point on the route, again protected with cable.

Now descend more easily in a stunning setting to the superbly situated **Rifugio Fonda Savio**, reached in around 2hr from the top of the chairlift. Just above the rifugio, at a prominent sign turn left, still following path 117 signed to Forcella Rinbianco and Rifugio Auronzo. This descends easy ground with intermittent cable to reach **Forcella Rinbianco** at 2176m, where path 119 branches off to the left. Keep right, continuing on path 117 and heading generally north.

LAGO DI MISURINA

The magical ambience of Lago Misurina has given rise to countless stories, myths and legends detailing the origination of the beautiful waters. The most widely told of these concerns an insatiable little princess named Misurina and her adoring grandfather King Sorapiss. One day Misurina demanded a magic mirror to add to her impressive collection of personal effects; unable to refuse her, Sorapiss approached the only person with the power to grant such an item – the evil witch Cristallo. However, the price for the mirror was the king's life and when Misurina discovered his sacrifice she cried until a lake was created from her tears. In despair she cast the mirror into the waters, and that's why Lago di Misurina still provides magical reflections to this day.

Reach the final protected section and continue more easily, now with superb views of the Tre Cime straight ahead. Continue on level ground across the grassy shoulder of **Monte Campedelle** to reach **Rifugio Auronzo** and the end of the route.

Other possibilities
This route can be done in either direction; in terms of logistics, one of the easiest ways to confront the route is to take the bus from Misurina to Rifugio Auronzo in the morning, completing the route in the opposite direction to the one described here and walking down below the Col de Varda chairlift at the end of the day, negating the need to rush to meet public transport times.

ROUTE 63
Sentiero delle Forcelle

Start/Finish	Rifugio Auronzo
Distance	12.5km
Total ascent/descent	500m
Grade	1B
Time	5–6hr
Wire length	800m
Map	Tabacco 10
Parking	Rifugio Auronzo: 46.6128, 12.29328
Note	Headtorch required

Offering an opportunity to explore the wartime trenches and tunnels so prevalent in this area, Sentiero delle Forcelle is a short and intermittently protected route following a series of quite airy ledges. The route ends at Forcella del Camoscio, the midpoint of Route 64, and as such is best traversed in conjunction with the second half of that route. The route may be travelled in either direction but the east to west direction described here is more common.

Driving approach
From Cortina d'Ampezzo, follow the SS48 east, passing over the Passo Tre Croci and continuing down to a rather blind junction. Turn left here, following the road uphill to reach Lago di Misurina. Continue to the north end of the lake then shortly

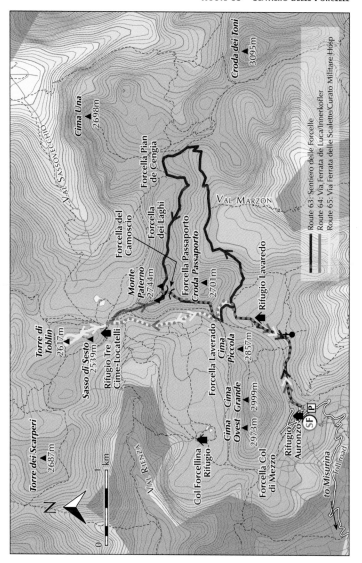

Croda dei Toni 3095m

Cima Una 2698m

VAL SASSOVECCHIO

Forcella Pian de Cengia

VAL MARZON

Route 63: Sentiero delle Forcelle
Route 64: Via Ferrata de Luca/Innerkofler
Route 65: Via Ferrata delle Scalette/Curato Militare Hösp

Forcella del Camoscio

Forcella dei Laghi

Monte Paterno 2744m

Forcella Passaporto
Croda Passaporto
2701m

Rifugio Lavaredo

Torre di Toblin 2617m

Sasso di Sesto 2539m

Rifugio Tre Cime-Locatelli

Torre dei Scarperi 2687m

Forcella Lavaredo

Cima Piccola 2857m

Cima Grande 2999m

Cima Ovest 2973m

Col Forcellina Rifugio

VAL RIENZA

Forcella Col di Mezzo

Rifugio Auronzo

SF P

to Misurina
Toll road

N

0   1 km

263

*The sun sets on the north faces
of the Tre Cime di Lavaredo*

after turn right, signed towards Rifugio Auronzo and the Tre Cime. Continue past
a campsite on the right and follow the road up a short series of hairpins to reach
Lago d'Antorno, then continue to reach the toll booth of the private (and very
expensive) road to Rifugio Auronzo. The road is steep but well surfaced, ascending hairpins for 7km to reach the large car park at the base of the towers.

From Rifugio Auronzo, follow the main path 101 north-east, passing a small chapel
and **Rifugio Lavaredo** before ascending towards Forcella Lavaredo. Before reaching the col, turn right onto path 104 and continue at length, passing a number of
small lakes before bearing north and north-west to reach **Forcella Pian de Cengia**.
The ferrata is well signed from the saddle; head south, descending slightly, then
bear right (west) to reach **Forcella dei Laghi** and the start of the ferrata.

Walk past some old wartime dugouts to reach a 10 metre-deep trench
equipped with a short ladder and protected by cables. Continue to ascend more
steeply for 100 metres up a scree slope to the true start of the route on a small
col; allow 2¼hr from Rifugio Auronzo to here. Follow the cable down to the start
of a series of broad ledges, traversing for around 30min to the end of the route at
Forcella del Camoscio.

The shortest descent is to follow the second half of Route 64; take the steep scree gully leading south from Forcella del Camoscio, marked with faded red triangular markers. This leads into Sentiero Attrezzato Forcella Passaporto, heading for the pronounced saddle of Forcella Passaporto, which separates Monte Paterno and Croda del Passaporto.

Follow a series of ledges and a small wooden bridge to reach the **saddle**, then continue along an exposed ledge. Descend a short gully then follow cables protecting the short wall in front. Pass through a short tunnel then follow the path along a ledge to the final short tunnel, descending to exit just above **Forcella Lavaredo**. From here, reverse the approach route on path 101 to return to **Rifugio Auronzo**.

Other possibilities

It is possible to continue north from Forcella dei Camosci, following the first half of Route 64 in the opposite direction to the one described.

ROUTE 64
Via Ferrata De Luca/Innerkofler

Start/Finish	Rifugio Auronzo
Distance	9km
Total ascent/descent	420m
Grade	2B
Time	5–6hr
Wire length	1000m
Map	Tabacco 10
Parking	Rifugio Auronzo: 46.6128, 12.29328
Note	Headtorch required. For route map see Route 63

The route is dedicated to two of the most famous protagonists of the Mountain War, Piero de Luca and Sepp Innerkofler, both accomplished mountaineers whose skills and local knowledge were vital to the military campaign. Innerkofler fell to his death during a skirmish on this mountain. The route provides an opportunity to explore a system of tunnels dating from the Mountain War and to ascend a peak offering unparalleled views of the surrounding mountains, notably the Tre Cime di Lavaredo.

Driving approach

From Cortina d'Ampezzo, follow the SS48 east, passing over the Passo Tre Croci and continuing down to a rather blind junction. Turn left here, following the road uphill to reach Lago di Misurina. Continue to the north end of the lake then shortly after turn right, signed towards Rifugio Auronzo and the Tre Cime. Continue past a campsite on the right and follow the road up a short series of hairpins to reach Lago d'Antorno, then continue to reach the toll booth of the private (and very expensive) road to Rifugio Auronzo. The road is steep but well surfaced, ascending hairpins for 7km to reach the large car park at the base of the towers.

From Rifugio Auronzo, follow the main path 101 north-east, passing a small chapel and **Rifugio Lavaredo** after 20min before ascending to **Forcella Lavaredo** and the first glimpses of the iconic north faces of the Tre Cime di Lavaredo in a further 30–40min. From the saddle, continue on one of the two parallel paths for 45min to **Rifugio Tre Cime-Locatelli**; the higher, easternmost path is quieter.

Watching the milky way from Rifugio Locatelli

From the rifugio, follow a good path to the south-east for 10min to reach the start of the route, just beyond the characteristic rock feature of Salsiccia di Francoforte, known more commonly as the Frankfurter Wurstel.

The route begins with a 600 metre-long tunnel complex, which climbs increasingly steeply and is often damp. While a number of windows provide some limited lighting, a torch is essential.

Exit the tunnels to reach a spacious shelf beneath a fairly steep wall; follow cables up the wall to reach easier terrain and continue to the pronounced saddle of **Forcella del Camoscio** and the junction with Sentiero delle Forcelle (Route 63) and an optional ascent to Monte Paterno (see 'Other possibilities'), reached in around 1hr from Rifugio Locatelli.

To continue the route, turn south and descend a steep scree gully, marked with faded red triangular markers. This leads into Sentiero Attrezzato Forcella Passaporto, heading for the pronounced saddle of Forcella Passaporto, which separates Monte Paterno and Croda del Passaporto.

Follow a series of spectacular ledges on the east side of the ridge, crossing a small wooden bridge to reach the **saddle**. Continue along an exposed ledge with intermittent protection, then descend a short gully. Climb the cables protecting the short wall in front then pass through a short tunnel. Continue along the ledge to reach a second short tunnel and descend to exit just above **Forcella Lavaredo**. From here, reverse the approach route for 45min on path 101 to return to **Rifugio Auronzo**.

Other possibilities

Ascent of Monte Paterno: from **Forcella del Camoscio**, ascend the first rather steep 15 metres to reach a series of scree-covered ledges leading easily to the **summit** in around 20min. Reverse the route to return to col, taking care not to dislodge loose rock onto the route below (100m ascent/descent)

ROUTE 65
Via Ferrata delle Scalette/Curato Militare Hosp

Start/Finish	Rifugio Auronzo
Distance	10km
Total ascent/descent	300m
Grade	3B
Time	5–6hr
Wire length	150m
Map	Tabacco 10
Parking	Rifugio Auronzo: 46.6128, 12.29328
Note	For route map see Route 63

Many via ferratas owe their existence, in some part, to the Mountain War of 1915–17 and this is particularly true of this route. The summit of Torre di Toblin (Toblinger Knoten) was an important Austrian observation post but could only be reached under cover of darkness, since the wartime access route – now the descent route – was exposed to Italian fire. The rather foreboding-looking north chimney, out of sight of the Italians, was therefore equipped as an alternative approach. The route is characterised by ladders and stemples, although the original wooden ladders (some remains of which can still be seen) have long since been replaced.

Driving approach

From Cortina d'Ampezzo, follow the SS48 east, passing over the Passo Tre Croci and continuing down to a rather blind junction. Turn left here, following the road uphill to reach Lago di Misurina. Continue to the north end of the lake then shortly after turn right, signed towards Rifugio Auronzo and the Tre Cime. Continue past a campsite on the right and follow the road up a short series of hairpins to reach Lago d'Antorno, then continue to reach the toll booth of the private (and very expensive) road to Rifugio Auronzo. The road is steep but well surfaced, ascending hairpins for 7km to reach the large car park at the base of the towers.

From Rifugio Auronzo, follow the main path 101 north-east, passing a small chapel and **Rifugio Lavaredo** after 20min before ascending to **Forcella Lavaredo** and the first glimpses of the iconic north faces of the Tre Cime di Lavaredo in a

Torre di Toblin
(2617m)

Sasso di Sesto
(2539m)

Rifugio
Tre Cime-Locatelli

Making a winter ascent of delle Scalette

further 30–40min. From the saddle, continue on one of the two parallel paths for 45min to **Rifugio Tre Cime-Locatelli**; the higher, easternmost path is quieter.

From the rifugio, take the prominent path leading due north towards the isolated tower of Torre di Toblin. Reach a saddle between this and Sasso di Sesto on the left then follow a good path around the left side of Torre Toblino, passing a wartime shelter and continuing along the ledge to the start of the route, marked by a plaque.

The route, which is well protected by cables throughout, climbs steeply up the back of the pronounced corner, on good but small holds, to reach the first in a series of ladders. Climb the ladders to reach a characteristic chimney, overcome by a ladder on left. Traverse left to reach an adjoining chimney, again equipped with ladders, before a cabled section leads left to a rock wall. Continue up exposed ladders to reach the small but dramatic **summit**, with a stunning view of the Tre Cime di Lavaredo north faces. The total ascent is completed in less than an hour.

The descent to Rifugio Tre Cime-Locatelli takes around 45min and follows the original access route to the old observation post, known as Sentiero del Curato Militare Hosp. Walk across the flat rock of the summit to reach the cables on the right, then begin a well-protected downclimb to reach the scree slope below. Follow a cairned path to rejoin the approach route and return easily to **Rifugio Tre Cime-Locatelli**.

From the rifugio, either reverse the route along path 101, or for a longer but more complete day follow path 105 south and then south-west, reaching **Forcella Col di Mezzo** at the west side of the Tre Cime before contouring back to **Rifugio Auronzo** around the south side.

Other possibilities

Torre di Toblin may also be ascended by the descent route; the ferrata is graded at 2A and is technically straightforward, but given the complications of encountering descending climbers, this option is not recommended.

9 SESTO

On Ferrata Nord – Croda Rossa di Sesto

SESTO

Located a mere 15km from the border with East Tyrol, the culture of the twin villages of Sesto/Sexten and Moso/Moos is emphatically Austrian. Like many other areas of the Dolomites, German is certainly the most commonly spoken language; according to the 2011 census, over 95% of the population named it their first language.

The attractive valley is a spur from Val Pusteria and forms the north-eastern boundary of the Dolomites, yet despite its outlying location it is also an excellent base offering good opportunities for via ferratas. The villages themselves are different in character, although they are now linked by a straggle of ribbon development along the road. As a holiday destination the area is very well served with accommodation of all standards: there are numerous hotels, guesthouses and holiday apartments, as well as a very luxurious campsite in Moos. The good range of shops includes several selling sports equipment, and there is no shortage of restaurants, bars and pizzerias.

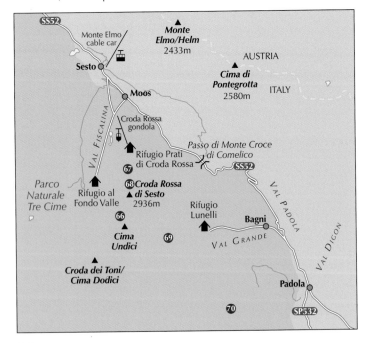

The villages are well served by public transport, with a good bus service from the larger towns of Val Pusteria (Pustertal). Access into the mountains is also reasonably good, with a cable car to the north-west flank of the Croda Rossa (Sextener Rotwand), and access by car or bus to the Dolomitenhof Hotel in Val Fiscalina (Fischleintal) and Passo di Montecroce di Comelico.

The routes in this chapter venture deep into the dramatic landscape of this border region of the Dolomites; Routes 66 and 67 are both technically straight-forward but immensely rewarding in terms of mountain scenery, while Routes 68 and 69 are long, more challenging routes. All five are long mountain days in a wonderful alpine setting, and there are various opportunities to combine the routes by spending the night in a rifugio.

It's worth noting that the routes in this area tend to hold snow late into the season; there's an Alpine Guides school in Sesto which is a useful resource for up-to-date information on route conditions (open 5pm–7pm year-round, with longer hours in high season: tel +39 0474 710375, www.alpinschule-dreizinnen.com).

ROUTE 66
Via Ferrata Strada degli Alpini

Start/Finish	Hotel Dolomitenhof
Distance	18km
Total ascent/descent	1400m
Grade	2B
Time	8–9hr
Wire length	2000m
Map	Tabacco 10
Parking	Hotel Dolomitenhof: 46.66703, 12.3534

A superbly scenic ledge traverse in the heart of the Dolomiti di Sesto, the Strada degli Alpini follows an old wartime route, crossing the dramatic and justifiably famous Cengia della Salvezza. The route was originally constructed in order to fortify and consolidate the Italian position on the summit of Cima Undici above Passo della Sentinella, at the time the border between the Italian and Austrian forces. Although technically very straightforward, it is a stunning route that is well worth exploring, both for its historical significance and for the unique views it offers into the Sesto range.

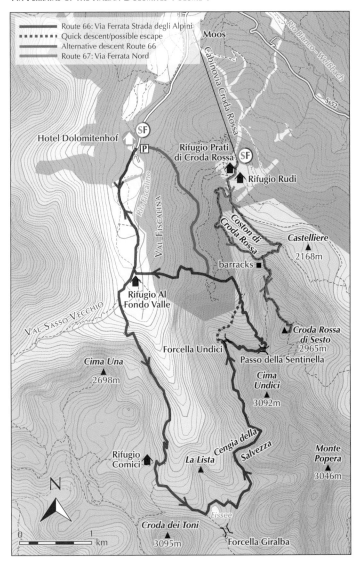

Route 66: Via Ferrata Strada degli Alpini
Quick descent/possible escape
Alternative descent Route 66
Route 67: Via Ferrata Nord

Moos

Rio Bianco – Weißbach

Cabinovia Croda Rossa

S52

SF

Hotel Dolomitenhof

P

SF

Rifugio Prati di Croda Rossa

Rifugio Rudi

Rio Fiscalino

VAL FISCALINA

Coston di Croda Rossa

Castelliere
2168m

barracks

VAL SASSO VECCHIO

Rifugio Al Fondo Valle

Croda Rossa di Sesto
2965m

Forcella Undici

Passo della Sentinella

Cima Una
2698m

Cima Undici
3092m

Rifugio Comici

La Lista

Cengia della Salvezza

Monte Popera
3046m

N

Fissee

Croda dei Toni
3095m

Forcella Giralba

0   1
⊢———————⊣ km

Labels on image: Cima Undici, Forcella Undici, La Mitria, La Lista, Rifugio Comici

Driving approach

From Sesto, follow the SS52 south-east to Moso/Moos. Just after Hotel Lowenwirt on the right, turn right onto Via Val Fiscalina and follow the road for 3km to reach a large paid parking area on the right, just before Hotel Dolomitenhof.

From the hotel follow path 102/103 south. Shortly after passing the luxurious **Rifugio Al Fondo Valle**, turn right onto path 103, following this south-east as it leads along the valley floor before switchbacks lead steadily up to a terrace. Follow this, still on path 103, to reach **Rifugio Comici**.

From the rifugio continue to ascend south, skirting alongside and around the back of La Lista to reach **Eissee**, a small lake. Before reaching the saddle of Forcella Giralba, take a path that cuts left alongside the lake, joining the more prominent path 101 now leading north. The path arrives quite suddenly at the dramatic **Cengia della Salvezza** and the start of the via ferrata (approximately 3hr from the car park).

The first part of the route is airy but well protected, with the ledge providing stunning situations without any technical difficulty. After around 1hr, the ledge exits into more open terrain, ascending steadily for another 30min over scree to reach **Forcella Undici**. At this point it is possible to escape to the left down the large scree gully (see 'Other possibilities').

To continue the route to Passo della Sentinella, follow the sign right, climbing over easy rock protected with cables. After 50 metres, move onto the north face

275

of Cima Undici, passing a commemorative plaque. The route now traverses on good ledges, with limited exposure, before reaching a short metal ladder. Climb this and continue up the groove above, ignoring (for the time being) the ledge on the left and continuing to traverse before a short scramble leads to **Passo della Sentinella** and the end of the ascent.

Reverse the final approach to the saddle to reach the ledge mentioned above and follow this to descend a gently sloping rib with numerous steep rock steps. At the top of the scree slope, turn left to descend into Vallon di Sentinella, eventually joining with path 124. Follow this right, skirting the rock walls and continuing to reach a fork.

Keep left at the fork, descending due west on path 124 to reach the junction with path 122; here either continue straight on along path 122 to return to **Rifugio Al Fondo Valle** to then follow the valley north back to **Hotel Dolomitenhof**, or alternatively turn right to follow path 124 along a terrace path, eventually keeping left to descend more directly to the parking area. Both options take around 1hr.

Other possibilities
To shorten the route, it's possible to avoid the ascent to Passo della Sentinella by descending directly into Vallon di Sentinella from **Forcella Undici**. This leads steeply down, initially protected by cable before joining the scree slope, to join path 124 below. Follow this right then continue as above.

ROUTE 67
Via Ferrata Nord

Start/Finish	Top of Cabinovia Croda Rossa gondola
Distance	8km
Total ascent/descent	1000m
Grade	2B
Time	5–6hr
Wire length	100m
Map	Tabacco 10
Parking	Cabinovia Croda Rossa: 46.68183, 12.36454
Note	For route map see Route 66

A technically unchallenging but enjoyable route, with short cabled sections and ladders interspersed with unprotected walking leading to the prominent summit of Croda Rossa di Sesto (Sextner Rotwand). Given the northerly aspect, snow is possible late into the season.

Driving approach
From Sesto, follow the SS52 south-east to Moso/Moos. Just after Hotel Lowenwirt on the right, turn right onto Via Val Fiscalina and continue to reach the gondola station of Cabinovia Croda Rossa on the left. Take the gondola to arrive at Rifugio Prati di Croda Rossa and Rifugio Rudi.

From the top of the gondola station, follow the main path across a grassy bowl to reach a junction, turning right (west) onto path 100. Follow this as it switchbacks steadily through sparse trees, dwarf pines and small rocky outcrops before climbing a series of wooden steps. About half an hour after leaving the gondola, reach a small saddle just beyond where a number of paths intersect; turn left here (south-east), following signs for the via ferrata.

277

Fantastic weather for a traverse of Via Ferrata Nord

Ascend over broken ground along the ridgeline of **Coston di Croda Rossa**, with superb views either side, and around half an hour from the previous junction reach the long ladder that marks the start of the route.

The most difficult sections are protected with cables and ladders, although the route is technically very straightforward. On reaching a large and slightly oppressive rocky combe, ignore the steep gully to the left (the original route that can be used in descent) and continue straight on, descending slightly past the remains of a wartime **barracks**, then continue to reach a large war memorial.

Easy ground leads to an area of slabby rock before encountering a steeper wall; this is easier than it appears and is well protected with cable. Continue across broken rock and scree to reach the end of the route at the large summit cross of **Croda Rossa di Sesto** (2965m). The ascent from the initial ladder to the summit takes around 2½hr.

To descend, reverse the route back to the barrack ruins and there, instead of climbing back down the Coston di Croda Rossa, turn right (north-east) through a narrow passage to descend the original route down a steep scree gully. This leads onto the broad ridgeline of Castelliere; turn left onto the well-marked path 15B to return easily to **Rifugio Prati di Croda Rossa**. Allow 2–2½hr for the total descent.

ROUTE 68
Via Ferrata Mario Zandonella

Start/Finish	Rifugio Lunelli
Distance	10km
Total ascent/descent	1500m
Grade	4C
Time	8–9hr
Wire length	1500m
Map	Tabacco 10
Parking	Rifugio Lunelli: 46.63346, 12.41815

A circular route in rugged and wild terrain. The approach is unpleasant and the rock is unfortunately rather loose, but the journey is satisfying and the via ferrata exits onto the Croda Rossa di Sesto (Sextner Rotwand) subsidiary summit, offering excellent (although not quite 360-degree) views. The route follows a system of ledges and broken chimneys and passes many wartime ruins.

Driving approach

From Sesto, take the SS52 south-east to reach the village of Moso/Moos. Keep left here, staying on the SS52 and passing over Passo di Montecroce di Comelico. Drive down the other side of the pass for 8km then turn right, signed towards Bagni, Terme di Valgrande and Rifugio Lunelli. Follow the small road past meadows before turning left, following signs to Rifugio Lunelli which is reached in a couple of minutes. There is ample parking by the rifugio but the area can be crowded in peak season.

From Rifugio Lunelli, ascend steeply up path 101 to **Rifugio Berti** (1950m; allow 1hr). Continue north-west up into the lunar landscape of **Vallon Popera**, still on path 101, to reach **Lago di Popera** (2142m), where path 124 joins from the right (an alternative approach route from Passo Montecroce Comelico joins here; see 'Other possibilities'). Continue north-west on path 101, ascending through moraine to where the path becomes less distinct as it climbs towards Passo della Sentinella. (A secondary, alternative path branches off to the left to skirt the lower

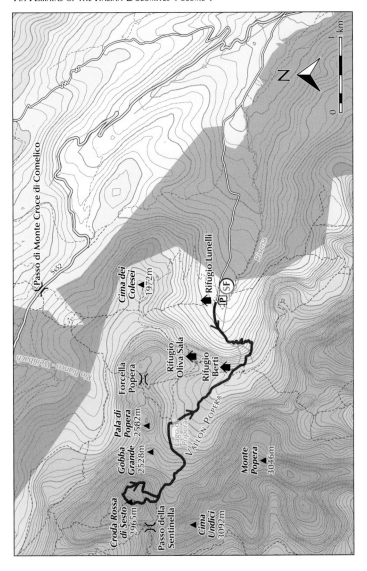

moraine bank before ascending steeply over scree to rejoin the pain path; this is unmarked on most maps but is well-cairned on the ground.)

The start of the route is visible to the right by an old shelter built into the base of the rock wall, located around 200 metres left (north-west) of the obvious gully of the descent route. At a large boulder marked with red and green waymarks (where the alternative and main paths join), branch right onto a smaller path leading up the scree, passing several large caves before reaching the shelter and the start of the via ferrata. Allow around 3hr for the ascent to this point.

Follow the cable easily before a rightward traverse leads to an unprotected ledge. Climb a short ladder up a steep wall then continue up steep and shattered rock to a second ladder. Climb this then pass a number of ruined wartime buildings set into the rock. Continue to traverse an intermittently protected ledge to the right, passing more wartime buildings, before a short scramble leads to a further rightward traverse on a broad scree-covered ledge.

At the end of the ledge, climb a corner and then continue up the steep but broken chimney above, soon reaching a notch in a subsidiary ridge with superb views of Sesto and Moso far below to the north-west. Descend 15 metres into a shallow rift in the rock, following cable to traverse for 100 metres until the summit cross comes into view. Scramble easily past more wartime dugouts to reach the subsidiary summit of **Croda Rossa di Sesto** and the end of the route.

The most satisfying descent is to take the South-East Variante; walk 50 metres to the east to pick up red and green triangular waymarking, just beyond which is a large red arrow pointing to the left into an obvious gap between two large rocks. The cable begins here and leads airily down a steep rib and a broken rock wall to reach the upper rim of a scree-filled cirque – which usually holds snow throughout the season so crampons can be useful.

Follow the cable up the steep buttress straight ahead (a red and green triangle in a small saddle to the left indicates an alternative scree descent into Vallon Popera, saving around 30min). Climb for 40 metres to reach a pronounced shoulder and an old observation position. From here follow a broad ledge to the south-west with intermittent protection, passing a number of old dugouts and the remains of an old field kitchen.

After about 300 metres reach a small saddle and follow cables down steeply to the scree slope below, reached in around 15min after leaving the summit. From here, a steep scree descent leads down to the Vallon Popera path and is rather unpleasant and loose; it's worth keeping a helmet on. Rejoin the path to return to **Rifugio Lunelli** in 2hr.

Traversing with splendid views over Val d'Ansiei

Other possibilities

The route can also be accessed from Passo Montecroce di Comelico: take path 15A-124, which departs around 100 metres north-west of the hotel on the crest of the pass, ascending through woodland and passing old fortifications from the war. After 30min pass a group of old farm buildings on the right and ascend through boulders to join the old dirt road ascending from Rifugio Lunelli. At the junction turn left onto path 124, signed to Rifugio Berti. Descend gently through beautiful scenery before climbing sharply to the abandoned **Rifugio Oliva Sala**, now an emergency bivouac. Follow the path alongside this then turn left towards **Forcella Popera**, continuing on path 124 to join the main route at **Lago di Popera** (7km, 700m ascent from Passo Montecroce di Comelico to the lake).

ROUTE 69
Via Ferrata Aldo Roghel/Cengia Gabriella

Start	Rifugio Lunelli
Finish	Hotel Dolomitenhof
Distance	20km
Total ascent	1600m
Total descent	1670m
Grade	4C/3C
Time	10–12hr
Wire length	400m/1500m
Map	Tabacco 10
Parking	Rifugio Lunelli: 46.63346, 12.41815

A combination of two via ferratas, this route enables a stunning traverse of the rarely travelled Popera group. The terrain is rugged, wild and scenically very impressive, while the climbing is interesting and varied. The routes could be attempted separately but as this would involve retracing the route in reverse, the traverse suggested here is a more complete option – although naturally the logistics of returning to the departure point must be considered. The route can also be combined with an overnight stay at Rifugio Carducci and a traverse of Strada degli Alpini (Route 66) – see 'Other possibilities'.

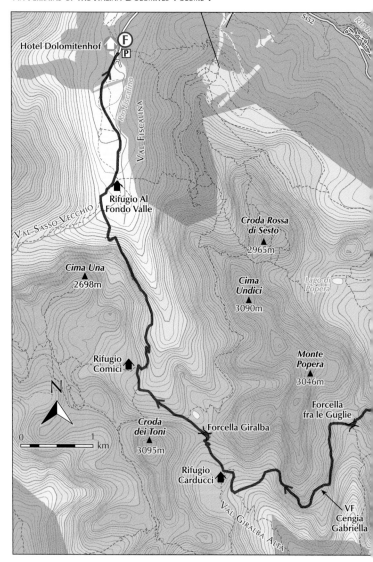

68: Via Ferrata Mario Zandonella   4C
69: Via Ferrata Aldo Roghel/Cengia Gabriella 4C/3C

Rifugio Berti

69   68

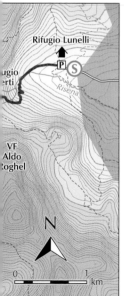

Rifugio Lunelli

ugio
rti

P S

Risena

VF
Aldo
loghel

N

0   1
km

Driving approach

From Sesto, take the SS52 south-east to reach the village of Moso/Moos. Keep left here, staying on the SS52 and passing over Passo di Montecroce di Comelico. Drive down the other side of the pass for 8km then turn right, signed towards Bagni, Terme di Valgrande and Rifugio Lunelli. Follow the small road past meadows before turning left, following signs to Rifugio Lunelli which is reached in a couple of minutes. There is ample parking by the rifugio but the area can be crowded in peak season.

From Rifugio Lunelli, ascend steeply up path 101 to **Rifugio Berti** (1950m; allow 1hr). From the rifugio, take path 109-152 south, initially losing height to cross a small stream. Around 300 metres beyond the stream, turn right onto path 109, signed to Rifugio Carducci and VF Roghel. This leads steeply up the scree slope to the south-west, with frequent but sometimes faded waymarks and cairns marking the often indistinct path. A short scramble leads up to the start

Superb rock and climbing is found throughout the route

of the first ferrata, Via Ferrata Aldo Roghel, around 45min after leaving Rifugio Berti.

Follow the cables to traverse easily to the right then climb back left. Climb a first steep wall protected with metal stemples then follow a broad scree ledge right to a steep crack leading into a damp gully. Ascend this on the steep right wall before making a traverse left back into the gully.

Stemples lead up the right wall again, re-entering the gully and finally exiting via the right wall to the saddle of **Forcella fra le Guglie**. (Given the north-easterly aspect, much of the first part of the route is in the shade and ice is possible at any time of year.)

From the saddle, descend for 40min to the foot of the rocks below, initially traversing down easy ground before a steeper section leads to a gully. From here, an easy protected scramble leads into Ciadin dei Stalata; turn right here to join the path leading around the scree bowl. Follow this easily for 40min before ascending a short and rather dirty gully, where easy angled rock and a steep gravel rake lead to the start of the second route, **Cengia Gabriella**.

The broad, sloping scree-covered ledge is the dominant feature of the route, with intermittent protection at the airiest sections. Follow the ledge for 30min to make an airy traverse across rock slabs. Continue along the ledge to reach a series of rock steps leading down into a shattered wall characterised by a large natural cave. Squeeze under an overhanging roof then begin to ascend steadily.

Another exposed traverse is followed by an ascent of a steep grassy slope along a gravel path, reaching an airy crest overlooking a shallow gully. Follow the path right along the ridge then descend into the gully, making a 100-metre leftward traverse protected by cable.

Climb easy rock to a shattered corner, then cross a shallow gully to broken rock slabs. Cross these before ascending a gentle gully to a broad grassy shoulder and the high point of the route. Continue along the broad ledge for 30min to begin descending steeply towards Val Giralba Alta. After a short traverse, down-climb a steep corner to reach a dirty and often snow-filled gully. Follow intermittent cable to exit into a large scree bowl.

To descend to Hotel Dolomitenhof, follow path 110 around the scree bowl to join with path 103. Follow this easily to **Rifugio Carducci**. Continue on path 103 as it switchbacks north to **Forcella Giralba**, then drop north-west to reach **Rifugio Comici**. From here a long but scenic walk down Val Fiscalina on path 103 leads to the road at **Hotel Dolomitenhof**.

Other possibilities

The route described here can be combined with Via Ferrata Strada degli Alpini (Route 66), spending the night at Rifugio Carducci. This combination enables a long traverse of the Dolomiti di Sesto, either returning to Hotel Dolomitenhof or, alternatively, making the ascent to Passo della Sentinella before descending the lower half of Via Ferrata Mario Zandonella (see Route 68) to return to Rifugio Lunelli. The latter option avoids the logistical complications of returning to the car but is a long and committing two-day route requiring stamina and good fitness.

ROUTE 70
Via Ferrata Mazzetta

Start/Finish	Acque Rosse, Padola
Distance	11km
Total ascent/descent	1200m
Grade	2C
Time	7–8hr
Wire length	150m
Map	Tabacco 17
Parking	Acque Rosse: 46.59893, 12.46827

This remote via ferrata can't be wholly recommended as it's difficult to make a complete circuit and doesn't contain enough interest to warrant doing the route as an out-and-back itinerary. While it is possible to create a circuit descending east from Forcella de Ambata and then taking path 164 back south, this requires an extremely confident party as the descent is loose, unprotected and exposed (beware of Tabacco maps marking this descent as a large path). Alternatively you can descend path 123, which leads south down Val de Ambata to the village of Villanova on the outskirts of Auronzo – although this does create logistical difficulties returning to Padola. All in all this is a route that will appeal to those seeking adventurous terrain well and truly off the beaten track; for everyone else there are better and more accessible routes nearby.

Driving approach
The route starts from the small village of Padola, situated equidistant between Sesto and Auronzo. From Sesto follow the SS52 south-east for 17km to reach the village. Once in Padola, follow signs to Malga Aiarmola, driving up Via Ajarmola and continuing along Via Al Castella to the end of the surfaced road and a large parking area at Acque Rosse.

From the car park follow path 152 as it leads steeply uphill, initially on a jeep track and then on a path. Eventually the path meets a forestry road; follow this

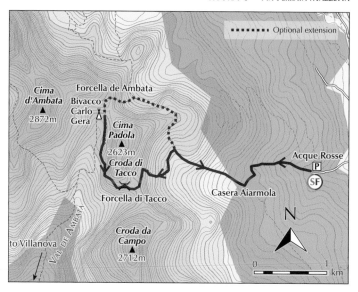

One of the few protected sections found on the route

for a few minutes to reach **Casera Aiarmola** (1600m), where there are some old stables and a welcoming (especially on a hot day!) trough with running water.

Continue along path 152 as it continues uphill, following signs to Bivacco Carlo Gera and then Forcella di Tacco and ignoring right-hand turn-offs to paths 164 and 153. The path continues through trees before exiting onto the scree of Giao Glauzei, then enters back into the trees before glacial moraine and steep slopes on grass lead just under Forcella di Tacco.

The ferrata wire starts just below the saddle on the east side, and after a few metres of climbing leads to the **forcella** itself. This offers excellent views into the bowl below and a distant panorama of Marmorole and Sorapiss.

From the forcella, descend north-west on good cables for about 150 metres before following easier ground down into the scree bowl below Croda di Tacco. A further 10min of scrambling across gravely ledges with intermittent protection leads to **Bivacco Carlo Gera** (2240m), roughly 40min after leaving the forcella.

Retrace your steps to return the car park at **Acque Rosse** (or see 'Other possibilities').

Other possibilities
- To continue via Forcella de Ambata, continue due north up scree (there are several small intermittent paths) to arrive at the **forcella** in 30min. Follow intermittent path markings and cairns north and then east down steep and exceptionally loose terrain with several exposed passages to eventually rejoin the woods. Turn right onto path 164, which heads south (lots of forestry work and re-routed paths at time of writing) back to **Casera Aiarmola** before reversing the route back to **Acque Rosse**.
- To descend via Val de Ambata, from Bivacco Carlo Gera reverse the route for 600 metres and then turn off right onto path 123 and follow intermittent path markers down **Val de Ambata** to Villanova. From here either arrange a taxi or during peak season take a bus back to Padola.

10 AURONZO

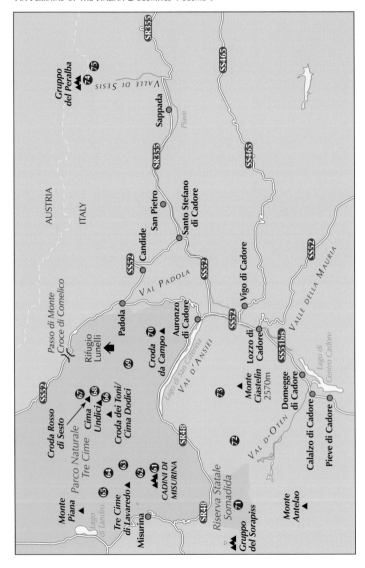

AURONZO

Auronzo di Cadore is a sizeable town along the banks of Lago Santa Caterina and the Ansiei river. The town enjoys a splendid position beneath the Marmarole group to the south and the Sesto group to the north, with more dramatic views up the valley to the north-west towards the iconic Tre Cime di Lavaredo.

Given its location on the edge of the main mountain groups, tourism is slightly less prevalent here and the atmosphere is more authentically northern Italian; somewhat unusually for the Dolomites, Italian is the principle language. Nonetheless the town still forms a good holiday base; the tourist office is very helpful, there is a good range of accommodation options and plenty of shops, bars and restaurants.

Auronzo is also quite easily accessible on public transport; a bus runs from Calalzo di Cadore, which can be reached by train from Venice and Belluno or by bus from Cortina. Unfortunately however, the routes in this chapter generally depart from rather remote subsidiary valleys and as such private transport is still essential.

The mountains in this area have a quiet, almost lonely feel to them, as they are frequently ignored in favour of their slightly higher or more dramatic neighbours (the proximity of the Tre Cime no doubt a factor here). The via ferratas are not particularly technical, but Routes 71 and 72 are long, committing and exposed mountain days regardless of the low grade. Routes 73 and 74 are shorter days, while Route 75 combines two short via ferratas and can also be combined with the previous route to make a long and complete day.

ROUTE 71
Sentiero Cengia del Doge

Start/Finish	Somadida Forest Nature Reserve car park, Ponte degli Alberi
Distance	17km
Total ascent/descent	980m
Grade	1C
Time	7–8hr
Wire length	150m
Map	Tabacco 17
Parking	Somadida Forest Nature Reserve car park: 46.53073, 12.28255

Sentiero Cengia del Doge is a spectacular ledge route traversing the north side of the distinctive Corno del Doge. Despite the low grade, there is a considerable amount of exposure, long sections of unprotected airy ledge walking and a substantial ascent and descent, so stamina and surefootedness are essential. The effort is, however, rewarded with stunning, untouched Dolomitic scenery away from the crowds of the better-known Sesto and Cortina d'Ampezzo groups.

Driving approach
From Auronzo take the SS48 along Val d'Ansiei, following signs to Misurina. After 12km, shortly after Albergo Palus San Marco, park in a small car park by Ponte degli Alberi on the left side of the road by the entrance to the Somadida Forest Nature Reserve.

Cross the bridge and follow the dirt road right alongside the river. Keep left at the fork, following path 226 to cross the bridge of **Ponte Piccolo** then soon after keep right to follow the track running parallel to the Rio di San Vido. At a junction just before the track ends, turn left onto a smaller path, still following waymarks for path 226.

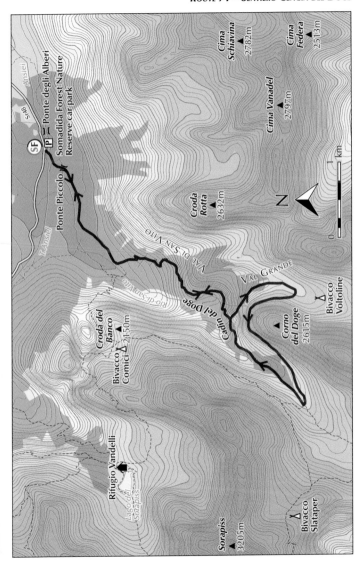

The sun sets on Monte Antelao, the 'King of the Dolomites'

Ascend steep switchbacks through the sparse woodland. After around 1hr, exit from the trees to descend slightly to a large amphitheater, with stunning views of Corno del Doge straight ahead and an impressive waterfall at **Cadin del Doge**.

The ascent continues over scree to reach the junction with path 278, now directly below the distinctive profile of Corno del Doge; turn left here to make a short traverse before a short section of cable, and continue up more scree slopes to exit into **Val Grande** – a stunning high-level glacial valley.

Around 1½hr from joining path 278, reach a junction with Alta Via 5 and a sign for Biv. Musatti to the left. Ignore this and continue for 100 metres to join path 280, now with the red box of Bivacco Voltoline straight ahead perched high among the rocks.

The ascent to the shelter is worthwhile in order to appreciate its wild and remote setting, but to continue the route, turn right following a sign to Val di S Vito/Forcella Grande. The path leads due north and is initially quite indistinct, winding through boulders and dwarf pines before becoming very narrow and exposed. After around 10min reach the first cable protection; the ledge is narrow with intermittent wire, on often shattered rock with some significant exposure.

After around 30min the terrain becomes easier, exiting the ledge and descending into the beautiful Val di San Vito. Where the paths intersect, turn right onto path 226, descending easily down the valley to Cadin del Doge and reversing the approach path to return to the **car park**.

ROUTE 72
Sentiero degli Alpini

Start/Finish	Ristorante alla Pineta, Val d'Oten
Distance	17km
Total ascent/descent	1600m
Grade	2C
Time	8–9hr
Wire length	450m
Map	Tabacco 16
Parking	Ristorante alla Pineta: 46.47218, 12.33845

A technically straightforward route in remote mountainous terrain. The protection is intermittent and the waymarking not always clear, while the ascent and descent are considerable; on the other hand, the length of both the approach and the route itself often ensure solitude and the views are excellent.

Driving approach

From Auronzo, follow the SS52 south, keeping right at the junction to join the SS51 bis and continuing to Calalzo di Cadore, 17km from Auronzo. From Calalzo, follow signs for Val d'Oten, turning into a hamlet and following the road north-west for 6km to reach Ristorante alla Pineta.

From the restaurant, follow the vehicle track north for just under a kilometre to reach a junction; turn right here, following signs for Rifugio Chiggiato and ascending steeply through the trees for 2–2½hr.

From **Rifugio Chiggiato**, continue north on path 260/Alta Via 5 to quickly reach **Forcella Sacu**. Turn left here, following a series of terrace paths along the south-west flank of Cima Salina. The waymarking is not always clear as the route ascends through dwarf pines, crossing a dirty gully and finally switchbacking up to the start of the ferrata, reached in around 1½–2hr from Rifugio Chiggiato.

Follow easy but loose rocky ground, intermittently protected with cable and a short ladder. Continue to reach the broad gully below a prominent saddle and

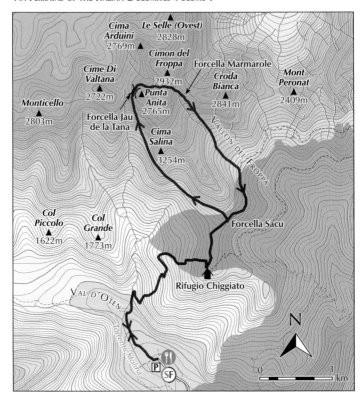

ascend this on its right side to reach **Forcella Jau de la Tana** in around 2½hr, affording excellent views of Cristallo and the Tre Cime di Lavaredo.

From the saddle keep right, cutting diagonally across a broad scree slope. Continue to reach a short section of wire along a ledge and ascend to Forcella Froppa and the highest point of the route (1hr from Forcella Jau de la Tana).

From the saddle, descend the opposite side (east) for 10min to **Forcella Marmarole** below, then turn right (south-east) to descend a steep, loose and unpleasant scree slope towards Vallon del Froppa. The terrain becomes more stable after around 15min; continue to descend through dwarf pines to intersect path 262. Turn right here, returning easily to **Forcella Sacu** above Rifugio Chiaggiato and reversing the approach route back to the **restaurant**.

ROUTE 73
Sentiero Attrezzato Amalio da Pra

Start/Finish	Pian dei Buoi, Lozzo di Cadore
Distance	7km
Total ascent/descent	550m
Grade	2B
Time	4–5hr
Wire length	200m
Map	Tabacco 16
Parking	Pian dei Buoi: 46.50752, 12.40576

A short circular route encircling Monte Ciareido, protected with short sections of wire on the most exposed sections. As the route weaves through sheltered gullies, late-lying snow is possible throughout the season and an axe and crampons are recommended early in the summer. Although possible in either direction, the anti-clockwise circuit described here is recommended.

Driving approach
From Auronzo, follow the SS52 south, keeping right to join the SS51 bis. Shortly after the junction, turn right into Lozzo di Cadore and follow signs to Pian dei Buoi. In high season the road beyond Le Spesse on the north-west side of the village has controlled access; it is open to uphill traffic between 9am and 1pm, and open to downhill traffic between 2pm and 5pm. The road is steep and narrow but reasonably well surfaced. Where the tarmac ends, continue for 1.5km to a large parking area at Pian dei Buoi.

From Pian dei Buoi, follow the vehicle track, waymarked 28, to reach **Rifugio Ciareido** in around 30min. Just beyond the rifugio, reach the junction with path 272 and turn right (north) then turn left (west) to ascend to **Forcella San Lorenzo**, reached in around 45min from the rifugio.

From the saddle descend briefly to the west, following a large ledge under **Torre Pian dei Buoi**, taking care of loose rock underfoot and falling stones from above. From here there is a wonderful panorama of the Dolomiti di Sesto to the

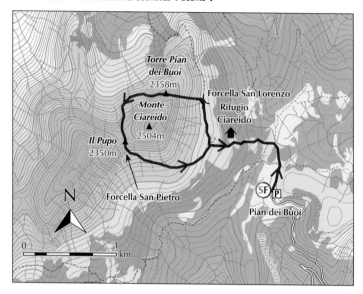

north and Monte Ciareido rising above to the south. Continue for 20min before descending cables, easily at first and then quite steeply, for 25 metres.

After crossing a gully, climb for around 80 metres to gain a rock spur then traverse through two small saddles towards Forcella San Pietro, dominated by the striking view of a large rock pillar, **Il Pupo** (2350m). The route from Forcella San Lorenzo to Forcella San Pietro takes around 1¾hr.

From the saddle, descend initially steeply before the terrain levels out somewhat. Keep left at the fork to continue contouring the hillside to the east to return to **Rifugio Ciareido**, reversing the approach route easily to the parking area at **Pian dei Buoi**.

ROUTE 74
Via Ferrata Sartor

Start/Finish	Car park 750 metres before Rifugio Sorgenti
Distance	8.5km
Total ascent/descent	880m
Grade	2B
Time	4–5hr
Wire length	250m
Map	Tabacco 01
Parking	Car park 750 metres before Rifugio Sorgenti: 46.62026, 12.71626

A straightforward but pleasant route that can be easily climbed in isolation or combined with Route 75 for a long mountain day. When climbed on its own, it's an enjoyable route that can be recommended to families or those without via ferrata or scrambling experience. The view from Monte Peralba is exceptional, giving a glimpse into this little-known border region of the Dolomites.

Monte Peralba (2694m)

Rifugio Calvi

Driving approach

From Auronzo, take the SS52 north-east to St Stefano di Cadore then turn right onto the SS355 to Cima Sappada. Just after crossing a bridge over the River Piave, turn left following signs to Rifugio Sorgenti del Piave and follow the narrow but well-surfaced road for 8km to reach a large parking area around 750 metres below the rifugio.

From the parking area, ascend a vehicle track waymarked 132 steeply to reach **Rifugio Calvi** in less than 1hr. Monte Peralba is to the left (north-west) of the rifugio. Follow path 131 leading north at a steep gradient for 15min to reach a sign for 'Ferrata Sartor'. Turn left here, traversing the hillside before switchbacks lead to the start of the route in around 30min from the rifugio.

The ferrata itself takes around 30min and develops on good rock, offering good positions and excellent views down the valley. After 15–20min reach a fork; the right branch is steeper and slightly harder, but both branches rejoin shortly after. Follow the red waymarks for a further 30min to reach the summit of **Monte Peralba** (2694m).

Climbing the stemples at the start of the route

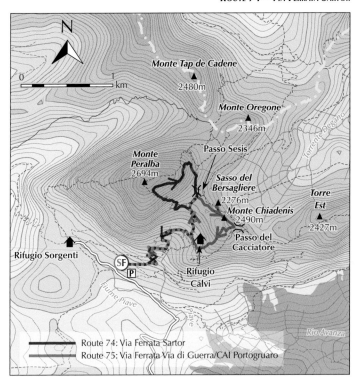

To descend, follow waymarks east to reach an arrow pointing north down a steep gully. The upper part is protected with cables, although these are often buried by snow early in the season. As the gully broadens out, continue down to reach a path that traverses east then south across the hillside to **Passo Sesis**, reached around 1hr from the summit. From here descend path 132 to return to **Rifugio Calvi** in around 20min then reverse the approach route to return to the **car park** below Rifugio Sorgenti.

Other possibilities

This route is easily combined with Route 75; from Passo Sesis, continue towards Passo del Cacciatori to join with the route to **Monte Chiadenis**. The combination of the two routes takes a total of 8hr.

ROUTE 75
Via Ferrata Via di Guerra/CAI Portogruaro

Start/Finish	Car park 750 metres before Rifugio Sorgenti
Distance	8km
Total ascent/descent	650m
Grade	3B/2B
Time	4–5hr
Wire length	700m
Map	Tabacco 01
Parking	Car park 750 metres before Rifugio Sorgenti: 46.62026, 12.71626
Note	For route map see Route 74

A circular route combining two worthwhile via ferratas on Monte Chiadenis. The route given here ascends the harder way from Passo del Cacciatori and descends the easier south-west ridge. For a longer day, the route may also be combined with Route 74, reaching two excellent summits in one day.

Monte Peralba (2694m)

74: Via Ferrata Sartor   2B
75: Via Ferrata Via di Guerra/CAI Portogruaro   3B/2B

Monte Chiadenis (2490m)

Passo Sesis

74

75

Rifugio Calvi

Parking area   75

*Spectacular 360-degree views await on
the summit ridge of Monte Chiadenis*

Driving approach

From Auronzo, take the SS52 north-east to St Stefano di Cadore then turn right onto the SS355 to Cima Sappada. Just after crossing a bridge over the River Piave, turn left following signs to Rifugio Sorgenti del Piave and follow the narrow but well-surfaced road for 8km to reach a large parking area around 750 metres below the rifugio.

From the parking area, ascend a vehicle track waymarked 132 steeply to reach **Rifugio Calvi** in less than 1hr, then follow path 131/132/140, ascending fairly steeply for 15min, and taking the right fork at the sign for Ferrata Sartor.

The gradient eases as the path bears north-east towards **Passo Sesis** (2312m), taking less than 30min in total from the rifugio. Now follow path 173 towards Passo del Cacciatori, reaching a sign in 15min pointing right for Via Ferrata Chiadenis. Follow this to reach the first section of cable.

The ascent is fairly steep in places and the cables are rather loose as the route leads to a wedged boulder before descending to the left to reach a gully. Climb the gully, with a number of quite challenging moves up a series of short walls and chimneys. After around 1hr, traverse along ledges with intermittent protection, avoiding Pic Chiadenis and passing a number of wartime caves to reach the summit of **Monte Chiadenis** (2490m) in around 10min.

To descend, follow the path south-west, with intermittent protection and some short sections of scrambling. The final 30 metres of downclimbing are quite steep but well protected. Reach a saddle to the south of Rifugio Calvi, marked by a number of wartime fortifications, then return to the **rifugio** and follow the jeep track or the well-waymarked Sentiero delle Marmotte back to the **car park** below Rifugio Sorgenti.

APPENDIX A
Useful contacts

Emergency numbers
Carabinieri/rescue 112

Police 113

Fire service 115

Road rescue 116

Mountain rescue/ambulance 118

General
www.visitdolomites.com
Overview site of the Dolomites
covering history, culture, sports and
accommodation

www.dolomitisupersummer.com/en
The primary resource for summer
walking, via ferrata and lift information

www.dolomites.org
Overview site with a focus on
accommodation

www.accommodation-dolomites.com
Accommodation search resource

Weather resources
Veneto area
www.arpa.veneto.it

Bolzano area
www.provincia.bz.it/meteo

Trento area
www.meteotrentino.it

Tourist information
Val di Fassa
tel +39 0462 609500
www.fassa.com

Val Gardena
tel +39 0471 777900
www.valgardena.it

Alta Badia
tel +39 0471 836176
www.altabadia.org

Arabba
tel +39 0436 79130
www.arabba.it

Val Fiorentina
tel +39 0437 720243
www.valfiorentina.it

Cortina and Misurina
tel +39 0436 866252
www.dolomiti.org/it/cortina

Sesto
tel +39 0474 710310
www.drei-zinnen.info

Auronzo
tel +39 0435 408056
www.auronzomisurina.it

Mountain guide offices
Guide Alpine Dolomiti (Val di Fassa)
www.guidealpinedolomiti.net

Guide Alpine Val di Fassa (Val di Fassa)
www.guidealpinevaldifassa.com

Association of Mountain Guides
(Val Gardena)
www.gardenaguides.it

Alta Badia Guides (Corvara)
www.altabadiaguides.com

Proguide (Corvara)
www.proguide.it

Guide Alpine Scuola di Alpinismo
(Cortina)
www.guidecortina.com

Guide Tre Cime (Misurina)
www.guidetrecimedilavaredo.it

Tre Cime Scuola di Alpinismo (Sesto)
www.alpinschule-dreizinnen.com

Associazione Guide Alpine Tre Cime
(Auronzo)
www.guidetrecimedilavaredo.it

Cosley and Houston Alpine Guides
(International)
www.cosleyhouston.com

Taxi companies

Canazei and Arabba
Taxi Autosella
tel +39 0471 790033

Desilvestro Taxi e Viaggi
tel +39 335 760 5170

Taxi Arabba
tel +39 339 705 7095

Ortisei and Selva
Viaggi Gardena
tel +39 0471 795150

Taxi Val Gardena Taxileo
tel +39 335 841 0330

Corvara
Taxi Vico Alta Badia
tel +39 335 611 6528

Taxi Corvara
tel +39 339 881 7965

San Martino
Autoservizi Bruno Tavernaro
tel +39 0439 68227

San Cassiano
Taxi Renato
tel +39 345 639 3680

Selva di Cadore
Radio Taxi
tel +39 0436 860888

Taxi Roby
tel +39 328 712 8813

Pecol
Dolomiti Autonoleggio Taxi Alleghe
tel +39 340 679 6016

Cortina and Misurina
Taxi Cortina Sci
tel +39 338 488 9793

Taxi Cortina Autonoleggio con
Conducente
tel +39 335 637 1419

Auronzo
Taxi Pieve di Cadore
tel +39 338 355 4518

Sesto
Taxi Holzer Remo
tel +39 0474 710650

Bus companies
Cortina Express
tel +39 0436 867350
www.cortinaexpress.it
In addition to offering airport transfers,
it offers local services between Cortina
and the Alta Badia.

Dolomiti bus
tel +39 0437 217111
www.dolomitibus.it
Public service serving the Belluno and
Cadore regions

SAD bus
tel +39 0471 450111
www.sad.it
Public service serving Bolzano,
Brunico, the Alta Badia, Val Gardena
and Cortina

Trentino Transporti
www.ttesercizio.it

Airport transfer services

www.altoadigebus.com
Transfer service from Munich,
Innsbruck, Bergamo and Milan airports

www.busgroup.eu
Transfer service from Milan, Bergamo
and Munich airports

www.cortinaexpress.it
Transfer services from Treviso and
Venice airports

Sports shops

Canazei and Arabba

Amplatz Sport
Via Dolomites, 109
38032 Canazei
tel +39 0462 601605

Sport Samont
Via Boè, 26
32020 Arabba
tel +39 0436 79142

Ortisei and Selva

Sport Gardena
Strada Rezia, 110
39046 Ortisei
tel +39 0471 796522

Sport Bruno Riffeser
Via Meisules, 131
Selva di Val Gardena
tel +39 0471 795141

Corvara

Sport Kostner
Str Col Alt, 97
39033 Corvara in Badia
tel +39 0471 836933

Sport Tony
Strada Colz, 56
39030 La Villa Badia
tel +39 0471 847622

Cortina and Misurina

K2 Sport
Via Cesare Battisti, 32
32043 Cortina
tel +39 0436 863706

Sesto

Sport Mode Kiniger
Via Dolomiti, 39
39030 Sesto
tel +39 0474 710433

Auronzo

Kiwi Sports House
Via Corte, 17
32041 Auronzo di Cadore
tel +39 329 655 9171

**Manufacturers of via ferrata
climbing equipment**

Black Diamond
eu.blackdiamondequipment.com/en-eu

Camp
www.camp.it

Edelrid
www.edelrid.de

Kong
www.kong.it

LACD
www.lacd.de

Mammut
www.mammut.ch

Petzl
www.petzl.com

Salewa
www.salewa.co.uk

Map suppliers

Tabacco www.tabaccoeditrice.it

Kompass www.kompass.de

Standfords www.stanfords.co.uk

The Map Shop www.themapshop.co.uk/

APPENDIX B
Glossary of mountain terms

Italian	German	English
ago	*Nadel*	needle, pinnacle
alpe, malga	*Alp*	alp, upland meadow
alta via	*Hohenweg*	high-level path
alto	*hoch*	high
arva, pala e sonda	*LVS-Gerät, Lawinenschaufel, Lawinensonde*	transceiver, shovel and probe
attacchi	*Bindungen*	bindings
attrezzato	*klettersteig*	protected
baita	*Berghütte*	mountain hut
bastoncini	*Stöcke*	poles
bianco	*weiss*	white
biglietto	*Fahrkarte*	ticket
bivacco	*Biwak*	bivouac hut
bocca	*Sattel*	pass, saddle
bocchetta	*kleine Scharte*	small pass, gap
bosco	*Wald*	forest
cabinovia, telecabina	*Gondelbahn*	gondola lift
caduta di sassi	*Steinschlag*	stone-fall
camere libre	*Zimmer frei*	rooms to let
canale	*Rinne*	gully
canalone	*Schlucht*	gorge
carta	*Karte*	map
cengia	*Band*	ledge
chiuso	*geschlossen*	closed
ciaspe/ciaspole/racchette da neve	*Schneeschuhe*	snowshoes

Italian	German	English
cima	Spitze	summit
col, colle	Hügel	hill
corda	Seil, Kabel	rope
cresta	Grat	ridge
croce	Kreuz	cross
croda	Felswand	wall, cliff
curve di livello	Hohenlinien	contour lines
destra	rechts	right
difficile	schwierig	difficult
diritto	geradeaus	straight ahead
discesa, giu	Absteig	descent, down
dislivello	Hohenunterscheid	altitude difference
esposto	exponiert	exposed
est	osten	east
estate	Sommer	summer
fiume	Fluss, Strom	river
forcella	Scharte	gap, small pass
frana	Erdlawine	landslide
funivia	Seilbahn	cable car
fuori pista	abseits der Piste	off-piste
ghiaio	Schutt, Geroll	scree
ghiacciaio	Gletscher	glacier
ghiaccio	Eis	ice
gradini	Klammern	stemples, iron rungs
grande	gross	large
gruppo	Gruppe	massif, group
impianti	Aufsteigsanlagen	lift system
lago	See	lake
lavina/slavina	Lawine	snowslide

Italian	German	English
lontano	weit	far
marcia	Tritt	foot-hold
montagna	Berg	mountain
mugo	Latschen	small pine bushes
nebbia	Nebel	fog
neve polverosa/neve fresca	Puderschnee	powder snow
nord	norden	north
noleggio	verleihen	to hire
occidentale	westlich	western
orientale	östlich	eastern
ovest	westen	west
parco naturale	Naturpark	natural park
parete	Wand	wall, cliff
parcheggio	Parkplatz	parking
passo	Joch	pass
pelli di foca	Skifelle	skins
pensione	Gasthof	guest house
percorso	Wanderweg	path
pericolo	Gefahr	danger
pericoloso	gefährlich	dangerous
piano	Ebene, Hochfläche	level ground, plateau
piccolo	klein	small
pista	Piste	piste
piz, punta	Gipfel, Spitze	summit
ponte	Brücke	bridge
rallentare	langsam	slow down
rifugio	Hütte	mountain hut
rio	Bach	stream, brook
ripido	steil	steep

Italian	German	English
rosso	rot	red
salire	aufsteigen	ascend
salita	Aufsteig	ascent
sasso	Fels, Stein	stone
scala	Leiter	ladder
scendere	absteigen	descend
sci	Ski	ski
scialpinismo	Skibergsteigen	ski mountaineering
sci escursionismo	Skitouren	ski touring
sci nordico/sci di fondo	Skilanglauf	cross-country skiing
segnalazione	Bezeichnung	waymarks
seggiovia	Sessellift	chairlift
sella	Sattel	saddle
sentiero	Fussweg	footpath
sinsistra	links	left
soccorso	Bergrettung	rescue
strada	Strasse	road
sud	Süden, süd	south
tempo	Wetter, Zeit	weather or time
torrente	Sturzbach	mountain stream
traversata	Uberquerung	crossing
ultima	letzte	last
valanga	Lawine	avalanche
val, valle	Tal	valley
vedretta	Gletscher	glacier
vento	Wind	wind
via	Weg	way, route
vietato	verboten	not permitted

APPENDIX C
Further reading

Books

Francesco Cappellari, *Ferrate a Cortina* (Idea Montagna, 2011)

Graham Fletcher & John Smith, *Via Ferratas of the Italian Dolomites: Vol 1* (Cicerone, 2014)

Graham Fletcher & John Smith, *Via Ferratas of the Italian Dolomites: Vol 2* (Cicerone, 2015)

Andrea Greci & Federico Rossetti, *Ferrate nelle Dolomiti Centrali* (Idea Montagna, 2016)

Eugen E. Hüsler, *Leichte Klettersteige Dolomiten* (Bruckmann, 2008)

Christjan Ladurner, *Klettersteige in den Dolomiten* (Tappeiner, 2013)

Libby Peter, *Rock Climbing: Essential Skills & Techniques* (Mountain Training UK, 2011)

Plan y Brenin, *International Mountain Trekking: A Practical Manual for Trekkers & Leaders* (Mountain Training UK, 2013)

James Rushforth, *The Dolomites – Rock Climbs and Via Ferrata* (Rockfax, 2014)

Websites and DVDs

Axel Jentzsch-Rabl, Dieter Wissekal, Andreas Jentzsch, *Klettersteigführer DVD, Dolomiten: Südtirol – Gardasee* (Alpinverlag, 2015)

James Rushforth, *The Dolomites – Via Ferrata*, www.ukclimbing.com/articles/page.php?id=6918 (2015)

BMC & Plas y Brenin, *Rock Climbing Essentials DVD* (British Mountaineering Council, 2012)

NOTES

NOTES

NOTES

LISTING OF CICERONE GUIDES

BRITISH ISLES CHALLENGES, COLLECTIONS AND ACTIVITIES

Cycling Land's End to John o' Groats
Great Walks on the England Coast Path
The Big Rounds
The Book of the Bivvy
The Book of the Bothy
The Mountains of England & Wales:
    Vol 1 Wales
    Vol 2 England
The National Trails
Walking the End to End Trail

SHORT WALKS SERIES

Short Walks Hadrian's Wall
Short Walks in Arnside and Silverdale
Short Walks in Dumfries and Galloway
Short Walks in Nidderdale
Short Walks in the Lake District:
    Windermere Ambleside and Grasmere
Short Walks on the Malvern Hills
Short Walks in the Surrey Hills
Short Walks Winchester

SCOTLAND

Ben Nevis and Glen Coe
Cycle Touring in Northern Scotland
Cycling in the Hebrides
Great Mountain Days in Scotland
Mountain Biking in Southern and Central Scotland
Mountain Biking in West and North West Scotland
Not the West Highland Way Scotland
Scotland's Best Small Mountains
Scotland's Mountain Ridges
Scottish Wild Country Backpacking
Skye's Cuillin Ridge Traverse
The Borders Abbeys Way
The Great Glen Way
The Great Glen Way Map Booklet
The Hebridean Way
The Hebrides
The Isle of Mull
The Isle of Skye
The Skye Trail
The Southern Upland Way
The West Highland Way
The West Highland Way Map Booklet
Walking Ben Lawers, Rannoch and Atholl
Walking in the Cairngorms
Walking in the Pentland Hills
Walking in the Scottish Borders
Walking in the Southern Uplands

Walking in Torridon, Fisherfield, Fannichs and An Teallach
Walking Loch Lomond and the Trossachs
Walking on Arran
Walking on Harris and Lewis
Walking on Jura, Islay and Colonsay
Walking on Rum and the Small Isles
Walking on the Orkney and Shetland Isles
Walking on Uist and Barra
Walking the Cape Wrath Trail
Walking the Corbetts
    Vol 1 South of the Great Glen
    Vol 2 North of the Great Glen
Walking the Galloway Hills
Walking the John o' Groats Trail
Walking the Munros
    Vol 1 – Southern, Central and Western Highlands
    Vol 2 – Northern Highlands and the Cairngorms
Winter Climbs: Ben Nevis and Glen Coe

NORTHERN ENGLAND ROUTES

Cycling the Reivers Route
Cycling the Way of the Roses
Hadrian's Cycleway
Hadrian's Wall Path
Hadrian's Wall Path Map Booklet
The Coast to Coast Cycle Route
The Coast to Coast Walk
The Coast to Coast Walk Map Booklet
The Pennine Way
The Pennine Way Map Booklet
Walking the Dales Way
Walking the Dales Way Map Booklet

NORTH-EAST ENGLAND, YORKSHIRE DALES AND PENNINES

Cycling in the Yorkshire Dales
Great Mountain Days in the Pennines
Mountain Biking in the Yorkshire Dales
The Cleveland Way and the Yorkshire Wolds Way
The Cleveland Way Map Booklet
The North York Moors
The Reivers Way
Trail and Fell Running in the Yorkshire Dales
Walking in County Durham
Walking in Northumberland
Walking in the North Pennines
Walking in the Yorkshire Dales: North and East

Walking in the Yorkshire Dales: South and West
Walking St Cuthbert's Way
Walking St Oswald's Way and Northumberland Coast Path

NORTH-WEST ENGLAND AND THE ISLE OF MAN

Cycling the Pennine Bridleway
Isle of Man Coastal Path
The Lancashire Cycleway
The Lune Valley and Howgills
Walking in Cumbria's Eden Valley
Walking in Lancashire
Walking in the Forest of Bowland and Pendle
Walking on the Isle of Man
Walking on the West Pennine Moors
Walking the Ribble Way
Walks in Silverdale and Arnside

LAKE DISTRICT

Bikepacking in the Lake District
Cycling in the Lake District
Great Mountain Days in the Lake District
Joss Naylor's Lakes, Meres and Waters of the Lake District
Lake District Winter Climbs
Lake District:
    High Level and Fell Walks
Lake District:
    Low Level and Lake Walks
Mountain Biking in the Lake District
Outdoor Adventures with Children – Lake District
Scrambles in the Lake District – North
Scrambles in the Lake District – South
Trail and Fell Running in the Lake District
Walking The Cumbria Way
Walking the Lake District Fells –
    Borrowdale
    Buttermere
    Coniston
    Keswick
    Langdale
    Mardale and the Far East
    Patterdale
    Wasdale
Walking the Tour of the Lake District

DERBYSHIRE, PEAK DISTRICT AND MIDLANDS

Cycling in the Peak District
Dark Peak Walks
Scrambles in the Dark Peak
Walking in Derbyshire
Walking in the Peak District – White Peak East

For full information on all our guides,
books and eBooks,
visit our website:
www.cicerone.co.uk

CICERONE

Trust Cicerone to guide your next adventure, wherever it may be around the world...

Discover guides for hiking, mountain walking, backpacking, trekking, trail running, cycling and mountain biking, ski touring, climbing and scrambling in Britain, Europe and worldwide.

Connect with Cicerone online and find inspiration.

- buy books and ebooks
- articles, advice and trip reports
- podcasts and live events
- GPX files and updates
- regular newsletter

cicerone.co.uk